The Blind St

The Blind Storyteller

How We Reason About Human Nature

IRIS BERENT

OXFORD
UNIVERSITY PRESS

OXFORD
UNIVERSITY PRESS

Oxford University Press is a department of the University of Oxford. It furthers the University's objective of excellence in research, scholarship, and education by publishing worldwide. Oxford is a registered trade mark of Oxford University Press in the UK and certain other countries.

Published in the United States of America by Oxford University Press
198 Madison Avenue, New York, NY 10016, United States of America.

Library of Congress Cataloging-in-Publication Data
Names: Berent, Iris, 1960– author.
Title: The blind storyteller : how we reason about human nature / Iris Berent.
Description: New York, NY : Oxford University Press, [2020] |
Includes bibliographical references and index.
Identifiers: LCCN 2019047229 (print) | LCCN 2019047230 (ebook) |
ISBN 9780190061920 (hardback) | ISBN 9780190061944 (epub) |
ISBN 9780190061951 (online)
Subjects: LCSH: Mind and body. | Thought and thinking. | Consciousness.
Classification: LCC BF161.B4745 2020 (print) | LCC BF161 (ebook) |
DDC 128/.2—dc23
LC record available at https://lccn.loc.gov/2019047229
LC ebook record available at https://lccn.loc.gov/2019047230

1 3 5 7 9 8 6 4 2

Printed by Sheridan Books, Inc., United States of America

With my love, for Saul, Amir, and Alma

Contents

Preface

This book was born on a sunny December day in the magnificent marshes of the Everglades. Walking through the sea of lush green under the bright blue sky, I was pondering the usual—life and work, the self and others. In my line of business, people are both the play and the players, the topic of inquiry and the inquirer. And as a psychoanalyst friend aptly observed, "People are a problem."

Those leisurely hours in nature gave rise to a dangerous idea. It concerned a series of seemingly irrational attitudes I'd detected in people (myself and others) when reasoning about a broad range of topics—*How do we know what we know? How do brains "think"? What happens to us when we die?* All of these topics relate to human nature and people's reactions to them made no sense. People, it appeared, suffer from a selective but chronic blindness toward aspects of themselves. I wondered whether this was indeed the case and, if so, why. Could our strange view of human nature arise from human nature itself?

As an experimental psychologist, I couldn't resist the urge to go to the lab and find out. In short order, the data came pouring back, and the results all checked out. I spent the next few months talking about these ideas over dinners with friends, including Ralph Scully and Merav Socolovsky, Karina Meiri and Jim Schwob, Stephen Harrison and Tommy Kirchhausen, all of them prominent life scientists. Their sharp comments and nonchalant attitudes toward innate ideas (a notion that many cognitive scientists find too threatening to even confront) strengthened my confidence and helped push me forward.

The subsequent development of the manuscript and the research described therein benefited from the advice and support of many colleagues. Steven Pinker, Noam Chomsky, and Paul Bloom generously offered helpful comments and support early on; Gary Marcus provided valuable advice.

I'm also grateful for comments from Woo-Kyoung Ahn, Robyn Carston, Peter Carruthers, Dave DeSteno, Jane Epstein, Lisa Feldman Barrett, Erol Franco, Lila Gleitman, Benjamin Juárez, Frank Keil, Nancy Kim, Joshua Knobe, Barbara Landau, Lori Lefkovitz, Joanne Miller, Elizabeth Spelke,

Santo Tarantino, and Edward Zalta. Special thanks to Alfonso Caramazza, Peter Carruthers, Veronique Izard, and Joshua Knobe for their detailed critiques of portions of the manuscript and to Claudio Lomnitz, who educated me about Mexico's Day of the Dead. Work on this project was generously supported by a Humanities Fellowship from Northeastern University, for which I'm immensely grateful. My talented lab team—Rachel Aronovitz, Melanie Platt, and Gwendolyn Sandoboe—helped carry out the experimental program. Melanie Platt also assisted in multiple administrative tasks and drew the illustrations for some of the chapters, for which I thank her deeply.

I'm indebted to my editor, Arthur Goldwag, for his sharp mind, skillful editorial hand, and warm heart; Arthur helped give birth to this book with his comments and advice. I'm also grateful to Joan Bossert from Oxford for her valuable insights and my agent, Jim Levine, for his assistance, advice, and support. Last but not least, my love and gratitude to my tour partners in the Everglades as in life: my husband Saul Bitran, and my children, Amir and Alma, the physicist and the humanist.

1

Know Thyself

Remy, the Harvard Humanities cat, has an orange coat, a focused agenda, and a strong interdisciplinary mission. He spends his mornings poring over the philosophy texts in the Yenching library, his busy afternoons at the Lyman Laboratory of Physics, evenings at the Divinity School, and, at times, he has even been known to pull all-nighters at the Law School (see Figure 1.1).

No, Remy isn't grappling with the "hard problem of consciousness" and the origins of knowledge. He doesn't investigate particle physics or worry about free will and legal responsibility. It is precisely for this reason that his thousands of Facebook followers (mostly Harvard students) are so enchanted by his adventures—because of the incongruity of a cat being so at home amid their austere academic surroundings.

Remy's fans recognize that Remy's feline condition is different than their own, and the reason is no mystery: they were born human, while Remy the cat was not. It's not just their physical and sensory experiences that differ. Yes, it's weird to imagine what it must feel like to navigate the maze of narrow library corridors with a tail hanging behind you and whiskers spreading out from your face, to be covered with thick fur and driven by the instincts of a cat. Weirder yet is the likelihood that Remy—a creature they've grown to know and love—thinks in a manner that is utterly incommensurable with their own cognition. Remy will never ponder his ontological and epistemo-logical condition—that he exists in the world, that his life is short, and that his understanding of it is so limited. Remy will likely live and die without ever gaining an understanding of himself.

It doesn't take much effort for us humans to grasp that being born a cat predestines Remy to certain cognitive constraints. By "constraints" I don't simply refer to his limited memory and narrow attention span. The little we have been able to learn about feline cognition (they are the least cooperative experimental subjects ever) suggests that cats do learn and think.[1] But there are fundamental qualitative differences between the kinds of conclusions

The Blind Storyteller. Iris Berent, Oxford University Press (2020). © Iris Berent, 2020.
DOI: 10.1093/oso/9780190061920.001.0001

Figure 1.1. Remy the Harvard Humanities cat.
Photo by Taylor Renee Joyce, used with permission.

that Remy extracts from his residence at Harvard and the ones that his human Facebook followers do. Remy views the world through the prism of his inborn cognitive capacities. What lies beyond that prism will always be beyond his grasp.

That a pet might experience a certain level of cognitive blindness is an idea we human beings accept with equanimity. But we are far less comfortable with the thought that we might suffer from similar cognitive limitations ourselves. Logic, however, compels us to entertain this as a distinct possibility. Having recognized that biology can innately limit other species' cognitions and that we too are biological kinds, blindness could very well obscure human minds.

Once again, I'm not referring here to "quantitative" limitations: there are obviously limits to the number of facts we can hold in our heads at once, the length of sentences we can parse and understand, and the frequencies of auditory stimuli that we can hear. What I really worry about is blindness to things that are in plain sight. The information is within our reach, but the inferences we draw from it are partial, systematically biased, and wrong. As a result, we are predestined to lives of blindness—partial or full—about who we really are. And that blindness exists for no other reason than that we are born human.

***

Having given birth to two humans and buried the two others who brought me into the world, I can attest to the fact that, when it comes to the origins and the end of cognitive life, my understanding is just as blurry as Remy's. When my kids were born, I was too tired and busy to spend much time thinking, and I still don't really get it in retrospect. *How could a tiny piece of matter—those two cells in my womb—have given rise to two unique individuals who think, talk, and laugh and who are utterly distinct from each other and from my own self?*

My parents' deaths allowed me more time to think, but granted me no clearer understanding. In my father's case, the end began one fateful Saturday morning, when he was taking his daily walk and the neighbor's dog caught sight of him. Although my father was 84, he was physically active and in robust health. But the dog, who was excited to see a familiar face so early in the morning, was big and fast, and when he jumped up on my father to greet him, he knocked him to the ground. My father picked himself up and walked home. But after an hour or two, he called me to say that he wasn't feeling well, and I took him to the hospital. His bald head did not show even a scratch, but a CT scan revealed massive brain bleeding (a known risk associated with the blood thinner he took for his heart arrythmia).

Hours later, the young neurosurgeon who was on call proudly declared my father's operation a success and showed me a picture he had taken with his cell phone of my father's exposed brain. He had good reason to be proud—the surgery was unusually long and risky, and he had worked skillfully and diligently. But it's never a good thing to have a picture of your brain on a surgeon's cellphone. At the end, the ordeal felt distinctly like a botched car repair. The parts of the engine all worked, but the car still wouldn't quite start.

Thanks to my training in neuroscience, I could see the ravaged areas of my father's brain in his CT scans, and yes, of course, I also know how babies are born. But "understanding" happens at multiple levels. My analytical cognition provided me with a detailed analysis of what newborn infants know from birth and what damaged brains can no longer understand. But voices from other parts of my mind protested. *How could my father's or my child's essence boil down to those pieces of meat in their skulls turning "on" and "off" like some light switch? How is it possible that meat really* thinks?

No matter how strongly I tried to hold to reason, those other voices were insistent. As I've begun to pay closer attention to them, reading the scientific literature, and conducting my own research, it's become evident that those "voices" are not just my own, and they are not only the consequences of grief or childbirth. In all likelihood, they reflect the normal operation of human brains. But their twisted messages can seriously derail our understanding of nearly every aspect of who we are.

I'm not only talking about the "big questions" like what happens when we die or whether we are endowed with free will. Yes, I will consider those matters, but let's start with the mundane. If you are holding a coffee cup in your hand as you read, you probably think you have a pretty solid notion of a what a "cup" is, right? Inspecting your surroundings further, you might see a familiar face, and at the sight of it you might feel flooded with a "warm" affect, perhaps love. What are those concepts and emotions, and where do they come from? Do you have to learn them from others over multiple encounters, or are they already ingrained in us when we are born? Can a newborn infant, for instance, recognize an object as such? Would they recognize love in a human face?

Science offers us detailed answers to each of these questions, and we will review them in due course. Most people, however, don't follow the technical literature, and even if they do, they don't refer to it while they go about their daily activities. When you hold your newborn child for the first time, you act on your instinctive beliefs regarding what this creature can grasp and feel. Similar beliefs guide your inferences about every one of your daily actions, why you did them, and, indeed, who you think you are. Each of these convictions is informed by those instinctive little "voices" that you hear in your head. But many of their conclusions are seriously tainted. Just as Remy sees Harvard Yard through the biased prism of his feline brain, you see your own existence through yours, and your vision is often blurred or skewed by what those irrational "voices" tell you about what you're seeing.

***

Who are those "voices," you might wonder? Where do they come from, and why do they so viciously derail our self-understanding? Before we can identify them, we need to understand the lay of the land of human cognition.

We tend to think of our cognition as a single unitary capacity that we typically identify with the rational mechanisms we use to solve problems (*"How will I make it to my flight on time?"*; *"Where will I get the cash I need to pay my mortgage?*") or "slow cognition," to use Daniel's Kahneman's term.[2] It's no wonder that this aspect of our mind stands out—it's precisely because it's slow and deliberate that it is salient to our conscious understanding. But cognition is not unitary; it is really an orchestra with many different instruments playing different parts. Most of them operate unconsciously, entirely "under the radar." And some of those "players" appear to be quite ancient. Not only do we apparently possess them at birth, so did some of our nonhuman ancestors. These principles form our core knowledge.

Core knowledge is not merely a "container," a space in which to hold the facts supplied by our experience. Rather, core knowledge *is* the facts. It provides us with some rudimentary principles that determine what objects, agents, and living things are. These notions, to reiterate, are implicit—we aren't consciously aware of the fact that we are applying them to what we see. We also don't need to learn them; they are hardwired within us from birth. Finally (and importantly), core knowledge refers to what we cognize; its contents are not necessarily true.

One principle—Dualism—governs how we think about agents and objects.[3] Briefly, Dualism makes you think that agents possess an immaterial mind that is distinct from their bodies, just like the philosopher René Descartes (1596–1650) suspected. Another principle—Essentialism—concerns living things.[4,5] Essentialism suggests to you that every living thing is what it is because it is born with some special material "essence" that defines it as such. Remy, for example, is what he is because he has the material essence of a cat.

These two cognitive principles—Dualism and Essentialism—appear pretty harmless, and as we will see, they are quite useful. If you are a chick (or a human baby, for that matter), you might want to immediately recognize that your mother is a single entity, not a collection of separate body parts. Core knowledge automatically leads you to draw this inference. So, core knowledge likely exists for good evolutionary reasons. It guides our understanding of physical objects, the minds of others, and other living kinds. But core cognition comes with a heavy price, as it is also a prism through which we unconsciously inspect our reality—both our psychological and our external reality. And this prism distorts our sight and sometimes blinds us altogether.

***

Psychological blindness, of course, is literally the stuff of Greek tragedy. Consider *Oedipus Rex*.[6] The Oracle of Delphi tells Oedipus' father, King Laius of Thebes, that his newborn son is destined to kill him and marry his widow. To avert this catastrophe, the king leaves the infant on a mountainside to die. A shepherd rescues him and takes him to Corinth, where he is adopted by King Polybus and Queen Merope. When Oedipus grows up, the Oracle tells him what she'd told his father, so Oedipus flees Corinth to escape his fate. In the course of his travels, he quarrels with an old man and kills him. When he comes to Thebes, he frees the city from the Sphinx and becomes its king, winning the hand of its widowed queen. But as he soon discovers, Queen Jocasta is in fact his birth mother, and the stranger he had killed was his birth father, Thebes' late king. In despair, Oedipus gouges out his eyes.

Plato recounts another allegory of blindness, a tale about prisoners who are shackled in a cave with their backs to its entrance.[7] All that they can see are shadows on the cave's wall, which they believe are reality. Like Oedipus, they are trapped in an illusion—a blind life.

Blindness stories shake us to our core because they touch on our fear that all that we think we know—the fingers on our hands, the faces of our friends—are so many shadows on the walls of our own internal caves, that all that we think we know about nature—that the sun will rise tomorrow, that a falling object accelerates at a rate of 32 feet per second—are the products of our own minds and not objective realities. What if our minds are not clear glass but blinding prisms? Worse yet, what if these prisms distort our views of our own psyches—our very selves?

Psychological blindness robs us of our dearest possession—the story of our mental lives. We tell tales about distant strangers, friends, and kin and, of course, about our favorite topic—ourselves: who we are, what we know, and who we want to be. We depend on these stories. They define us, whether we think we are lucky or wronged, have overcome adversity or succumbed to failure, or are heading toward growth or demise. Our stories also color our understanding of our social world. *Are people essentially good? Should we trust a friend or a stranger? Who will offer us a hand in our moment of need? Who will share our joy and feel compassion for us when we are sad?* Through these stories, we form our understanding of the nature of humankind. But what if our stories about human nature are false? What if we can't see the truth, even if we are told about it?

Recall that Oedipus's problem stemmed not so much from what he didn't know—the Oracle, after all, warned him of his fate—but from what he *thought* he knew. He was certain that Queen Merope was his birth mother. Had he considered the possibility that she might not be, he could have adopted a life of celibacy. Oedipus, however, trusted his knowledge—he was blind to the possibility that his view of the world and his place in it could be wrong. It was that internal blindness that caused his calamity. Blindness, then, is dangerous precisely to the extent that we don't recognize it. And as the Greeks feared, internal blindness is our fate. It is for this reason that they bequeathed us the maxim, "Know thyself."

People routinely make inferences about what they know and, quite often, our bets turn out to be wrong. Some of our errors are random and inconsequential—a slip of the mind makes us forget where we left our keys. Other errors arise from memory and attention—the "container" and "spotlight" of cognition. Kahneman has famously shown how we jump to a dazzling array of false inferences and irrational choices, simply because our logical thinking is slower and demands more attention relative to our intuitive unconscious thinking.[2] But other mistakes are systematic and profound; they are not easily remedied by facts. Our minds follow those tracks instinctively, much like birds migrate south.

This book explores some of our most profound mistakes—the systematic errors we make in reasoning about our own human nature. Like Oedipus, we are often oblivious to our ignorance, and our oblivion exacts a steep price, personal and social. Unlike Oedipus, however, our obliviousness is not due to our arrogance or hubris, nor is it due to the limited capacity of our cognitive "containers" and "spotlight." Rather, our blindness is deeply rooted in the contents of those "containers"—in the principles of core cognition. I will argue that the same notions that guide our normal grasp of external reality—the core mechanisms that make our minds tick—are also responsible for our psychological blindness. And those principles are probably innate. In other words, *our blindness to human nature is rooted in human nature itself.*

The first part of the book explores *what we think we know.* We examine whether certain ideas are available to us just because we are born human (just as other capacities are available to Remy simply because he's a cat). For example, are infants born with a specific notion of what "objects" are like, without ever having to learn it from their experience (e.g., through interactions with specific objects, like cups and balls)? As we will see, there is a striking contrast between what science tells us about where ideas come from and what laypeople believe about such matters. Science gives us good reasons to suspect that infants are born with detailed core knowledge about objects, agents, number, and language. Laypeople, however, insist that ideas cannot be innate. Moreover, these biases against ideas are quite selective: most people are perfectly happy to accept that emotions, for instance, are innate, but they assert that ideas are not. Why does the notion of innate ideas seem like an oxymoron? We will engage in some detective work, and in short order, the evidence will point right back at core knowledge itself. It is our innate ideas (specifically, the twin forces of Dualism and Essentialism) that interfere with our ability to grasp that ideas can be innate.

These findings pave the road to a journey that explores how our blindness to our own nature shapes other stories we tell about ourselves. Part II investigates *who we think we are*. As noted, we hold opposite misconceptions about concepts and emotions. "Cold" concepts (tacit notions, such as "object," "cup," and "chair") seem immaterial and disembodied to us, whereas our "warm" emotions seem to reside in our bodies (*I can sense my anxiety in the nervous rumbling of my stomach*). These two sets of misconceptions—that emotions are embodied, whereas concepts are not—generate endless tensions and puzzlement. *How can an immaterial thought* ("I need an energy boost") *move my very material body toward the coffeemaker? How can neuroimaging experiments miraculously make such immaterial notions light up my physical brain like a Christmas tree?*

Our misconceptions about human nature are not just a personal affair; our blindness has vast social consequences. Since we believe we are all born with the same set of embodied emotions, we (wrongly) conclude that we can accurately read others' feelings off their faces—we think we can tell whether a twitch of muscle in someone's lip signals an amused smile or contempt, contentment or pain. A jury believes they detected anger on a defendant's face—his aggression, in their minds, was a sure sign of guilt, but in reality, this innocent person was fearful and anguished. Tragically, the myth of innate embodied emotions leads us to presume that affective psychiatric disorders like major depression are destiny, whereas for cognitive disorders such as dyslexia, we wrongly assume the opposite—that these disorders are "just in our heads" (rather than "really in our brains"). These misconceptions give rise to prejudice in laypeople, professionals (clinicians and teachers), and policymakers; they rob affected individuals of a better understanding of their condition and its potential for remediation.

The two final chapters explore our errors in moral reasoning while we're here on earth, and our beliefs about what happens once we're no more. We will see how our core knowledge sways our notion of free will, derailing our understanding of criminal justice and responsibility and distorting our very notion of the moral self. Finally, we consider our curious views about the afterlife. What happens after we die is a matter of debate. Some of us assert that life persists after death; others contend that it ends here and now. But no matter what we say, deep down, we all secretly believe that the dead still think. Who is to blame for this? Once again, the footprints lead right back to our two (inborn) "friends"—Dualism and Essentialism.

As we embark on this journey, a word of qualified hope is in order. Although our blindness may well be inborn, it is not necessarily full or inevitable. Core knowledge, to reiterate, is only one player in our cognitive "orchestra." Other cognitive "instruments" allow us to think rationally, and we can use them to dampen the sounds of our false beliefs. In this regard, we are more similar to Oedipus Rex than to Remy the cat, who is a slave to his feline instincts. Reason presents us with a path out of our cognitive "cave," just as the Oracle's pronouncement provided Oedipus with an escape hatch. Yet blindness is hard to counteract. Oedipus did not escape his destiny, and as we will see in this book, we, too, often fall victims to ours. All our blind stories, whether they are about the natural or the supernatural world or our own minds, spring from a common origin: the human nature of the storyteller, ourselves.

References

1. Vitale Shreve KR, Udell MAR. What's inside your cat's head? A review of cat (Felis silvestris catus) cognition research past, present and future. *Animal Cognition*. 2015;18(6):1195–1206.
2. Kahneman D. *Thinking, fast and slow*. 1st ed. New York, NY: Farrar, Straus and Giroux; 2011.
3. Bloom P. *Descartes' baby: how the science of child development explains what makes us human*. New York, NY: Basic Books; 2004.
4. Keil FC. The acquisition of natural kind and artifact term. In: Demopoulos W, Marras A, eds. *Language Learning and Concept Acquisition*. Norwood, NJ: Ablex: Norwood; 1986:133–153.
5. Gelman SA. *The essential child: origins of essentialism in everyday thought*. New York, NY: Oxford University Press; 2003.
6. Sophocles. Oedipus Rex. Mulroy DD, Moon WG, eds. Madison, WI: University of Wisconsin Press; 2011.
7. Plato. (1892). *The republic* (B. Jowett, Trans.): Auckland, New Zealand: Floating Press. (Original work published ca. 380 B.C.).

PART I

WHAT WE KNOW

A. Who's Afraid of Innate Ideas?

2

Innateness Stories

How do you make small talk with a newborn baby? The question arose when my newborn son, Amir, was returned to me at the maternity ward. I had never been much of a "baby person"—I had not stopped to admire other people's babies on the street, and when I did meet an infant, I greeted them with the proper respect; no cooing and cuddling. So when I was finally reunited with my own baby, I wasn't quite sure about protocol.

What are you supposed to say to a little person? There were no instructions attached to his back, and baby talk seemed totally inappropriate. Amir was staring right at me, wide awake, entirely present, and well within his faculties. In fact, his gaze then did not seem much different from his look right now, a couple of decades later.

Small talk is a trusted icebreaker in novel social situations, but small talk only works when you and your interlocutor share a sum of common knowledge. And I had no idea what infants know. Ultimately, I turned to the classical FM radio station, and that was a winning bet. Amir's reaction was immediate and unmistakable. His large eyes opened yet larger, and he seemed to be listening intently. It was no surprise that he turned out to be a musician.

Music comes to us naturally, it requires no words, and it touches us right at our core. We "hear" happiness or melancholy, exhilaration or longing. But music "gets" us precisely because listening to it is an active process *that does* rely on knowledge and lots of it. I'm not referring here to trivia like the composer's name and era or to the technical knowledge you acquire from years of training at Juilliard or a PhD program in musicology. I'm referring to tacit musical principles that people—even those with no formal musical training—grasp intuitively.

Music has a structure that you sense implicitly, even if you have never held an instrument or heard that particular piece before.[1] The proof is in your behavior: you can tap your foot to the rhythm, you can tell when the tune is about to end, and you might even notice that the performer has landed on a

The Blind Storyteller. Iris Berent, Oxford University Press (2020). © Iris Berent, 2020.
DOI: 10.1093/oso/9780190061920.001.0001

couple of wrong notes. All these things that people notice (and which ulti-mately give rise to their emotional reactions[2]) rely on a knowledge of tacit musical principles. If you detect a "wrong note," it means you know what the right one could be, and you know that even if you've never heard the piece be-fore, because you implicitly recognize that it was composed in a musical key. Now, how plausible is it that a newborn baby would know any of this stuff?

***

Don't ask the mother! Scientists work hard to unveil the capacities of new-born infants; we will discuss some of their findings in Chapters 3 to 5 of this book. Most people, however, think this pursuit is, well, silly. Infants' minds, in their views, are akin to sponges: empty, fluffy, and eager to absorb. The possibility that infants come into the world pre-equipped with *knowledge* seems utterly ridiculous.

But is it? Let's examine some of the truths we hold dear. We often say, "I know that this is right like I know that 1 + 1 is 2." Well, what makes us believe that 1 + 1 is always 2? Or how about our knowledge of language, a fundamental capacity that is apparently unique to the human species? It is self-evident that English speakers *blog*, but not *lbog*, and that they know not to *drive* and *drink*, rather than to *rdive* and *rdink*. How do we know these things? And finally, consider the foundations of our moral reasoning. We all know that we should help our neighbors and not hurt them. But why? What is the origin of our moral beliefs? Keep in mind that my concern, for the mo-ment, is with laypeople's intuitive beliefs about the origins of knowledge, as opposed to scientists' interpretations of experimental data.

For many people, these questions have a simple answer: *we know these things because we learned them*, primarily from other people—our parents, teachers, and peers. You might indeed recall your first arithmetic lesson in kindergarten, the many grammar and spelling corrections on your home-work, and an early discussion with a parent about the value of kindness and sharing. Such knowledge, you might reason, must have been instilled in our minds by learning via social interactions. And in some sense, this is of course true. People certainly learn about numbers, language, and moral values from relevant experiences and formal instruction.

But stating that people *can* learn *some* of these facts is quite different than asserting that they *must*. To reiterate, there is no doubt that *some* knowledge is learned. The real question at hand is whether laypeople intuitively be-lieve that such core concepts as "number," "syllable," and "goodness" must be learned *in their entirety,* or if they are open to the idea that some part of them are inborn. To get at this, my lab asked a sample of laypeople to consider a thought experiment.[3] Suppose, we told them, it was possible to test the cognitive capacities of newborn infants in a laboratory. Obviously, the infants wouldn't be required to state the rules of grammar or solve calculus problems. Rather, by tracking subtle changes in the infants' behavior, the experimenters would be able to discern whether they possessed a rudimentary inborn grasp of number, language, and morality. What would the results of such experiments be? For example, would the infants be able to distinguish two objects from four? Would they prefer listening to syllables like *blog* over *lbog*? And when presented with social interactions featuring one character helping or hindering another, would they favor the helper characters over the hinderers?

The answers we got ranged from a resounding "no" to a weak "maybe." A large majority of the people we asked (80%) stated that infants lack the ability to discern number and that they are devoid of moral sense. When it comes to language, people's opinions were completely random. Some people did predict that infants would have an innate preference for real words over nonsense syllables, but most of them attributed it to the sensory qualities of the sounds (*blog* "sounds" more natural) rather than to any innate linguistic capacities per se.

Here is another thought experiment. Suppose a group of infants were raised on a desert island. Suppose it was further possible to care for all their needs—that they could be well-fed, loved, and nurtured. But critically, let us assume that the infants would never be exposed to adult humans, that they would never hear a language, be exposed to numbers, or be tutored on moral values. Once those children have matured, would they have any sense of number? Would they favor "right" over "wrong"? Would they communicate using a system that resembles a human language?

As with the neonate experiment, participants thought that the desert-islanders would know of no such things, and they maintained this belief even when they were provided with information suggesting that the relevant trait *is* in fact innate (e.g., because it is universal to all humans and emerges in early development). Participants stated unequivocally that, absent exposure to an adult community, those desert-islanders would lack any knowledge of numbers and that they would have no moral values or human language—certainly, they wouldn't be able to produce any complex sentences. Although, with time and experience, the stranded kids might begin to favor "well-doers" over "evil-doers," those preferences would be the result of their later social interactions, not anything innate in the human mind.

These results suggest that laypeople hold firm beliefs about the origin of knowledge. We believe that without learning, children will lack the foundations of human cognition, that learning is the *only* way that the concepts of number, language, and ethics are written on our blank slates. Knowledge is a human invention, and people are the proud sole authors of their intellects.

But our naïve notions of ourselves are a myth. As we will see in the next chapters, scientific experiments have indeed shown that neonates possess a rich understanding of some concepts that are apparently inborn. In particular, young infants can reliably encode the precise number of objects (provided the number of objects is small, up to about four).[4,5] Newborn brains also process syllables like *bla* more readily than *lba*.[6] And finally, infants as young as 3 months of age already show a rudimentary preference toward puppet characters that appear to help others.[7,8] These results suggest that young infants possess the scaffolding for adult beliefs concerning number, morality, and language and that they arrive in the world equipped with notions such as "1 + 1 is 2." In other words, infants possess a set of *innate ideas* that they have not learned.[9,10] Just as females don't need to "learn" to grow breasts, certain notions are inborn. Some of those traits are present at birth, and this is helpful, because in such cases, learning is easier to rule out. So the discovery that human infants converge on certain notions spontaneously, without learning them from others, provides strong evidence for innate ideas. And these facts are starkly at odds with our intuitive understanding of human nature.

Like Oedipus, we are doubly blind. Not only are we oblivious to how knowledge actually emerges, we are blissfully unaware of our obliviousness. Rather than simply pleading ignorance about the workings of cognition, people incorrectly believe that they know where their knowledge comes from.

In reality, human cognition is part invention and part discovery. Our rational capacities allow us to venture far beyond the principles of core cognition—that is the "invention" part of our cognitive lives. But core cognition paves some of our cognitive paths, and when we instinctively follow those trails, we engage in cognitive discovery, not invention. We are partners in a collaborative project between human nature and human nurture. We, however, incorrectly credit culture, not biology, as the sole sire of our beliefs.

***

Why is our naïve understanding of our cognitive life so distorted? Before I consider this question, allow me a few more words of personal introduction. I am a cognitive scientist. I study how the mind works, and I am particularly interested in the basis of the human capacity for language. Why is it that my daughter, Alma, for instance, has readily acquired English (in fact, she is a native speaker of Spanish and Hebrew too, as is my son Amir; our household is trilingual), whereas her cat Lia, who arrived at our home shortly after Alma's birth, has never managed to utter a single word? In other words, I am asking whether our capacity for language is partly innate.

To address this question, my lab examines what people know about language tacitly and instinctively, without having had the opportunity to learn it. We infer this knowledge from people's behavioral responses to language (for example, the speed with which they press buttons after hearing different words) as well as the measured activities of their brains. With my many collaborators, I study speakers of different languages, both spoken and signed, adults, children and even newborns. So, while my research question might seem abstract, my approach is quite concrete and familiar—I employ the tools of science.

The research I conduct in my lab is not much different from the work that my biologist friends carry out in theirs. My friends and I both ask questions about innateness. I study innate cognitive capacities of the brain, while they examine the innate design of the rest of the body. We design experiments, observe what happens, make inferences, and plan our next move (you guessed it—it's yet another experiment!).

For example, I'm friends with a couple who are both biologists. The wife explores how red blood cells are normally formed from stem cells and why this process is disrupted in leukemia; her husband studies the faulty mechanism of genetic repair leading to breast cancer. When they come over for dinner, we often discuss "what's cooking" in our respective labs. They tell me about their astonishing discoveries (they truly are), and I tell them what I have found. Questions about inborn capacities are their bread and butter. As we talk over a glass of wine, they might ask how we arrived at our conclusions and what we plan to do next. Their main concern (like mine) is to make sure we get the answer right. But the question, *Is any knowledge innate?* is never up for discussion. They don't think it's the slightest bit exotic or unique.

This, however, is not the reaction I get from most people. Ironically, it is not the reaction of most of my colleagues in cognitive science and psychology, either. "Innate" is a loaded word in my field. To paraphrase Queen Elizabeth II (another monarch who's had her share of rough times), it is the *verbum horribile* (Latin for a "horrible word"). My colleagues and I were all trained under its shadow, entrusted with the enormous task of unveiling human nature. "Innateness studies" is precisely what we were supposed to do. Yet whenever the word is uttered out loud, people get visibly uncomfortable. You see a sudden shiver in their faces, a slight twist of the lip or eyelid. Discussions about it often start out civilly, but within a matter of minutes, the blood starts boiling, palms get sweaty, and voices are raised. So lethal are some of my peers' reaction to the idea of innateness that I have had coauthors veto our use of the *i*-word altogether. When I submit my papers for publication in scientific journals, editors and reviewers often demand that I refrain from using it in print.

Why so much fuss about what is simply human nature? Innateness is everywhere in our daily lives: we live in the era of the genome. Curious about your ancestry? No problem—for a modest fee, there is 23andMe! Concerned about a wrongful criminal conviction? DNA may set you free! And "smart medicine," individually tailored to your own genome, can offer effective treatments for a number of diseases. So why do people get so upset about the concept of innateness when it's applied to ideas? Why do we systematically shift the responsibility for our intellectual capacities toward human nurture and experience, denying the role that nature and biology also play? And, most critically, why are we so blind to this tendency? Why aren't we aware of the deep biases that distort the narratives we construct about our own psyches?

***

These questions, no doubt, have not a single right answer but many. One possibility is that our errors are simply due to the limitations of our comprehension. Most laypeople are not aware of the body of science that attests to the amazing intellectual lives of infants. Additionally, our life experiences present us with ample evidence of learning. We know that the language we speak depends on the language of our family and community; that children learn about numbers in school, and that parents preach to their children about right and wrong. So perhaps our intuitive grasp of our own psychology is faulty simply because on the one hand we lack the requisite knowledge of it and, on the other, because we are overly focused on our own experiences with learning.

Articulating this sentiment, the philosopher Peter Carruthers suggests that people are victims of our obsession with our own minds.[11] We constantly interpret people's actions—both our own and others'—by "reading" their minds. We conclude that *John left the room* because he *wanted* to get a coffee, or that *Mary opened the window* because she *felt* warm. All this *want* and *feel* stuff are mental states that we ascribe to people. And in our implicit "theories" of minds, beliefs are the product of three processes: experience (*People typically go to Starbucks to get coffee*), communication (*John said he went to Starbucks*) and inference (*If Starbucks customers typically seek coffee and John went to Starbucks, then John was probably seeking coffee*). These three modes of belief fixation (experience, communication, and inference) serve us pretty well, so according to Carruthers, we feel no need to consider a fourth "Baroque" route—the possibility that some beliefs are innate. People, then, are just blissfully content in their ignorance. Perhaps, but that still doesn't account for the vehemence of our denial.

Another answer is that our innate instincts might be inherently impenetrable. As the evolutionary psychologists Leda Tooby and John Cosmides have pointed out,[12] to recognize first-hand that reasoning is guided by innate knowledge, one must gain access to the inner workings of our minds. But instincts are notoriously inconspicuous. Like your favorite glasses, they are so familiar that when you try to find them, you fail to notice that they are sitting right on (or rather, in) your head.

Optical illusions can help us find our "mental glasses." At first glance, the white lines in Figure 2.1 appear to be two different lengths. In reality, however, they are the same—you can verify this by measuring them, or by seeing how they match up to the two vertical lines, which are parallel. Visual illusions show us that our perceptions of the visual world are not faithful "photos" taken by our senses but active constructions of our minds, based on principles that are innate. But we are so used to experiencing reality through these mental lenses that we are blind to their existence. We believe that they faithfully reveal external reality, rather than partly reflect our inner selves.

I certainly agree with these arguments. Many of our cognitive capacities are inaccessible to our conscious minds, and our reasoning about their internal workings could be further compromised by our personal experiences and the gaps in our scientific knowledge. I nonetheless doubt that these are the sole reasons for our blindness to human nature. If this were the case, then people would easily shift their views once they were presented with good evidence for innate knowledge.

Figure 2.1. An optical illusion.
Drawing by Mario Ponzo, licensed under Creative Commons; gray lines are added.

But most people, even highly educated ones, who have been exposed to precisely such evidence, greet the notion of innate ideas with extreme skepticism. When the Harvard biologist E. O. Wilson suggested that some aspects of human social behavior, like the social behaviors of ants and other animals, can be partly explained by the workings of evolutionary biology,[13] the popular reaction was deeply emotional and quite vocal. People seem to actively *resist* the very notion of innate ideas.

Why do we insist that our minds must be blank slates, born free of any pre-existing content? Why do we believe it is only experience, not human nature, that inscribes our intellectual fates? In his book *The Blank Slate*,[14] the psychologist Steven Pinker attributed this resistance to the social and moral implications of innateness.

The notion that some mental capacities are innate could exacerbate racism and sexism and even justify some forms of discrimination. Testing—and even worse, confirming—innate cognitive differences between groups of people can't but encourage prejudice, many people believe. Even if we stick to the seemingly less-charged question of the differences between the genders, innateness seems to threaten the notion of equality that forms the foundation of liberal society. If males are more likely to excel in math and spatial reasoning than women, for example, then perhaps, some will conclude, our limited resources for math and engineering education should be invested exclusively in boys, and high-tech companies should continue to favor male over female job applicants. If, on the other hand, males are more prone to aggression, then perhaps only female criminal offenders should be eligible for rehabilitation services and early parole.

But, as Pinker notes, such arguments are based on several fallacies. First, the genetic differences between populations of distinct ancestries are small, and they mostly concern physical adaptations to climate, such as skin pigment and eyelid folds. It is in principle possible that distinct populations could show subtle and limited differences in certain cognitive capacities that are genetically based (the processing of linguistic tones in languages such as Mandarin Chinese is possibly a case in point, as the prevalence of tones has been linked to certain geographic conditions and to the frequency of certain genetic alleles in the people who live in those places[15,16]). But systematic differences in aptitude are quite another matter. As Pinker notes, such genetic differences are not expected on theoretical grounds, nor are they found.

Gender differences are another matter, however, as males and females have different reproductive roles, which could have led to the evolution of cognitive and personality characteristics that affect their mating and parenting behaviors. Indeed, males do outperform females on spatial skills, although several recent studies found no reliable gender differences in mathematical abilities.[17,18] But even if males, on average, were slightly more mathematical than females, this would still leave wide open the possibility that some women will be outstanding mathematicians (the late Maryam Mirzakhani, the winner of the 2014 Fields Medal, informally known as the Nobel Prize for Math, attests to that) and that a good number of women will have mathematical capacities that outstrip those of most men.

Most important, the recognition of differences between groups does not justify discrimination against individuals. We all agree that the identification of genetic risk factors for disease should not be grounds for denying anyone their healthcare coverage. On the contrary, such information can be used to promote life-saving measures. For example, the discovery that certain mutations to BRCA1 and BRCA2 genes present a significant risk for breast cancer allows women who carry those mutations to protect themselves by early screening and elective mastectomies. There is no reason that innate cognitive differences should be treated any differently.

Finally, recognizing some of the darker innate aspects of human nature does not mean we must succumb to them. In fact, we *know* we can overcome them. The human mind includes a plethora of cognitive attributes and capacities. Some—our instinctive suspicion of outsiders, for example—might push us toward the darkness, but others allow us to reason, reflect on our instincts, and subject them to checks and balances. As Pinker argues, these are the "better angels" that guide us on the path toward enlightenment.[19,20] Identifying our darker instincts does not make us more evil, any more than recognizing a higher risk for cancer makes us get sick. In fact, it gives us our best chance for a cure. So not only does the study of innate ideas not threaten liberalism, it can be its guardian angel and protector, a beacon for progress and hope. But for people who believe otherwise, the notion of a blank slate—of minds that are born without biases or unequal capacities—seems to offer a bulwark against such imaginary dangers to individual freedom. By rejecting nativism (the notion that some aspects of our mind are innate), they hope to eliminate all unjust disparities between individuals and ultimately erase every trace of aggression, prejudice, and greed.

Pinker is right to note that our resistance to nativism stems from an active revulsion to it, not just passive ignorance, and he is also right to underscore our worries about the dangerous social and moral implications of nativism gone awry. But I think that these social and philosophical considerations only scratch the surface of why we are so uncomfortable with the notion of innate ideas.

For one thing, our moral and social resistance to innateness should make us resistant to every form of nativism. We should be particularly averse to the innate emotions and personality traits that are associated with aggression, which is the most obvious precursor for social digression and harm. Compared to those, innate ideas about number should seem relatively innocuous. But, in fact, people seem to be *more* willing to grant the existence of innate emotions than innate ideas; in fact, they insist that emotions are innate, even when they are told that they are actually learned from experience (more on this in Chapter 10). Moreover, when people justify their aversion to innateness, they do not always cite their social and moral reservations. Some of the most ardent opponents of nativism appeal not to ethics but to ontology—the philosophical analysis of the nature of being. In the words of the right-wing gadfly Tom Bethell, a vehement opponent of E. O. Wilson's sociobiology:

> Wilson's lifelong "dream of a unifying theory" materialized between hard covers in his 1998 bestseller *Consilience*, [which argues that] . . . everything is material, everything can be reduced to the laws of physics, everything that is alive ipso facto evolved. Mind is matter.[21]

Make no mistake—I vehemently disagree with Bethell on most matters (the author of *The Politically Incorrect Guide to Science*, he has argued that Darwin's theory of evolution is bad science and that "intelligent design" is not). But I find his reasoning instructive, as it vividly demonstrates why people resist the possibility that knowledge is inborn. In Bethell's view, the innateness of human nature is inconceivable *because it obliterates the distinction between mind and matter.*

Bethell's words reflect a broadly shared assumption that mind and matter are distinct entities. Philosophically, this is known as Dualism—the idea, famously articulated by René Descartes (1596–1690) in his *Sixth Meditation*, that "inasmuch as [the body] is only an extended and unthinking thing, it is certain that this I (that is to say, my soul by which I am what I am), is entirely and absolutely distinct from my body, and can exist without it."[22p28]

For Descartes, Dualism is an ontological claim about what entities exist in reality. Bodies and minds are distinct, he declares, and he arrives at this conclusion as a result of a deliberate process of reasoning. But Dualism is also a psychological principle that our brains instinctively impose on our representation of reality. Much as your brain tricks you into believing that the two lines in Figure 2.1 are different lengths, so does it lead you to believe that bodies and minds must be comprised of different substances. In the psychological sense, Dualism describes how we view reality instinctively (as distinct from the nature of reality itself, inferred by scientific and philosophical reflection).[23]

We instinctively believe that our bodies are material—comprised of living cells, made of molecules of matter—and that bodily functions like breathing and digestion proceed according to the laws of physics. But our minds seem different to us. We tend to view thinking, belief, memory, and planning as immaterial. If you believe that the earth is round or that God is almighty, you don't ascribe this belief to some chemical reaction in your brain. Some cultures believe that the mind exists prior to the birth of the body and that it will remain thereafter (and, as we'll see in Chapter 14, many secular Westerners believe this too).

This instinctive Dualist bias helps us understand why we recoil at the notion of innate ideas. For Bethell, Dualism is a fundamental truth. So strong is his belief in the mind–body dichotomy that the mere hint of its obliteration ("mind is matter") seems to violate an immutable law of nature. Since Bethell believes that nature is the creation of a deity, Wilson's materialism is blasphemous and hence evil.

But Dualism is a psychological bias, rather than a position grounded in science. Most cognitive scientists do attribute our mental lives to the workings of our brains. When you hold a belief (*The building is on fire!*) that mental state corresponds to some physical state of the brain that is different from what it would be if you held a contrary opinion (*It's just a drill*). Scientists nonetheless choose to couch their explanations of our mental behaviors in terms of cognition (what we *think* and *remember*) because they still have only a rudimentary understanding of the workings of our brains. So at least for now, the cognitive level provides a more convenient level of analysis.

That is not an unusual scientific choice. Many aspects of nature can be described at multiple levels. Chemical reactions, for instance, can be described at the level of atoms and molecules (in chemistry) or as the forces at play between subatomic quarks and strings (in physics). When chemists choose to couch their explanation at the molecular level, they do so because this level of explanation provides the simplest and richest account of the phenomenon of interest. Cognitive scientists choose to construct their explanations at the cognitive (mental) level for similar pragmatic reasons, not because they believe "mind" and "brain" are distinct scientific entities.

Dualism is likewise not grounded in ethics. Contrary to Bethell's fears, the unification of mind and body does not make us the same as any other material thing. When I state that both you and your cell phone are made of matter, I am not saying that we should license updates of human systems and recycle old ones. Nor does this view obliterate the self by reducing us all to zombies that are indistinguishable from one another or threaten our individual rights and values. On the contrary, having a material view of our minds protects our individuality and human dignity. If a loved one were to lose their memory to Alzheimer's or their personality to profound depression, we would still regard them as themselves and eagerly accept any medical fix that would restore them by manipulating the physical properties of their bodies.

But it is precisely because Bethell's indignation is devoid of any scientific or ethical basis that it is so revealing. His rage emanates from the depths of his psychological cave, and it speaks in the voice of the blind prisoners trapped within it. At root, Dualism is a strong intuitive conviction that underpins our naïve understanding of our psyches. And as I will explain below (and in much more detail in subsequent chapters), its hold on us is part and parcel of our gut resistance to the possibility of innate knowledge.

***

Here, in a nutshell, is the gist of what I will argue. I believe that our resistance to innate ideas is but one of many examples of our blindness to our own human nature. And I suggest that all of these cases of self-blindness arise from the collision between two titanic forces that are buried deep within our psyches. Both, ironically, are likely to be innate ideas. The first is our instinctive belief in Dualism—the notion that our minds are immaterial, distinct, and separable from our material bodies. The other is our deep-seated belief in Essentialism—the idea that living things are each defined by some innate, immutable, but necessarily material essence. I have briefly introduced these two principles in Chapter 1—let me now elaborate a bit more.

Infants are natural Dualists. They recognize that bodies are material entities that are governed by the laws of physics. Agents, in contrast, follow goals, set by their beliefs and desires, which are immaterial mental states. Laboratory experiments have borne this out. When presented with a stationary ball, an infant expects it to move only if it is contacted by another moving object in line with the laws of physics that apply to all material objects (we can infer this by judging their reactions when their expectations are violated by having the stationary ball initiate its movement not immediately after its contact with the moving object, but only after a slight delay; I will have more to say about this in Chapter 3).[5,24,25] But when infants are presented with a self-propelled object, they will view it as agentive and interpret its movement based on psychological principles such as "goal," rather than by purely physical principles. For example, when an infant sees a rectangle hop continuously over obstacles as it approaches a circle (see Figure 2.2a), he or she will assume that the rectangle is driven by its goal of reaching the circle. Once the obstacle is removed, the infant will expect the rectangle to change its trajectory and approach its goal in the simplest possible way—along a straight line (see Figure 2.2b), rather than by hopping (as it did before).[26] Dualism is an

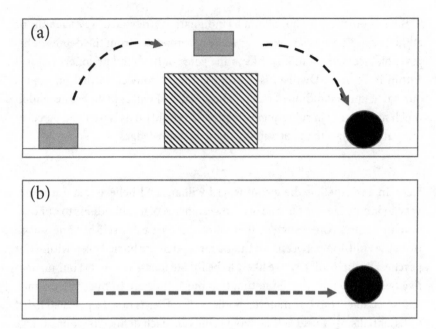

Figure 2.2. A test of goal-oriented movement.
Redrawn from Scholl and Tremoulet (2000),[27] with permission.

innate psychological principle; to paraphrase the psychologist Paul Bloom, we are all Descartes' babies.[23]

But people are also instinctive Essentialists. When we reason about what renders cats distinct from dogs and raccoons from skunks, we assume that these living things are each defined by some innate immutable essence that must be material. Even if we know nothing about genetics, we still assume that these species possess distinct material essences that are transmitted to them from their mothers.

These two innate principles—about the material essence of living things and the immaterial basis of knowledge—collide whenever people reason about innate cognition. Think about it: if innate traits must be material (as per Essentialism), and knowledge must be immaterial (per Dualism), then it follows syllogistically that knowledge (cognition) cannot be innate.

Our resistance to the notion of innate ideas, including knowledge, beliefs, and goals, is neither a result of passive ignorance nor an active, logically constructed philosophical/social stance. People actively resist the notion of innate ideas not only because nonnativist modes of belief formation are salient (per Carruthers' view), because our cognitive instincts are opaque to us (per Cosmides and Tooby's proposal) or because they are threatening (per Pinker). It's not that people are not willing to consider the possibility of innate knowledge. It is rather that, in a way, they *cannot*. Doing so contradicts the basic workings of their psyches.

To be clear, these twin core principles—Dualism and Essentialism—do not account for the entire arsenal of our cognitive capacities by any stretch of the imagination. People are certainly capable of engaging in deliberate analysis, and it is this capacity that explains how some philosophers and psychologists are able to consider the innate nature of the human mind, and why my biologist friends (who are adept at thinking about the innate design of organisms) are more open to the possibility of innate ideas than many of my psychologist colleagues, who are typically trained in a different intellectual tradition. But these conclusions, the products of effortful deliberations, are distinct from what our core cognition whispers in our ears. Our gut instinct is that knowledge cannot be innate.

Just as Bethell fears, to acknowledge innate knowledge is to erase the dichotomy between mind and matter. And while the proposition that "mind is matter" is both scientifically plausible and ethically defensible, it is one that is exceedingly uncomfortable for humans to hold, because it violates the core principles of Dualism and Essentialism that guide the inner workings of our cognition. Just as the ancient Greeks feared, when it comes to ideas, our blindness to our nature is inscribed in our nature. People are innately antinativist.

***

The consequences of this blindness cannot be overestimated. How we come to know what we know is a question that has preoccupied humanity from the dawn of history. The discovery that our reasoning about innate knowledge is systematically biased challenges centuries of academic debate and much of the current received wisdom in numerous academic disciplines, while at the same time shedding new light on many of our everyday concerns.

Early discussions of the origins of knowledge took place within philosophy. These sought to determine what knowledge is and how it is obtained. The first question—*What is knowledge?*—concerns what statements we can ascertain to be true. Can I ascertain that my cat is gray or that the sun will rise tomorrow? And what about inferences? If you knew that all cats are gray, could you be certain that this would hold for your own cat or mine? "What we know," however, is intimately linked to our account of how knowledge is obtained. "Rationalist" philosophers, such as Plato (roughly 423–348 BCE), Descartes, and Immanuel Kant (1724–1804), asserted that knowledge can only be grasped by reasoning, rather than by our senses; consequently, knowledge must be innate to the human mind. The Empiricists—most notably, the British philosophers John Locke (1632–1704), George Berkeley (1685–1753), and David Hume (1711–1776)—credited knowledge to experience. Let's briefly consider some of their arguments.

In Plato's view, knowledge is infallible—it is always true, absolute, and unchanging: "Those who see the absolute and eternal and immutable may be said to know"[28BkVp399]. But the impressions of our senses are neither reliable nor eternal. The prisoners in Plato's allegory of the cave were deceived by their eyes; they believed that the shades on the cave's wall were real. As I am looking at my cat, he appears gray, but under party lights, he will turn green and orange. Since my visual impression of this particular instance (my own cat, as opposed to the concept of CAT generally) is transitory, contradictory, and relative, it cannot be the basis of knowledge:

> All things are said to be relative; you cannot rightly call anything by any name, such as great or small, heavy or light, for the great will be small and the heavy light—there is no single thing or quality, but out of motion and change and admixture all things are becoming relatively to one another.[29p8]

Knowledge, on the other hand, concerns universals (the concept of CAT generally, rather than my cat or yours), so it cannot be acquired from the experience of the senses. It thus follows that all knowledge exists in advance of sensory experience—it must be innate.

To demonstrate this point, Plato describes a dialogue between Socrates and a slave boy who had no prior instruction in geometry. Remarkably, the boy is shown to possess knowledge related to the Pythagorean theorem (to double the area of a square, one must draw a square on the diagonal of the original square). Socrates coaxes the boy's inborn knowledge out into the light through systematic questioning, much as a midwife helps a mother deliver an infant into the world.[29] He does not teach the child so much as he helps him recollect what he already knew.[30]

John Locke, the founder of Empiricism, challenges this conclusion. For Locke, "reason" consists not just of statements that can be ascertained to be true but also of ones that are probably true.[31] The grounds of probability are either "conformity with our experience, or the testimony of others' experience."[31ch15§4] Locke, however, sees no reason "to believe, that the soul thinks before the senses have furnished it with ideas to think on."[32Bk2Ch1p20] In fact, he ridicules the notion of innate ideas. "It is evident," he wrote, "that all children and idiots have not the least apprehension or thought of them."[32Ch2§5] The fact that uneducated people (such as Plato's slave boy) can assent to statements that they have never learned presents no evidence of innateness, "since men never fail, after they have once understood the words, to acknowledge them for undoubted truths."[32§17] He offers yet another challenge to innate ideas by counterexamples, showing that those putative universal notions are not universal at all. Even the belief in God is not held universally, as there are entire nations who are devoid of any sense of the divine.[32Ch4§8] In the light of such observations, Locke concludes that knowledge emerged only from experience. In his famous words, the mind is like a blank sheet of paper:

> Let us then suppose the mind to be, as we say, white paper void of all character, without any ideas. How come it to be furnished? Whence comes it by that vast store which the busy and boundless fancy of man has painted on it with an almost endless variety? Whence has it all the materials of reason and knowledge? To this I answer, in one word: from experience.[32Bk2Ch1§2]

Locke's position is implicit in much research in the social sciences and humanities (these discussions are concerned with the origin of human beliefs, rather than with their truth, but for simplicity, I will continue to use the term "knowledge" to refer to them). For example, the anthropologist Margaret Mead states: "We are forced to conclude that human nature is almost unbelievably malleable, responding accurately and contrastingly to cultural conditions."[33p262] Emile Durkheim, the father of sociology, asserted that our major conceptual categories are shaped by religion, which is a social construct. It thus follows that those categories are likewise constructed:

> At the root of our judgment, there are certain fundamental notions that dominate our entire intellectual life. It is these ideas that philosophers, beginning with Aristotle, have called the categories of understanding: notions of time, space, number, cause substance, personality. . . . Now, when we analyze primitive religious beliefs methodically, one naturally finds the principal categories among them. They are born in and from religion: they are

a product of religious thought. . . . Religion is an eminently social thing. Religious representations are collective representations that express collective realities. . . . But if the categories are religion: They, too, must be social things, products of collective thoughts.[34pp8-9]

The linguist/anthropologist Daniel Everett follows suit:

In what follows I propose a model of how we become who we are as individuals and societies, based on the acquisition and organization of particulars. But these particulars do not include the building blocks of some grander theories—I am not concerned directly with such familiar anthropological themes as totemism, animism, ethics, religion, folk theories of health and reproduction, and so on. That is because I believe that none of these are basic, but derivative, based upon more primitive building blocks that emerge naturally from living. They require no psychic unity of man, no nativism, and, especially, they require no innate content or concepts.[35pviii]

And the historian Yuval Noah Harari suggests that the confines of biology may no longer define human destiny:

Natural selection may have provided Homo sapiens with a much larger playing field than it has given to any other organism, but the field has still had its boundaries. The implication has been that, no matter what their efforts and achievements, Sapiens are incapable of breaking free of their biologically determined limits.

But at the dawn of the twenty-first century, this is no longer true. Homo sapiens is transcending those limits. It is now beginning to break the laws of natural selection, replacing them with the laws of intelligent design.[36p397]

Many psychologists and cognitive scientists share Locke's aversion to innate ideas. Linda Smith, for instance, states:

Many theorists of cognitive development have looked at the diversity of human knowledge and at the certainty with which children acquire it all and have come to the conclusion that the building blocks of knowledge are made of knowledge itself, that babies begin the task of cognitive development with enabling concepts and principles. . . . As the saying goes, one cannot get something from nothing. These theorists are mistaken, however.

One can get something from nothing, or at least, something much much more from something much much less. A chain of moment-to-moment mundane causes and effects can over time create something that did not exist before. This is developmental process.[37p133]

Lawrence Barsalou goes even farther. In his view, not only are there no innate abstract concepts; there are no abstract concepts at all. We encode only the details of specific sensory and motor interactions:

> Standard theories of cognition assume that knowledge resides in a semantic memory system separate from the brain's modal systems for perception (e.g., vision, audition), action (e.g., movement, proprioception), and introspection (e.g., mental states, affect). . . . Conceptions of grounded cognition take many different forms (Gibbs 2006, Wilson 2002). In general, however, they reject the standard view that amodal symbols represent knowledge in semantic memory. . . . As an experience occurs (e.g., easing into a chair), the brain captures states across the modalities and integrates them with a multimodal representation stored in memory (e.g., how a chair looks and feels, the action of sitting, introspections of comfort and relaxation). Later, when knowledge is needed to represent a category (e.g., chair), multimodal representations captured during experiences with its instances are reactivated to simulate how the brain represented perception, action, and introspection associated with it.[38p618]

My colleague Lisa Feldman-Barrett challenges the nativist account of emotions. In her view, "emotion perception is not innate but constructed."[39p52]

Similar reservations about innateness are expressed with respect to the origins of language. The linguist Noam Chomsky has famously suggested that language is a capacity we possess innately.[40–42] We are not born knowing English or French. Rather, we innately possess a set of universal tacit rules that are common to all human language—a Universal Grammar. Steven Pinker further suggested that language is a human instinct and, along with Paul Bloom, argued that language is shaped by natural selection.[43,44] But many psychologists and linguists believe that proposal is dead wrong. In a paper entitled "Universal Grammar Is Dead," the psychologist Michael Tomasello states"

> The idea of a biologically evolved Universal Grammar with linguistic content is a myth, perpetuated by three spurious explanatory strategies

of generative linguists. To make progress in understanding human linguistic competence, cognitive scientists must abandon the idea of an innate Universal Grammar and instead try to build theories that explain both linguistic universals and diversity and how they emerge.[45p470]

Similarly, the psychologists Moreton Christiansen and Nick Chater suggest that the structure of language is not specified in our genes. Rather, it emerges spontaneously in the process of transmitting language from one generation of speakers to the next, much like the "telephone" game. "The origin of language requires no genetic leap, but the cumulative cultural evolution of language itself."[46p2]

Reading these quotes, you might think that the notion of innate knowledge is totally bankrupt—a mere philosophical speculation that lacks any grounding in modern science. But this is hardly the case. As we will see in the next chapters, a large scientific literature speaks to this very question, and the results suggest that people do, in fact, possess rich knowledge in multiple domains that they are not likely to have had an opportunity to learn from experience. Many of these concepts are present in newborns, and in some cases, we can trace their evolutionary precursors to nonhuman animals.

We saw earlier that laypeople hold similar opinions concerning the origins of their knowledge, that their beliefs are demonstrably biased, and that those biases can be traced to core cognitive mechanisms that shape all human minds. So why are the authors I quoted (and many others) so certain that the notion of innate ideas is wrong? Could these scientists be misled by those same biases?

This question is impossible to answer with absolute certainty. Scientific reasoning is different from the reasoning of the participants in our experiments, who were presented with scenarios that clearly portray traits that are innate. In real science, the facts are not always so clear-cut; it is not unusual for a single datum to give rise to multiple interpretations by different scientists. Showing that scholars disagree about whether human traits are innate is not, in and of itself, evidence that those leaning toward "nay" are biased in their assessments; neither does it prove that their conclusions are due to the effects of the twin forces of Dualism and Essentialism. In short, correlation (between the conclusions of scholars and laypeople) is not evidence of causation. But given the fact that scholars are human and that humans possess biases that demonstrably *do* interfere with their reasoning about these matters, we cannot rule out the possibility that those scientists and scholars

Does she look at history? (Non-western?)
Does she look @ cross-culturally?

might be biased either. This observation is a call to action for everyone involved in the innateness debate—an invitation to take a hard look within, identify our internal biases and, in so doing, put our blindness to human nature on check.

This book, however, is concerned not so much with the scientific debate about human nature as our intuitive reasoning about it. In the remainder of Part I, I will examine our errors in reasoning about *what we think we know*. To put our views in perspective, Chapters 3 to 5 first review what science tells us about the rich mental lives of infants. As we will see, there is good reason to suspect that some ideas are indeed innate. But when laypeople are invited to think about where knowledge comes from, they systematically resist that possibility; the evidence is described in Chapter 6. Having documented our discomfort with innate ideas, I will consider why we are so biased against them (in Chapter 7). Finally, in Chapter 8, I will test my conclusions in another series of experiments.

References

1. Lerdahl F, Jackendoff R. *A generative theory of tonal music.* Cambridge, MA: MIT Press; 1983.
2. Meyer LB. *Emotion and meaning in music.* Chicago, IL: Chicago University of Chicago Press; 1956.
3. Berent I, Platt M, Sandoboe GM. People's intuitions about innateness. *Open Mind: Discoveries in Cognitive Science.* 2019. doi:10.1162/opmi_a_00029
4. Izard V, Sann C, Spelke ES, Streri A. Newborn infants perceive abstract numbers. *PNAS, Proceedings of the National Academy of Sciences of the United States of America.* 2009;106(25):10382–10385.
5. Carey S. *The origin of concepts.* New York, NY: Oxford University Press; 2009.
6. Gómez DM, Berent I, Benavides-Varela S, et al. Language universals at birth. *Proceedings of the National Academy of Sciences of the United States of America.* 2014;111(16):5837–5341.
7. Hamlin JK, Wynn K, Bloom P. Social evaluation by preverbal infants. *Nature.* 2007;450(7169):557–559.
8. Hamlin JK, Wynn K, Bloom P. Three-month-olds show a negativity bias in their social evaluations. *Developmental Science.* 2010;13(6):923–929.
9. Samuels R. Innateness in cognitive science. *Trends Cognitive Sciences.* 2004; 8(3):136–141.
10. Samuels R. Is Innateness a confused concept. In: Carruthers P, Laurence S, Stich S, eds. *The innate mind: foundations and the future.* New York, NY: Oxford University Press; 2007:17–34.
11. Carruthers P. How mindreading might mislead cognitive science. *Journal of Consciousness Studies.* 2020.

12. Cosmides L, Tooby J. Beyond intuition and instinct blindness: toward an evolution-arily rigorous cognitive science. *Cognition*. 1994;50(1):41–77.

13. Wilson EO. *Sociobiology: the new synthesis*. Cambridge, MA: Belknap Press of Harvard University Press; 1975.

14. Pinker S. *The blank slate: the modern denial of human nature*. New York, NY: Viking; 2002.

15. Dediu D, Ladd DR. Linguistic tone is related to the population frequency of the adaptive haplogroups of two brain size genes, ASPM and Microcephalin. *Proceedings of the National Academy of Sciences of the United States of America*. 2007;104(26):10944–10949.

16. Everett C, Blasi DE, Roberts SG. Climate, vocal folds, and tonal languages: Connecting the physiological and geographic dots. *Proceedings of the National Academy of Sciences of the United States of America*. 2015;112(5):1322–1327.

17. Hyde JS. Sex and cognition: gender and cognitive functions. *Current Opinion In Neurobiology*. 2016;38:53–56.

18. Else-Quest NM, Hyde JS, Linn MC. Cross-national patterns of gender differences in mathematics: a meta-analysis. *Psychological Bulletin*. 2010;136(1):103–127.

19. Pinker S. *The better angels of our nature: why violence has declined*. New York, NY: Viking; 2011.

20. Pinker S. *Enlightenment now: the case for reason, science, humanism, and progress*. London, England; 2018.

21. Bethell T. Against sociobiology. 2001. https://www.firstthings.com/article/2001/01/against-sociobiology.

22. Descartes R. Meditations on first philosophy. In: Haldane ES., trans. *The Philosophical Works of Descartes*. Cambridge, England: Cambridge University Press; 1641/1996.

23. Bloom P. *Descartes' baby: how the science of child development explains what makes us human*. New York, NY: Basic Books; 2004.

24. Spelke ES, Kinzler KD. Core knowledge. *Developmental Science*. 2007;10(1):89–96.

25. Spelke ES, Phillips A, Woodward AL. Infants' knowledge of object motion and human action. In: Sperber D, Premack D, Premack AJ, Sperber D, Premack D, Premack AJ, eds. *Causal cognition: a multidisciplinary debate*. New York, NY: Oxford University Press; 1995:44–78.

26. Gergely G, Nádasdy Z, Csibra G, Bíró S. Taking the intentional stance at 12 months of age. *Cognition*. 1995;56(2):165–193.

27. Scholl BJ, Tremoulet PD. Perceptual causality and animacy. *Trends in Cognitive Sciences*. 2000;4(8):299–309.

28. Plato. (1892). *The republic* (B. Jowett, Trans.): Auckland, New Zealand: Floating Press. (Original work published ca. 380 B.C.).

29. Plato. (1990). *Theaetetus* (B. Jowett, Trans.): Raleigh, N.C.: Boulder, Colo. NetLibrary, Inc (Original work published ca. 380 B.C.).

30. Plato. (1990). *Meno* (B. Jowett, Trans.): Raleigh, N.C.: Boulder, Colo. NetLibrary, Inc (Original work published ca. 380 B.C.).

31. Russell B. *A history of Western philosophy*. New York, NY: Simon and Schuster; 1945.

32. Locke J. *The works of John Locke, in nine volumes*. 12th ed. London,: Printed for C. and J. Rivington etc; 1824.

33. Mead M. *Sex and temperament in three primitive societies*. New York:: Harper Collins; 1935/2001.

34. Durkheim E. *The elementary forms of religious life*. New York: Free Press; 1912/1995.

35. Everett DL. *Dark matter of the mind: the culturally articulated unconscious.* Chicago: University of Chicago Press; 2016.

36. Harari YN. *Sapiens: a brief history of humankind.* First U.S. ed: New York, NY: Harper; 2015.

37. Smith LB. Do infants possess innate knowledge structures? The con side. *Developmental Science.* 1999;2(2):133–144.

38. Barsalou LW. Grounded cognition. *Annual Review of Psychology.* 2008;59:617–645.

39. Barrett LF. *How emotions are made: the secret life of the brain.* Boston, MA: Houghton Mifflin Harcourt; 2017.

40. Chomsky N. *Syntactic structures.* The Hague, The Netherlands: Mouton; 1957.

41. Chomsky N. *Language and mind.* Enl. ed. New York, NY: Harcourt Brace Jovanovich; 1972.

42. Chomsky N. *Rules and representations.* New York, NY: Columbia University Press; 1980.

43. Pinker S, Bloom P. Natural language and natural selection. *Behavioral and Brain Sciences.* 1994;13(4):707–784.

44. Pinker S. *The Language instinct.* New York, NY: Morrow; 1994.

45. Tomasello M. Universal grammar is dead. *Behavioral and Brain Sciences.* 2009;32(5):470–471.

46. Christiansen M, H., Chater N. Towards an integrated science of language. *Nature Human Behaviour.* 2017;1.

B. The Rich Mental Lives of Infants

3

Object and Number

In the kingdom of darkness, no one is blind. If you were to spend your entire life in a dark cave, as the prisoners in Plato's allegory did, you would never know that your visual experience was lacking. Even if you never had the opportunity to see your own hand, only its shadow on the cave's wall, you wouldn't know that your visual world was confined. It is only once we step out into the light of day that we can recognize the extent of our blindness.

So, before we can recognize how blind we are to the workings of our innate psyches, we must first examine what science tells us about the origins of our ideas; specifically, about the core innate principles of our cognition. The rich mental lives of infants present the clearest evidence for innateness.

"Rich mental capacities" is not a notion one typically associates with infants. Infants eat and cry, but they do rather poorly on calculus and physics and show little appreciation for Shakespeare and Rembrandt. But infants can do other things, and some of those behaviors can help us unveil their inner psyches. When you get their attention by presenting them with a novel stimulus, they will often stare at it longer or suck harder on a pacifier. Similarly, when their minds are working "overtime," the blood flow to their brains increases, which can be detected by brain imaging methods. These various behavioral and brain responses indicate the infant's ability to detect differences, and once you can identify what infants consider to be "different," you can infer what cognitive distinctions they can make. All you have to do is present them with two conditions that contrast minimally and observe their response—for example, two types of words (say, *blog* vs. *lbog*) that differ only in the sequencing of their sounds (but share the same voice and intonation). If infants can encode this dimension, then once you change the condition (say, from *lbog* to *blog*), their response (in brain or behavior) should change. The precise directions of response—whether infants prefer to listen longer to an unusual syllable like *lbog* or would rather spend more time attending to the more pleasant *blog*—is secondary (and is not always predictable). What

The Blind Storyteller. Iris Berent, Oxford University Press (2020). © Iris Berent, 2020.
DOI: 10.1093/oso/9780190061920.001.0001

matters, for us, is that their response *changes*. If it does, then the infant must have encoded this notion.

What's more, such experiments can further tell us *how* infants encode those distinctions: whether they only register sensory qualities, such as changes in sight, sound, smell, scent, and touch, or whether they draw on abstract notions, such as "object," "agent," and perhaps even "syllable" (I will explain exactly how this is done later).

The experimental results we will discuss in the next three chapters suggest that infants already possess a rich set of concepts within the first weeks or months of life. Some of those concepts are even evident at birth. To illustrate this, Chapter 3 examines our core understanding of object and number; Chapter 4 moves to the social realm; and Chapter 5 explores the dawn of language.

These three chapters are not intended to provide an exhaustive account of the full cognitive capacities of infants. Instead, by focusing on a few select cases, I will show that, from their first hours on earth, infants display a rich knowledge of concepts and principles that are likely innate. Before we start, a word of caution: some of these discussions can get quite technical and their link to my main argument is indirect. My main goal, you might recall, is to demonstrate that we are blind to innate knowledge. I include this review to show that, contrary to what we believe, knowledge may well be innate. You the reader can pick and choose the extent to which you wish to engage with this material, depending on your own interests.

The Makings of an Object: Cohesion, Contact, Continuity

Like most winter days in Florida, the morning of January 28, 1986 was clear and sunny. Following the countdown, the space shuttle Challenger lifted off with immense thrust and fury. But less than two minutes into its flight, the enormous metal object disintegrated. Millions of bewildered viewers witnessed the catastrophe, on television and in person. It took them a fraction of a second to recognize exactly what had happened, but even before they could grasp the horrific implications for the Challenger's seven crew members, their reaction was utter shock.

Solid objects are supposed to stay that way. We expect them to move as *cohesive* bounded wholes, not as a bundle of distinct fragments. This expectation is mostly tacit, but it is nonetheless there, and it guides our interpretation of reality. The possibility that the moving space shuttle was comprised of thousands of distinct pieces never even crosses our minds. Our surprise when these expectations are violated, the horror that we feel, even before we've consciously processed the event, is indicative of just how powerful our concept of a solid object is.

Remarkably, this concept is abstract, distinct from the impressions of our senses. To recognize this fact, consider how you interpret a moving object that is partially occluded. Imagine that the diagonal black rod in Figure 3.1A were to move back and forth behind the occluding horizontal gray rod (as indicated by the arrow). Now, suppose the occluding horizontal rod is removed to reveal the blue rod in full view. What would you expect it to look like?

Clearly, you would expect to see the cohesive object in C (Figure 3.1), rather than the fragmented one in B. But this expectation is not supported by your sensory experience. At no point did your retina register any continuity between the top and bottom parts of the diagonal black object—the tiny blank section separating the upper and lower parts in B was never seen as black. Although you are certain you saw C, your sensory experience was actually consistent with B.

This expectation shows that your original understanding of the occluded object A (Figure 3.1) was determined by the notion that moving objects are *cohesive*; discontinuous objects such as B do not typically move as a whole. And since this notion has no support from the sensory information provided by your eyes, it must be abstract. In fact, our concept of the object applies

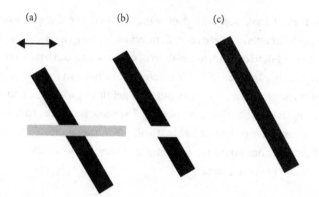

(a)　　　　　　(b)　　　　　(c)

Figure 3.1. A test of the cohesion of objects.
Redrawn, from Valenza et al. (2006).[1]

across multiple modalities. If, instead of seeing the complete object (C) we were to feel it with our hand, we would still link this tactile experience to the partially occluded object in A. This shows that the principle of cohesion is neither visual nor tactile. Rather it forms part and parcel of our notion of an object, and this notion is not sensory but abstract.

***

But where did this abstract concept come from? We, adults, have had countless interactions with moving objects—rods, airplanes, and space shuttles—and these experiences could have shaped our notion of objects. Perhaps we start our intellectual lives with no abstract notion of objects at all. If a newborn infant's first view of her mother is partly occluded by the rail of her crib, perhaps she might perceive two different objects, a head/torso and a pair of legs, rather than one. Similarly, the newborn would interpret the occluded object in Figure 3.1 as B, not C. Only later, through thousands of encounters with partly hidden visual objects, would she learn to associate their real forms with the fully visible object in C. Our initial understanding of the physical world could be guided only by the registry of our senses.

This account, as we saw in Chapter 2, corresponds to the view advocated by empiricist philosophers. The empiricists asserted that knowledge is obtained solely from the sum of our sensory experiences with the world. To the extent that we hold an abstract, multimodal notion of an object, this notion must have emerged through multiple sensory experiences. We can recognize how the rod in Figure 3.1A looks and feels because we have experienced it through multiple senses. In the words of the philosopher David Hume,

> If a man can't have some kind of sensation because there is something wrong with his eyes, ears etc., he will never be found to have corresponding ideas. A blind man can't form a notion of colours, or a deaf man a notion of sounds. If either is cured of his deafness or blindness, so that the sensations can get through to him, the ideas can then get through as well; and then he will find it easy to conceive these objects. The same is true for someone who has never experienced an object that will give a certain kind of sensation. A Laplander ... has no notion of the taste of wine because he has never had the sensation of tasting wine.[2pp8-9]

Rationalist philosophers, such as Plato, Descartes, and Kant, disagree; they argue that at least some concepts are inborn. We don't have to learn that the partial sensory impression in object A corresponds to the object C because the interpretation in B is immediately ruled out by our innate notion that moving objects are cohesive. Since this notion of an object is abstract, rather than strictly visual or tactile, it is conceivable that infants (and adults) could spontaneously generalize it across different sensory forms. So even if your experience of a particular object were solely haptic (i.e., tactile), you would still be able to recognize it once it was presented to you visually. In fact, you should be able to do so even if you have never had *any* visual experience at all.

An interesting test of this possibility was suggested by the philosopher William Molyneux (1656–1698), who wondered what a blind person would see if she were to suddenly gain sight. Here is the description of the problem (as recounted by the philosopher John Locke):

> Suppose a man born blind, and now adult, and taught by his touch to distinguish between a cube and a sphere of the same metal, and nighly of the same bigness, so as to tell, when he felt one and the other, which is the cube, which the sphere. Suppose then the cube and sphere placed on a table, and the blind man be made to see: quære, "whether by his sight, before he touched them, he could now distinguish and tell, which is the globe, which the cube?" [3p28]

The answer partly depends on our notion of an object. If it is strictly sensory (as the empiricists argue), then our first visual encounter with an object will be utterly unrelated to our past haptic experiences with the same object. This was reportedly Molyneux's own answer, which Locke wholeheartedly endorsed.[3] On the other hand, if our notion of an object, say a cube, is at least partly abstract, then it should be *in principle* possible to project it to the novel sensory input from sight.

I say "in principle" because in practice, the outcome of this thought experiment depends not only on our notion of an object (abstract or sensory) but also on neuroscience. Innateness concerns the inborn capacities of human brains. But Molyneux's conundrum concerns not a newborn but an adult. And the adult brain is not equivalent to that of a newborn child.

Blind people rely heavily on haptic and auditory information, and those experiences can "take over" some of the brain turf that is typically dedicated to visual processing. For example, my colleague, the neurologist Alvaro Pascual-Leone, has shown that blind people recruit the brain's visual system when they read Braille (a tactile process).[4] Another line of research, from the lab of Amir Amedi, has shown that the brain areas that are typically engaged by visual inputs can respond to sound. These experiments created auditory "soundscapes" of visual objects and letters by systematically mapping their spatial coordinates onto the frequency and loudness of auditory tones. The rising stroke of a T, for instance, is indicated by a rising tone, the horizontal line corresponds to a flat tone, etc. Remarkably, when presented to blind people, these auditory landscapes activate brain areas that are typically associated with vision.[5]

These results suggest that Molyneux grossly underestimated the complexity of visual perception. Tacit in Molyneux's problem is the assumption that vision is a sensory process that shares nothing with audition and touch. But the picture that is emerging from modern neuroscience suggests that the "visual" brain system is not strictly visual, inasmuch as those same areas also respond to inputs that are haptic and auditory. Visual processing, then, is defined not only by the sensory input (typically optic) but also by the abstract computations it effects (recognizing the abstract shape of a square, or the right angle in a T). And those computations, apparently, are not confined to sight.

Molyneux further underestimated the challenge facing the blind. He implicitly assumed that if a blind person gained sight, their visual system would be fully functional immediately, as is the case with a newborn child. But modern scientific findings suggest that blindness causes the visual system to be reorganized as brain areas associated with vision are reassigned to nonoptical inputs (like the soundscapes of visual objects), and even to computations that are utterly unrelated to vision, such as the extraction of syntactic organization in language.[6] The "take-over" of those visual turfs can occur quite rapidly. Sighted individuals begin to show these changes after being blindfolded for just five days.[7] For this reason, it is unclear whether a newly sighted individual could immediately recognize objects by sight even if our notion of an object is abstract and innate.

The most recent evidence from newly sighted individuals is indeed mixed. The findings come from congenitally blind people who underwent successful cataract surgery. One such study reported data from five Indian children (mostly teenagers) who were tested 48 hours after their surgeries.[8] First, they were invited to explore an object using either sight or touch. Next, they were presented with two objects, either visually or haptically, and asked to determine which of the two matched the original objects. Results showed that they were able to perfectly identify the objects when the target and test were presented in the same modality (either visually or haptically), but they were unable to link the information across modalities (e.g., from touch to sight). In another study, a 3-year-old Tibetan child had reportedly recognized her hand immediately after the removal of her eye patch after surgery. When tested 3 days after surgery, she was further able to successfully identify a visual target that she had previously both touched and seen. But unlike the older children in the previous study (who were *only* able to identify objects *within* modality), this younger girl was unable to accomplish the task by relying on a single modality––either by sight only or by touch only.[9]

So, the conclusions emerging from these studies are akin to a partly full glass. The "half full" perspective is that children in both studies were able to identify visual objects almost immediately after the onset of vision; the "half empty" take is that these children showed a limited capacity to connect sight to touch. But given their long period of blindness prior to surgery, there is no reason to expect their brains to match those of sighted children. So, sadly, Molyneux's test may not be able to determine whether our notion of an object is innately abstract.

Newborn infants, in contrast, can be tested more directly, though I should point out that they are not devoid of sensory experience when they come into the world. By the third trimester of gestation, a fetus can hear her mother's voice[10] and can even contrast distinct light configurations that are shone on her mother's abdomen.[11] But since light and sound must pass through thick tissue, the sensory information is highly degraded and impoverished. Newborns have never seen a square or a triangle, and their acoustic experience in utero is probably too coarse to distinguish linguistic sounds like *b* and *p* (more on this in Chapter 5). So, while newborns are not sensory blank slates, their experiences are nonetheless highly limited. And consequently, their behavior can shed light on the origins of concepts.

If our concept of an object is innate and abstract, then a newborn's response to an object should not depend solely on its sensory qualities. Similarly, when given the opportunity to touch an object, newborns should be able to immediately recognize it by sight. Suppose, for example, the infant discovered a pacifier hidden under a blanket and explored it with her mouth. If her mother were to next show her the same pacifier, along with another one that was different in shape and touch, the infant would immediately be able to tell by sight which one is the familiar pacifier and which one is not. (This has been tested under laboratory conditions, as will be seen below).

***

For many centuries, the origins of knowledge and the capacities of newborns were strictly the purview of philosophical rather than scientific inquiry, as they could only be approached via thought as opposed to laboratory experiments. But now we can test newborns using a variety of experimental techniques, some of which were described earlier in this chapter. And the results speak directly to their innate mental capacities.

To determine whether prior experience with an object is necessary before a concept can be formed of it, one can examine the expectations of a newborn infant who is likely viewing it for the first time. Do newborns know that moving objects are cohesive? Are they surprised when this notion (for which they have had no evidence) is violated?

It turns out that they are. In a study by Eloisa Valenza, Irene Leo, Lucia Gava, and Francesca Simion,[1] newborn infants were first presented with a movie featuring a diagonal moving rod that is partly occluded behind a horizontal bar, similar to the one shown in Figure 3.1 (to overcome the limitations of the immature visual systems of newborns, the movement was stroboscopic, such that the rod "jumped" back and forth, rather than moved continuously). Next, infants were presented simultaneously with two objects, B and C, one on each side of the screen. If newborns expect the occluded object to be cohesive, then when presented with the two options, B and C, they should be more interested in the novel fragmented object (B) compared to the expected cohesive object (C).

This is exactly what they did. This did not happen because the fragmented object B is inherently more interesting. When another group of infants was presented with the two options, B and C, without having previously seen the occlusion event (in A), they showed no special interest in the fragmented object B. This shows that the fragmented object is not more interesting in and of itself. Rather, newborns in the original experiment were more interested in the fragmented object because the cohesive object C was what they expected to see—it matched their representation of the previous occlusion event. But critically, this expectation is based on neither sensory input (remember, our eye never registers an occluded object as cohesive) nor experience—these newborns have never had the chance to see occluded geometric shapes before. So, these results suggest that newborn infants spontaneously interpret their visual sensory experience as an abstract object, and assume (without evidence) that moving objects must be cohesive.

Could the infant have induced this notion from seeing her partially occluded hand in utero? This possibility cannot be entirely ruled out, but it begs the question of how such induction arises. *Why* should the newborn categorize disparately distinct experiences, such as her hand (familiar also by touch, taste, and proprioceptive feedback) and a moving rod (an utterly novel shape, experienced only visually) as a single class—"objects"? Why should she consider her tasty hand more similar to a rod (an object) than to, say, milk (which is not an object but stuff)? Of course, if the child *had* a notion of an "object," then these questions would be trivial. But the problem for the empiricist story is that this is precisely what the infant has to acquire. And when the sample size informing the induction is limited, it is unclear how it would arise.

Animal research presents additional clues to this mystery. Newborn chicks also interpret moving objects as cohesive, even when they are partly occluded. Now, I realize that this might sound a bit strange. Talk of abstract concepts in infants is hard enough to swallow; chick cognition sounds like a joke from a Far Side cartoon.

But remember, we are not talking about conscious philosophical deliberation, but about our instinctive representations of reality. If human infants are innately equipped to view moving objects as cohesive, then this concept must be there for some good evolutionary reason—because a species that possesses this notion is better fit to represent its natural world. And humans are not the only species who benefit from such knowledge. If our notion of "object" is innate, then there is every reason to expect this notion to be shared with other species—even chicks.

And it turns out that it is. Researchers Lucia Regolin and Giorgio Vallortigara[12] designed an experiment around the instinctive tendency of chicks to follow objects with which they are familiarized immediately after hatching (known as "imprinting"). Typically, this moving object is the chick's mother, so imprinting prompts the chick to follow its mother, rather than a running dog. But precisely because instincts are tailored to meet a particular evolutionary challenge, they can also be rather dumb. The imprinting instinct concerns not mothers specifically, but any moving object seen after hatching. When mothers are replaced by humans, or even by a moving cardboard triangle, the chick will follow them. And this gives us the opportunity to determine what chicks consider "the same object"—whether their notion of a moving object is defined by cohesion.

To find out, the researchers first familiarized the hatching chicks with a cohesive moving object—a triangle (Figure 3.2A). Next, they compared their responses to three objects. One was the original cohesive triangle A;

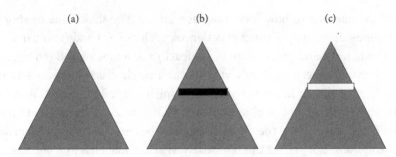

Figure 3.2. A test of the cohesion of objects.
Redrawn from Regolin and Vallortigara, (1995).[12]

the other two objects were novel: a partly occluded triangle B (a possible representation of the original "imprinted" object) and a fragmented triangle C (an impossible representation of the original triangle). Of interest is which of the two novel objects the chicks would interpret as equivalent to the original imprinting object. If it was B, the partly occluded triangle, then when presented with the pair of novel objects, the chicks would be more likely to approach the partly occluded triangle (a possible representation of the original triangle) than the impossible fragmented triangle, which is exactly what they did. In fact, the chicks' preference for the occluded object was indistinguishable from their preference for the original one. So, like humans, chicks hold an abstract notion of an object that requires it to be cohesive. The convergence of this notion across species—humans and chicks—is significant because is consistent with the possibility that this innate notion is an ancient evolutionary instinct.

***

Cohesion—the notion that moving objects are bounded wholes—is one of three requirements that we impose on objects, known as the three Cs. The other two are *contact* and *continuity*.

To appreciate those constraints, consider this thought experiment that follows the pioneering work of the Belgian psychologist Albert Michotte (1881–1965).[13] Imagine two balls on a billiard table, balls A and B. If you were to launch ball A and it were to contact ball B, then you would expect B to launch immediately and to follow A's path. But if ball B were to move without immediate contact—either spontaneously or after a brief delay, you would be surprised. Likewise, if B were to venture off in an entirely different direction than the path of A, you would be highly intrigued. We are surprised because we expect a launching ball to move only by immediate contact with another moving ball, and once contacted, we expect it to follow continuously on the same path. Remarkably, so do newborn infants.

In these experiments, Elena Mascalzoni and her colleagues compared the responses of newborn infants to possible and impossible launching events (Figure 3.3).[14] In the possible event (i), ball A moved toward ball B, which in turn, started to move immediately along the same path as A. The impossible event delayed the movement of the second ball B by a second. The researchers reasoned that if the infants' looking preference is only

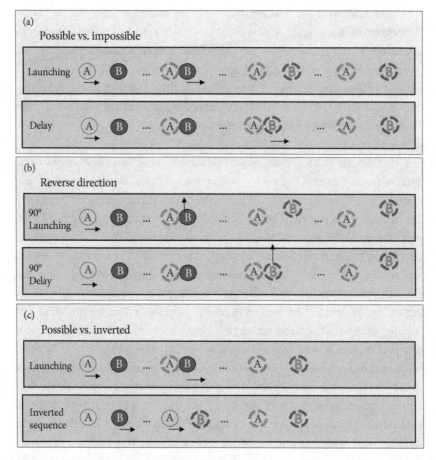

Figure 3.3. Possible and impossible launches.
Redrawn, from Mascalzoni et al. (2015).[14]

guided by their visual sense, then they should prefer looking at the impossible event, as this discontinuous motion can be perceived more readily by their immature visual system. But if the infants know that objects should only move after immediate contact, then they should prefer looking at the possible event over the impossible one. This was indeed what they observed.

Infants did not find the delayed launching event uninteresting in and of itself. In another experiment, infants actually preferred to look longer at the delayed event compared to the immediate one when these events were both impossible (because A approached B horizontally, but B was launched vertically, either immediately or after a delay; see (ii)). In yet another impossible launching condition (iii), the spatial contingencies between the two events (A contacts B) were maintained, but the order of events was reversed, as the movement of B preceded A; this event was compared to a normal launching event in which B moves following its contact with A. Although the temporal properties of these possible and impossible events were similar, infants were far more likely to stare at the possible launching event than the reversed-sequence alternative. Thus, newborn infants expect moving objects to launch by immediate contact, and once contacted, they expect the object to continue on the same path.

Other results (with slightly older infants, two months of age) suggest that infants further expect the path of a moving object to be unobstructed and connected. When a moving ball encounters an obstacle along its trajectory, the ball comes to rest right before the obstacle; it does not miraculously traverse the obstacle and rest behind it. To demonstrate this knowledge, the psychologist Elizabeth Spelke and her colleagues presented infants with a ball rolling horizontally toward an obstacle; midway throughout the event, the ball's trajectory was occluded by a screen (the "habituation" phase, see Figure 3.4).[15] Next, the screen was raised, to reveal either an outcome that is consistent with the habituation (the possible outcome) or the impossible one that is inconsistent with the launch. Results showed that infants looked longer at the inconsistent (impossible) outcome compared to the consistent (possible) one. A control experiment compared the same scenarios (the ball landing before or after the obstacle) except that now the ball was dropped vertically, so both outcomes were excepted. Here, no reliable differences in looking time were expected, nor were they found. Together, these results suggest that young infants know that the path of a moving object must be continuous and unobstructed.

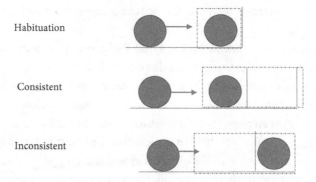

Habituation

Consistent

Inconsistent

Figure 3.4. Consistent vs. inconsistent outcomes for a launching event.
Redrawn, from Spelke et al. (1992).[15]

You might have noticed that the direction of preferences in the occlusion studies (toward the impossible event) is opposite to the one in the studies with visible launching events (where possible events were the ones to attract the infants' attention). As noted earlier, this is not unusual, given that the two types of displays differed. In the unoccluded events, infants witness impossible launching events, whereas in the occluded scenarios, these impossible events are inferred. Additionally, Mascalzoni and colleagues noted that the discontinuous motion in the impossible event was inherently more interesting for infants. Accordingly, the specific direction of preference can only be interpreted in the context of the specific procedure. In other words, we are interested in the *difference* in response to possible and impossible events, not in its specific direction. What matters is that within a given procedure, impossible launching events consistently elicit the same response (e.g., see (i)–(iii) in Figure 3.3). All of these results show that newborn infants know that objects should move immediately after contact, and they should continuously follow the same path.

***

Before we conclude this section, we ought to briefly return to Molyneux's problem—at least insofar as it applies to infant cognition. The results reviewed so far suggest that infants' initial understanding of objects is abstract inasmuch as it organizes their perception according to notions such as cohesion, contact and continuity—principles that are not supported by their senses. Molyneux's original problem, however, concerned the transfer of knowledge across sensory modalities. He wondered whether an object that is familiar to us haptically would also be recognizable in a novel sensory modality of sight.

The psychologist Andrew Meltzoff and Richard Borton tested this question with 29-day-old infants.[16] To this end, the infants were first allowed to explore a pacifier only orally (by touch), without seeing it (Figure 3.5). Next, they were presented with the pacifier as well as a slightly different one. If the infants' notion of an object is strictly sensory, then the tactile experience with the object should offer little help in recognizing the object in the visual realm. But if the infants' notion of the object is abstract, then it should be possible for it to generalize to the visual modality. Consequently, infants would be more likely to look at the matching shape compared to the novel one. And this is exactly what the infants in these experiments did. Subsequent research reported that newborns can recognize objects visually after first being allowed to explore them with their hands.[17] Other results show that cross modal transfer is informed not only by the shape of an object but by its cohesion. When given the opportunity to haptically explore two rings that move independently of each other, infants recognized them as two distinct objects. But when the two rings were connected by a rod, in such a way that they could not move independently of each other, infants recognized them as a single visual object.[18]

I should note that cross-modal transfer presents a rather conservative test for abstraction. It is indeed conceivable that infants could hold an abstract notion of an object, but fail to project it across modalities (e.g., due to differences in sensory inputs). On the other hand, if infants do show cross modal transfer, then their notion of the object is likely abstract. In other words, cross-modal transfer is sufficient, but not necessary to support the abstraction hypothesis. Finding that infants can overcome the sensory

Figure 3.5. A test of multisensory object perception in infants.
From Meltzoff and Borton (1975),[16] with permission.

differences between sight and touch and transfer their knowledge across modalities presents strong evidence that our early notions of objects are abstract.

Together, these results suggest that, from birth, infants have an abstract notion of an object. This notion requires moving objects to be cohesive and to move continuously, only by immediate contact. This notion is demonstrably distinct from the information provided by the visual sense, is evident close to birth (before the infant has had sensory experience with launching events), and matches the instinctive interpretations of non-human animals. While it is perhaps conceivable that the perceived cohesion of occluded objects could be partly informed by experiences of occluded body parts in utero, as noted, it is far from clear how this notion would be learned. And these challenges are even greater for contact and continuity, which are far less likely to be experienced prenatally. Further evidence for the abstract notion of object is presented by the ability of newborn infants to recognize a visual object they had previously explored haptically. The most likely explanation is that this abstract concept reflects knowledge that is innate.

Number

Let us consider again the newborn infant in the first hours after birth. She is lying in her crib, alert, watching her surroundings with bewildered eyes. For the first time, her two parents enter the room to marvel at their child. The parents, no doubt, recognize the infant. But what does the infant see?

Earlier, we noted that the infant is innately equipped with the capacity to identify visual objects, so, thankfully, she can recognize that each of her parents has a body (rather than a haphazard collection of torsos and legs), even if they are partly occluded by the bars of the crib. But can she tell that there are two people looking at her, rather than one, or three?

It turns out that she can. Her number sense, at this point, is quite rudimentary, distinct from the one we use in algebra—infants are by no means able to do calculus or compute square roots. But infants (and other animals) can nonetheless keep track of small sets of objects (up to about four), and they can also compare the magnitude of larger sets (say, 10 vs. 20 dots) by tracking their ratio. These two capacities are supported by distinct systems that we will consider next.

Objects Count

As any gamer can tell you, it's hard to withstand an invasion of multiple ene-mies. Whether you are trying to protect your turf from a bunch of zombies or invading enemy aircraft, tracking various objects in parallel is difficult and the difficulty increases with the size of the set. If you are facing a single ob-ject/invader, no problem. Two objects are easy to manage. But once there are more than three or four, you can no longer keep track of them all.

But let's consider what happens when you still have the upper hand. As long as you remain within the sweet spot of up to about three to four objects, you can typically do quite well. You can tell if one of the enemies disappears off the screen or a new one pops up. So although you do not encode the number of objects explicitly—at no point do you need to tell yourself "now there are three zombies," implicitly, you represent that fact or else you wouldn't be able to detect that one creature disappeared and another has just appeared.

Tracking multiple objects in parallel is a basic capacity of our visual system[19-21] that allows us to implicitly keep track of number.[22] And quite as-tonishingly, we can do this in our first days of life, well before we have learned the words for "one" or "two." So can many other animals that will never utter a word in their lives. To reiterate, this is not to say that monkeys can per-form algebra or calculus. For one thing, our adult number system is infi-nite, whereas our object tracking mechanism is strictly limited in size—we can only deal with about four objects in parallel, and this size limit sharply contrasts this system from our mature concept of number. But as long as you remain within the small set of roughly four objects, infants and animals can keep track of number, and they can even do some rudimentary operations of addition and subtraction.

This has been borne out by numerous studies. In one, the researchers Sue Ellen Antell and Daniel Keating examined the numeric capacity of new-born infants (aged 54 hours, on average).[23] First, they presented infants with two sets of dots. The number of dots in the two sets was identical, but they differed in their spatial arrangement (to make sure the infants were tracking number and not just visual configurations). The infants looked at the dis-play until they lost interest. Next, they were presented with a test set with a different numerosity (say, three dots), arranged so as to combine the visual attributes of the two previous sets. If newborn infants can extract the number of dots, then they should regain interest in the test display. This was indeed the case. But infants were only able to track the number of small sets: they were sensitive to the contrast between two and three objects, but they utterly failed to distinguish four and six dots.

Other experiments by Lisa Feigenson and her colleagues documented these capacities by tracing the reaching behavior of older infants.[24] Here, Graham crackers were placed in two containers, one cracker at a time. When 10- to 12-month-old infants were given the opportunity to approach the containers, they reliably favored the one with the larger number of crackers. And since the containers were opaque, infants had to have chosen by encoding the number of crackers, rather than simply by viewing the two quantities. But once again, set size matters. Infants preferred two crackers over one, and three over two or one. But when the total number of crackers in the containers reached four (or more), infants showed no reliable preference (in line with the behavior of newborns), and they remained indifferent to number even when the total ratio between the two sets was large (a choice between 4:2 or 6:3). As we will see shortly, infants can also estimate number by relying on a second cognitive system that computes magnitude based on ratios—the larger the ratio between two quantities, the greater the sensitivity, irrespective of set size. But since the cracker experiment used opaque containers, the magnitude of the set was not salient to the ratio system. (A control experiment confirmed that. Once the crackers were placed on open trays, infants indeed went for the larger set.) So, the finding that, with opaque containers, set size was critical whereas ratio did not matter is significant because it suggests that the object file system—the putative mechanism that guides this judgment—is distinct.

A parallel experiment with monkeys found just the same. In this experiment, free-ranging rhesus monkeys in the island of Cayo Santiago (Puerto Rico) saw two experimenters place slices of apples in two empty, opaque boxes. When given the opportunity to approach the boxes, the monkeys spontaneously preferred the one holding the larger set, and they did so on the first trial, without any possibility for learning. But like human infants, monkeys could only do so for small sets. They showed a reliable preference for the larger set for up to four objects (two vs. one, three vs. two, and four vs. three), but they showed no preference for larger sets, even when the ratio between the sets was as large as eight to three.[25]

Considering the studies discussed thus far, one might worry that infants (and monkeys) respond not to the number of objects but to unrelated aspects of the visual display—the configuration of dots (in the newborn studies)[23] or the overall amount of crackers/fruit in the toddler and monkey experiments.

To address this concern, other experiments explored infants' sensitivity to number across different modalities.

In one experiment, five-month-old infants were first familiarized with either two or three objects by touch. When they were next presented with a visual display of the objects, they looked longer when the number of visual objects mismatched the number of objects the infants had explored haptically.[26] Another set of experiments compared the numeric capacities of seven-month-old human infants to those of rhesus monkeys. Participants looked at two screens side by side while hearing the voices of either two or three individuals of their species. On one screen two conspecific faces uttered the sounds, the competing display featured three such faces. Results showed that participants—humans and monkeys alike—preferred to look at the visual display that was congruent with the number of vocalizations (e.g., if two voices were heard, they looked longer at the two faces).[27,28]

Although the direction of congruence effects differed across the visuohaptic and audiovisual procedures (this is not unexpected given the differences in tasks), both studies showed that young infants are sensitive to numeric congruence across modalities. These results cannot be explained by extent or configuration alone (e.g., the infants chose the larger amount of cookies). The parallels between human infants and monkeys further suggest that these capacities are based on the same mechanism. The object file system is thus evolutionarily ancient and innate in both species.

Not only can infants keep track of number; they can even add and subtract. The psychologist Karen Wynn has documented these abilities in five month-old infants.[29] In her study, infants saw a doll placed on a stage (see Figure 3.6). Infants then saw a screen come up, hiding the doll from view. Next, another doll was placed behind the screen. Finally, the screen dropped down to reveal either two dolls (the expected outcome) or one (the unexpected outcome). If infants can add, then they should look longer at the unexpected event (one doll) compared to the expected one (two).

To make sure that these results are not simply due to a preference for larger sets (more dolls), another condition presented the infants with the same choice (one or two dolls) in the context of a subtraction event. Here, infants first saw two dolls. Next, the screen came up and one doll was removed. The final event presented the infants with either one doll or two (the same choice as in the addition experiment), except that now, the expected outcome is one doll, rather than two. Results showed that infants' preference (for one doll vs. two dolls) shifted depending on the condition (addition vs. subtraction).

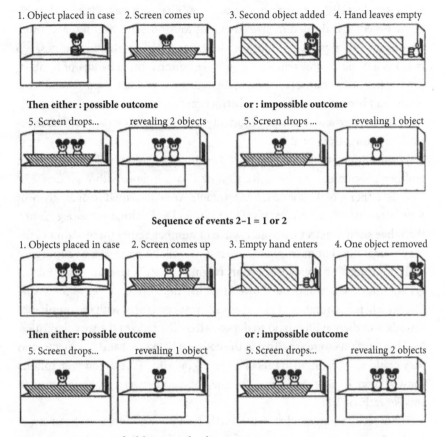

Figure 3.6. A test of addition and subtraction.
From Wynn (1992), with permission.

In each case, infants looked longer at the unexpected event. Similar abilities to add and subtract small sets have also been demonstrated in rhesus monkeys,[25,30] in newborn chicks[31] and even in bees,[32] suggesting that this innate capacity is ancient.

Numbers in Sound and Light

The findings reviewed thus far suggest that both infants and animals can keep track of small numbers of objects by capitalizing on their visual abilities and that they can do so already at birth. Impressive as it may be, this ability is nonetheless distinct from our mature number systems. First, and as already noted, it is limited in size (to about four objects). Second, and more significant, our algebraic numeric abilities can extend across modalities. A 3 is a 3 is a 3, no matter whether it is three sounds, three beams of light, or three touches on your screen. We recognize these various disparate events as equivalent because we rely on an abstract cardinal value of "three" that is distinct from a particular sensory modality. Can humans extract such abstract cardinal values from birth?

Within limits, they can. To show this, the psychologist Véronique Izard and her colleagues[33] first familiarized newborn infants with a sequence of sounds, either 4 or 12 sounds. Next, infants were presented with an array of four or twelve visual objects. If infants extract the cardinal value (e.g., four), then they should detect the congruence in number across these distinct sensory modalities. For example, "four sounds" will be perceived as congruent with "four dots," so congruent events might be more interesting than incongruent ones. Results indeed showed that infants looked longer at the visual display when the number of visual objects was congruent with the number of sounds. But their ability to do so depended on the ratio of the two quantities. Newborn infants were sensitive to the contrast between 4 and 12 objects, and they could also distinguish sets of 18 and 6 (a ratio of 3:1). However, infants showed a far weaker preference for the contrast between eight and four (a smaller ratio of 2:1).

These results suggest that, from birth, infants can represent the abstract cardinal value of events across different modalities. But this system of abstract number differs from the object tracking capacity in several ways. One difference is size: while object tracking is strictly limited to about three or four objects, the abstract number capacity seen in neonates can track up to 18 events. Ratio is another factor. Our abstract number sense is acutely sensitive to ratio. We are good at contrasting between large ratios (3:1), but fail at smaller ones (20:19), and you might recall that, when the ratio is favorable, newborn infants can detect numeric congruence between large sets of dots and sounds (12 vs. 4).[33]Remarkably, when the set size is small (six vs. two), newborns fail to detect numeric congruence between dots and sounds despite the fact that the ratio and procedure are identical to the ones used in the experiment with larger sets.[34] Similar results obtain with older children. Recall that 10- to 12-month-old infants prefer three crackers over one—when offered a choice, they approach a container with the larger number (these results were discussed in the previous section).[24] But when offered the choice between one and four crackers—a number that apparently falls beyond their object file limit—infants utterly fail to differentiate between the two sets.[35] In line with this analysis, the two systems also elicit distinct brain responses.[36]

So humans (and nonhuman animals) can encode number by relying on two distinct systems. Each of these capacities is limited in ways that distinguish it from the infinite numerical concept used in mathematics, but these capacities nonetheless allow humans to represent number, and they are apparently operative at birth. The innate principles that govern our understanding of number and object form the foundation of our initial understanding of the physical world. Chapters 4 and 5 very briefly explore two other sets of core knowledge principles—those that concern the social realm and the structure of language.

References

1. Valenza E, Leo I, Gava L, Simion F. Perceptual completion in newborn human infants. *Child Development*. 2006;77(6):1810–1821.
2. Hume D. An enquiry concerning human understanding. In: Millican PF, ed. *Oxford world's classics*. New York, NY: Oxford University Press; 1748/2007. Retrieved from http://ebookcentral.proquest.com/lib/northeastern-ebooks/detail. action?docID=415078
3. Locke J. *The works of John Locke, in nine volumes*. 12th ed. London, England: Printed for C. and J. Rivington etc; 1824.
4. Pascual-Leone A, Hamilton R. The metamodal organization of the brain. *Progress in Brain Research*. 2001;134:427–445.
5. Amedi A, Stern WM, Camprodon JA, et al. Shape conveyed by visual-to-auditory sensory substitution activates the lateral occipital complex. *Nature Neuroscience*. 2007;10(6):687–689.
6. Bedny M, Pascual-Leone A, Dodell-Feder D, Fedorenko E, Saxe R. Language processing in the occipital cortex of congenitally blind adults. *Proceedings of the National Academy of Sciences of the United States of America*. 2011;108(11):4429–4434.
7. Kauffman T, Théoret H, Pascual-Leone A. Braille character discrimination in blindfolded human subjects. *Neuroreport*. 2002;13(5):571–574.
8. Held R, Ostrovsky Y, de Gelder B, et al. The newly sighted fail to match seen with felt. *Nature Neuroscience*. 2011;14:551.
9. Chen J, Wu E-D, Chen X, et al. Rapid integration of tactile and visual information by a newly sighted child. *Current Biology*. 2016;26(8):1069–1074.
10. Kisilevsky BS, Hains SMJ, Brown CA, et al. Fetal sensitivity to properties of maternal speech and language. *Infant Behavior and Development*. 2009;32(1):59–71.

11. Reid VM, Dunn K, Young RJ, Amu J, Donovan T, Reissland N. The human fetus preferentially engages with face-like visual stimuli. *Current Biology*. 2017;27(12):1825–1828.e1823.

12. Regolin L, Vallortigara G. Perception of partly occluded objects by young chicks. *Perception & Psychophysics*. 1995;57(7):971–976.

13. Michotte A. *The perception of causality*. New York, NY: Basic Books; 1963.

14. Mascalzoni E, Regolin L, Vallortigara G, Simion F. The cradle of causal reasoning: newborns' preference for physical causality. *Developmental Science*. 2013;16(3):327–335.

15. Spelke ES, Breinlinger K, Macomber J, Jacobson K. Origins of knowledge. *Psychological Review*. 1992;99(4):605–632.

16. Meltzoff AN, Borton RW. Intermodal matching by human neonates. *Nature*. 1979;282(5737):403–404.

17. Sann C, Streri A. Perception of object shape and texture in human newborns: evidence from cross-modal transfer tasks. *Developmental Science*. 2007;10(3):399–410.

18. Streri A, Spelke ES. Effects of motion and figural goodness on haptic object perception in infancy. *Child Development*. 1989;60(5):1111.

19. Kahneman D, Treisman A, Gibbs BJ. The reviewing of object files: object-specific integration of information. *Cognitive Psychology*. 1992;24(2):175–219.

20. Pylyshyn ZW, Storm RW. Tracking multiple independent targets: evidence for a parallel tracking mechanism. *Spatial Vision*. 1988;3(3):179–197.

21. Scholl BJ. Objects and attention: the state of the art. *Cognition*. 2001;80(1-2):1–46.

22. Carey S. *The origin of concepts*. New York, NY: Oxford University Press; 2009.

23. Antell SE, Keating DP. Perception of numerical invariance in neonates. *Child Development*. 1983;54(3):695–701.

24. Feigenson L, Carey S, Hauser M. The representations underlying infants' choice of more: object files versus analog magnitudes. *Psychological Science*. 2002;13(2):150–156.

25. Hauser MD, Carey S, Hauser LB. Spontaneous number representation in semi-free-ranging rhesus monkeys. *Proceedings Biological Sciences*. 2000;267(1445):829.

26. Féron J, Gentaz E, Streri A. Evidence of amodal representation of small numbers across visuo-tactile modalities in 5-month-old infants. *Cognitive Development*. 2006;21(2):81–92.

27. Jordan KE, Brannon EM. The multisensory representation of number in infancy. *Proceedings of the National Academy of Sciences of the United States of America*. 2006;103(9):3486.

28. Jordan KE, Brannon EM, Logothetis NK, Ghazanfar AA. Monkeys match the number of voices they hear to the number of faces they see. *Current Biology*. 2005;15(11):1034–1038.

29. Wynn K. Addition and subtraction by human infants. *Nature*. 1992;358(6389):749–750.

30. Hauser MD, Carey S. Spontaneous representations of small numbers of objects by rhesus macaques: examinations of content and format. *Cognitive Psychology*. 2003;47(4):367–401.

31. Rugani R, Fontanari L, Simoni E, Regolin L, Vallortigara G. Arithmetic in newborn chicks. *Proceedings Biological sciences*. 2009;276(1666):2451.

32. Giurfa M. An insect's sense of number. *Trends in Cognitive Sciences*. 2019;23(9):720–722.

33. Izard V, Sann C, Spelke ES, Streri A. Newborn infants perceive abstract numbers. *Proceedings of the National Academy of Sciences of the United States of America.* 2009;106(25):10382–10385.
34. Coubart A, Izard V, Spelke ES, Marie J, Streri A. Dissociation between small and large numerosities in newborn infants. *Developmental Science.* 2014;17(1):11–22.
35. Feigenson L, Carey S. On the limits of infants' quantification of small object arrays. *Cognition.* 2005;97(3):295–313.
36. Hyde DC, Spelke ES. Neural signatures of number processing in human infants: evidence for two core systems underlying numerical cognition. *Developmental Science.* 2011;14(2):360–371.

4

The Social World

We all eagerly await the day when a self-propelled robot will take over our domestic chores—clearing the dishes, doing the laundry, and fishing out that lost sock from under the bed. But before you order your personal helper, you'd better be sure it won't put your cat in the washer like any old sweater or dust your child as if she were a lamp. No human cleaner would ever stop to think of such challenges, as humans draw sharp distinctions between inanimate objects and living agents. But do we do so instinctively, or is it something we learn? What is the initial social understanding of newborn infants?

In the previous chapter, we saw that newborn infants possess the basic concepts that define our adult understanding of the physical world, including notions of object and number. But human agents are a mystery. Viewed from the outside, they are solid material objects, like chairs and socks. But the principles that guide their behavior are quite different. Agents move spontaneously (you will occasionally rise up from your stationary position on the couch and approach the kitchen). They are driven not only by contact with other physical objects but by mental states—our goals (you'd like a glass of water) and beliefs (the glasses are in the cupboard). So, to understand the social realm, infants must partly suspend the principles that they extend to physical bodies (at least the principles of contact and continuity) and apply a whole set of new principles that appeal to agents' mental states—their knowledge, desires, goals, and beliefs.

How do infants draw this distinction? The answer to this question is not entirely clear. But what we do know for sure is that human newborns' reactions to other humans are qualitatively distinct from their reactions to objects. And within a couple of weeks, they seem to imbue social agents with a rich set of mental states. What follows are just a couple of appetizers from this rich literature.

The Blind Storyteller. Iris Berent, Oxford University Press (2020). © Iris Berent, 2020.
DOI: 10.1093/oso/9780190061920.001.0001

Agents Are Special, Distinct from Objects

One of the most striking demonstrations of newborns' selective responses to other humans is imitation. When newborns see a person stick out their tongue, they will do the same. When the person opens her mouth, they will likewise follow suit. And in each case, the behavior is selective: when they see an adult protrude their tongue, newborns are more likely to protrude their tongue than to open their mouth; when they see an adult open their mouth, the infant's most likely response is to open hers.[1-3]

Newborn infants do not generate these complex behaviors "on the fly." Ultrasound recordings of human fetuses shows that infants perform these orofacial gestures spontaneously, while they are still in utero.[4] So, when a newborn infant imitates the adult's tongue protrusion, she is calling upon a behavior that she has previously mastered. Remarkably, human newborns deploy these behaviors at will to mirror the actions of social agents. And like other newborn traits discussed in the previous section (e.g., the cohesion of objects), this mirroring capacity is also evident in nonhuman apes, such as rhesus macaques.[5] The long evolutionary history of this behavior provides further evidence to suggest that it is innate.

Another trick used by newborns to win the hearts of their exhausted mothers is to reciprocate her eye gaze. Infants are more likely to look at pictures of human faces that stare at them directly (compared to ones that avert their gaze), and these faces also elicit stronger brain responses.[6] Critically, newborns react differently to agents and objects. For example, newborns are more likely to move their fingers and flex their hand when they see their mother's face (compared to a moving ball that is designed to approximate an infant's view of a mother's head, which tends to elicit arm extensions).[7] This behavior strongly suggests that the distinction between human agents and objects is innate.

Within the next couple of weeks, infants seem to infer different causes for the behaviors of agents and objects. The launching events, described in the previous section, present a clear demonstration of this contrast. From birth, infants expect a stationary inanimate object to move only if it is contacted by another object. So, if they were to see a red ball approach a stationary blue ball and the stationary blue ball were to launch spontaneously (without contact with the moving red ball), infants would appear to be surprised (that is, they will stare longer at the display). Seven-month-old infants react similarly, even when the balls are replaced by two inanimate human-size objects. But when the scenario features human agents, the expectation for movement by contact is suspended. For example, when infants see a man walking toward a standing woman, they show no surprise if the woman were to move (without having first touched the man) compared to a "launching event" (the man approaches the woman and touches her, after which she moves).[8] This suggests that infants believe that, unlike inanimate objects, agents can move spontaneously, guided by their own goals.

Another study showed that infants expect agents to move according to goals rather than to follow the same path of motion.[9] So if infants see a hand grasp one of two objects (a ball, presented on the left, rather than a doll, on the right, see Figure 4.1A), they would next expect the hand to reach the same object (the ball) even when its location is switched—when the ball is now placed on the right. In fact, if the hand were to maintain its path and reach the doll (see Figure 4.1B), the infants would be surprised (as evident in their looking longer at the display). Critically, infants only expect this of agents. When the animate agent (suggested by the hand) was replaced by an inanimate moving object (a moving rod), infants showed the typical preference for path continuity over goal.

Agents can likewise hold beliefs, and these concepts could be either true or false. If I were to surreptitiously remove your car keys from their usual place

Figure 4.1. A test of the projection of goals to human agents.
Redrawn, from Woodward (1998).[9]

on the table and place them instead on the chair (don't you wonder whether this happens rather frequently?), you would likely futilely search for the keys on the table when you need them, as your action is guided by your belief that the keys should be where you left them. People would typically predict that this is precisely what you would do: you would follow your (false) belief, rather than the true facts (that are unknown to you).

The distinction between one's own beliefs and the (false) beliefs of others is not trivial, as people with autism struggle to keep those apart. When a child with autism is presented with an equivalent of the car key mystery, they expect the unsuspecting victim to look for the keys where they actually are, rather than where they believe they are.[10] This is because autistic children have trouble intuiting the thoughts and feelings of others. But remarkably, typical infants show understanding of the minds of others by 15 months of age.

In one experiment an infant saw an actor searching for a misplaced toy. In the first situation, the actor was aware of the misplacement (and the infant had seen them witness it); in another, the change was made "behind the scenes," when the infant knew the actor could not have possibly seen this event. If infants know that the actor's actions depend on his or her goals, then they should expect the actor to search for the toy where the actor *believes* it is, regardless of whether this belief is true or false. So if the actor were to look at the opposite location, infants should be surprised, irrespective of whether this location does actually contain the toy (in the false belief situation) or doesn't (in the true belief case). And this is exactly what they did. Infants thus expect the actor to search for a hidden object by following their beliefs about the object's location.[11] This suggests that infants expect that, unlike inanimate objects (which move according to the three Cs—cohesion, contact and continuity), agents' actions follow beliefs and goals.

You might have noticed, however, that most of the evidence for infants' ability to reason about the minds of agents obtains well after birth. So, one still wonders whether our intuitive psychology is an innate human instinct or is learned from social interactions. But recall that the onset of a trait in development is not necessarily indicative of its source. Human females, for instance, develop breasts at puberty, but no one would argue that "having breasts" is learned. Moreover, the ability to infer mental states seems to be an old evolutionary capacity that is shared with nonhuman primates. Research with rhesus monkeys suggests that monkeys can assess the reliability of their own knowledge, and they use this information in foraging for food. When they recognized that their knowledge about the food's location was imperfect (because their view was occluded), they would probe further for its location.[12] Other results show that rhesus monkeys follow the direction of an agent's gaze when the agent's goal is within the monkey's view, suggesting that they attribute a goal to the agent's looks.[13] These results open up the possibility that the ability to reason about one's own mind and the minds of others is an innate capacity that we share with other primates, and it is distinct from our core knowledge of objects.

Agents Can Be Good or Bad

To engage in the social world, infants must learn not only to contrast agents and objects but to distinguish among different kinds of agents. We prefer to associate with friends—typically, those who are likely to help us and do good—and to avoid foes, who do the opposite. But how do we form the notions of "good" and "bad"?

One possibility is that we learn them from experience. Having suffered from the inflictions of our enemies and benefitted from the benevolence of our friends, we learn to avoid the former and seek out the latter and, by extension, extract broader categories of "good" and "bad," which we codify in religion and law. The implication, then, is that moral categories such as "good" and "bad reflect not human nature—a moral instinct—but social conventions that are learned. The philosopher Thomas Hobbes (158–1679) expressed this view as follows:

> It is true, that certain living creatures, as Bees, and Ants, live sociably one with another, (which are therefore by Aristotle numbred amongst Politicall creatures;) and yet have no other direction, than their particular judgements and appetites; nor speech, whereby one of them can signifie to another, what he thinks expedient for the common benefit: and therefore some man may perhaps desire to know, why Man-kind cannot do the same. To which I answer . . . the agreement of these creatures is Naturall; that of men, is by Covenant only, which is Artificiall: and therefore it is no wonder if there be somewhat else required (besides Covenant) to make their Agreement constant and lasting; which is a Common Power, to keep them in awe, and to direct their actions to the Common Benefit.[14p394]

But research by the psychologists Paul Bloom, Karen Wynn, and their colleagues suggests an entirely different possibility. Their findings suggest that, by three months of age, infants spontaneously prefer good agents to bad ones, even when their actions do not concern the infants themselves.

In one set of experiments, three-month-old infants were shown a self-propelled triangle (equipped with eyes), attempting (but failing) to climb a steep hill (see Figure 4.2). Next, they were presented with two scenarios involving two additional geometric characters (which were likewise self-propelled and equipped with eyes). In one condition, a triangle (the helper) assisted the circle by pushing it up the hill; in a second condition, a rectangle (a hinderer) interfered with the circle's climb by pushing it in the opposite direction. Strikingly, when the infants were subsequently presented with the "helper" and the "hinderer," they looked longer at the "helper."[15-17]

When 6-month-old infants were shown the same scenarios and then given the opportunity to grab one of the two characters, they reliably chose the "helper." Another experiment confirmed that these older infants who grabbed the "helper" also tended to look at it longer. This suggests that the prolonged looking time of the younger infants reflected a preference.[16] These results, obtained across a variety of ages, characters, and scenarios, show that infants instinctively prefer the "good guy." Not only that, but when older infants (20 months) were offered the opportunity to reward the "helper" (by giving it a treat) and punish the "hinderer" (by taking a treat away), they reliably did so. [18] These early moral behaviors are linked to the social reasoning of the same children later in life. As the infants turned four, they were invited to return to the lab and tested on various aspects of their abilities to recognize the states, desires, and beliefs of others. Children who showed stronger moral preferences in infancy also tended to be more attuned to the minds of others when they were four.[19]

Figure 4.2. A test of infants' moral cognition F.
From Hamlin et al. (2007),[15] with permission.

As with theory of mind, the moral preferences of children are mostly evident well after birth—the earliest known demonstration of moral behavior is found around 3 months of age, and most of the literature on moral reasoning is obtained with older children. But there is reason to doubt that moral cognition is only a "social covenant," to use Hobbes's words. One challenge is to explain how an infant would come to construct abstract notions of "good" and "bad" from the sensory evidence available to her. A second is presented by the existence of moral universals. Although there can be no doubt that different societies vary on some specifics of their ethical beliefs, there is nonetheless convergence on the general types of behaviors that are considered "good" and "bad." [20] Finally, we are not the only moral species. Various species of monkeys will systematically reward other individuals, and at times, they will do so at a cost to themselves. Chimpanzees will help others reach a distant object or obtain food.[21] The universality of moral reasoning and its old evolutionary history point to the very strong possibility that it is at least partly innate.

In our eyes, then, agents are inherently distinct from objects. Agents' actions are guided not by laws of physics but by internal mental states, and from an early age, we tacitly view certain actions as good, and others as bad.

References

1. Meltzoff AN, Moore MK. Imitation of facial and manual gestures by human neonates. *Science.* 1977;198(4312):75–78.
2. Meltzoff AN, Murray L, Simpson E, et al. Re-examination of Oostenbroek et al. (2016): evidence for neonatal imitation of tongue protrusion. *Developmental Science.* 2018;21(4):e12609.
3. Nagy E, Pilling K, Orvos H, Molnar P. Imitation of tongue protrusion in human neonates: specificity of the response in a large sample. *Developmental Psychology.* 2013;49(9):1628–1638.
4. Keven N, Akins KA. Neonatal imitation in context: Sensorimotor development in the perinatal period. 2017;40:e38.
5. Ferrari PF, Visalberghi E, Paukner A, Fogassi L, Ruggiero A, Suomi SJ. Neonatal imitation in rhesus macaques. *PloS Biology.* 2006;4(9):e302–e302.
6. Farroni T, Csibra G, Simion F, Johnson MH. Eye contact detection in humans from birth. *Proceedings of the National Academy of Sciences of the United States of America.* 2002;99(14):9602–9605.
7. Rönnqvist L, von Hofsten C. Neonatal finger and arm movements as determined by a social and an object context. *Early Development and Parenting.* 1994;3(2):81–94.
8. Spelke ES, Phillips A, Woodward AL. Infants' knowledge of object motion and human action. In: Sperber D, Premack D, Premack AJ, Sperber D, Premack D, Premack AJ, eds. *Causal cognition: a multidisciplinary debate.* New York, NY: Oxford University Press; 1995:44–78.

9. Woodward AL. Infants selectively encode the goal object of an actor's reach. *Cognition*. 1998;69(1):1–34.

10. Baron-Cohen S, Leslie AM, Frith U. Does the autistic child have a "theory of mind"? *Cognition*. 1985;21(1):37–46.

11. Onishi KH, Baillargeon R. Do 15-month-old infants understand false beliefs? *Science*. 2005;308(5719):255–258.

12. Rosati AG, Santos LR. Spontaneous metacognition in rhesus monkeys. *Psychological Science*. 2016;27(9):1181–1191.

13. Bettle R, Rosati AG. Flexible gaze-following in rhesus monkeys. *Animal Cognition*. 2019;22: 673–686.

14. Hobbes T. *Leviathan, or, The matter, forme, & power of a common-wealth ecclesiasticall and civill*. Crooke A, Nodin J, eds. London, England: Printed for Andrew Ckooke i.e. Crooke, at the Green Dragon in St. Pauls Church-yard; 1651.

15. Hamlin JK, Wynn K, Bloom P. Social evaluation by preverbal infants. *Nature*. 2007;450(7169):557–559.

16. Hamlin JK, Wynn K, Bloom P. Three-month-olds show a negativity bias in their social evaluations. *Developmental Science*. 2010;13(6):923–929.

17. Bloom P. *Just babies: the origins of good and evil*. 1st ed: New York, NY: Crown; 2013.

18. Hamlin JK, Wynn K, Bloom P, Mahajan N. How infants and toddlers react to anti-social others. *Proceedings of the National Academy of Sciences of the United States of America*. 2011;108(50):19931–19936.

19. Yamaguchi M, Kuhlmeier VA, Wynn K, vanMarle K. Continuity in social cognition from infancy to childhood. *Developmental Science*. 2009;12(5):746–752.

20. Haidt J, Joseph C. Intuitive ethics: how innately prepared intuitions generate culturally variable virtues. *Daedalus*. 2004;133(4):55–66.

21. Sheskin M, Santos L. The evolution of morality: Which aspects of human moral concerns are shared with nonhuman primates? In: Vonk J, Shackelford TK, Vonk J, Shackelford TK, eds. *The Oxford handbook of comparative evolutionary psychology*. New York, NY: Oxford University Press; 2012:434–450.

5

The Dawn of Language

Newborn infants, it appears, are equipped with much of what they need to begin their social lives. They can recognize that their parents have cohesive bodies (rather than being haphazard collections of parts) and that they are social agents, which, unlike inanimate objects, are driven by mental states such as knowledge, desires, and goals. Each of these capacities is based on innate ideas.

Language is a quintessentially human capacity, and as such, it presents a critical test for the innateness hypothesis. Every human community relies on language as its primary form of communication. Furthermore, our capacity for language is different in kind from the communication systems used naturally by nonhuman animals. When I say that other species lack language, I mean no disrespect to their own systems of communication, which in some cases are quite complex. But just as our mode of locomotion differs from birds' (they fly; we cannot), our natural communication systems likewise differ in significant ways. Moreover, no other species has been shown to be able to fully master a natural language.[1-3] Nonhuman animals can acquire certain partial components of language—your dog, for example, can understand hundreds of words,[4] and your parrot can utter them.[5,6] But language goes far beyond words, and at its core, this capacity is uniquely ours.

What's unique about language is its architecture. Every language is constructed like a double-decker cake (see Figure 5.1). One layer (syntax) forms patterns of meaningful words. English speakers, for instance, generate sentences like *dogs bark*, but not *bark dogs*, and because word order matters in English, *cats scratch men* is news; the reverse isn't. A second layer of patterning (phonology) generates words by combining meaningless sounds, such as *c*, *a*, and *t*. Here, too, order matters, so a *cat* isn't an *act*. This also explains why English speakers *blog*, not *lbog*, and why it is wrong to *drink* and *drive* (not *rdink* and *rdive*). While distinct languages differ somewhat on the specific structure of their patterns (more on this below), the general architecture, known as duality of patterning, is universal.[7] As we will see shortly,

The Blind Storyteller. Iris Berent, Oxford University Press (2020). © Iris Berent, 2020.
DOI: 10.1093/oso/9780190061920.001.0001

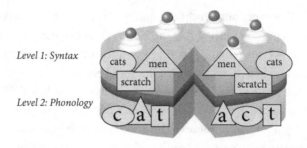

Level 1: Syntax

Level 2: Phonology

Figure 5.1. Duality of patterning.
Cake image courtesy of OpenClipart-Vectors from Pixabay.

some of the rules that govern the patterning within each level are possibly universal as well.

To be clear, it is not patterning per se that is uniquely human. Birds and whales form complex vocal patterns that are apparently meaningless (akin to our phonology)[8–12]; Campbell and Diana monkeys[13,14] combine meaningful calls (akin to our syntax). But all these examples reflect patterning at a single level only. No animal has been shown to exhibit *duality* of patterning (akin to syntax and phonology). And while nonhuman animals can certainly be trained to acquire some aspects of human language, none has attained a full command of it, even when raised with humans and even when some of the vocal demands associated with language use have been simplified (by using a sign language).

The chimpanzee Nim Chimpsky reportedly acquired numerous signs and was even able to form novel sign combinations (as would any child). But upon careful inspection, it turned out that many of Nim's novel sentences were in fact imitations of his caregivers', and his sentences were far shorter and simpler than the ones used by human children (with lots of repetitions, like "Nim eat Nim").[1,15] Another great ape, Kanzi the Bonobo, has been more productive in his use of language, but Kanzi expresses words by pointing to visual symbols—one whole symbol per word.[16] Impressive as this may be, Kanzi's communication includes only the single layer of patterning (syntax). Similarly, Alex the gray parrot, a prodigious language learner, was able to utter words and combine them, but it is unclear whether he encoded words as patterns of discrete elements or as unanalyzed wholes.[5] Duality of patterning—whether natural or acquired—has not been shown in nonhumans.

Why is it that every human child acquires a language, but no kitten, dog, or chimp has ever accomplished that same feat? Over 60 years ago, the linguist Noam Chomsky suggested a seemingly simple solution for the puzzle: language is a biological capacity of the human species.[17-19] People have language for the same reason they have hands, lungs, and hearts. The human genome determines the plan of our bodies and it sets the organization of the brain. Having a human genome means that as an embryo develops, its limbs will differentiate to give rise to hands and legs and 10 fingers and 10 toes. By the same token, the genome will also give rise to differentiation in its brain, resulting in diverse sensory and cognitive capacities—vision, audition, facial recognition, and kin detection. Each such system comes equipped with distinct principles of internal organization and function—for example, the principles by which we recognize visual objects are different from the ones guiding the recognition of musical sounds. Language is one such system—an organ of the mind.

This language organ, in Chomsky's view, endows the newborn child with an innate set of rules. By "rules," we mean nothing like the dictums of the language mavens, such as "Never end a sentence with a preposition" or "Don't split infinitives." Rather, these rules are pattern generators, tacit principles that your brain extracts implicitly and follows in an instinctive, unconscious fashion. And these rules are available to every human being, irrespective of age (infants have them) and education (yes, even illiterate people follow rules of language). In Steven Pinker's words,

> People know how to talk in more or less the sense that spiders know how to spin webs. Web-spinning was not invented by some unsung spider genius and does not depend on having had the right education or having an aptitude for architecture or the construction trades. Rather, spiders spin spider webs because they have spider brains, which give them the urge to spin and the competence to succeed.[1p18]

But the proposal that we are innately equipped with a universal set of rules has been met by fierce criticism. First, languages are diverse; in English *John ate sushi*, whereas in Japanese, it is roughly *John sushi ate*. Second, language is acquired gradually. Unlike our notion of an object or an agent, many aspects of language are not present at birth. And third, many of the regularities seen across languages are not arbitrary. Patterns like *blog* for instance, are easier for the speech system to produce and perceive.[20,21] So perhaps the patterns of a given language are for the most part the products of learning from experience, rather than any innate linguistic concepts. Perhaps the commonalities among languages emerge not because of abstract linguistic rules but because of the simple mechanics of speech—the physical constraints of our lips, tongues, and larynxes.[22-24]

Most discussions of innateness focus on syntax, so much so that many linguists use the term "grammar" (our tacit knowledge of the rules of language) and "syntax" (the rules concerning sentence structure) as synonyms. Here, instead, I'd like to focus on phonology. Since the sound patterns of language are closely aligned with the demands of speech, it is all too easy to jump to the conclusion that phonology *is* speech. But if phonology, which in some views is the stepchild of the language system, is abstract, then there is certainly reason to suspect that other aspects of language are abstract as well.

***

Our specific test case concerns the structure of the syllable. As noted, we *blog* not *lbog*, and we must not *drink* and *drive,* not *rdink* and *rdive.* This is not because syllables like *lbog* and *rdive* are impossible for humans to produce. Russian speakers, for instances, are perfectly comfortable with those syllables (e.g., *lva,* "lion" and *rzhan,* "zealous"). But across languages, they are nonetheless rare.[25,26] The question is why.

Linguists believe that the problem with *lbog* originates from its abstract structure. Very briefly, we know that people perceive speech sounds by categorizing them according to distinct abstract classes. So, when you hear sounds like *b* or *p*, you automatically assign them into one of two mental categories; a sound is either in the "b" bucket or the "p" bucket, but never in between. Within each such bucket, we treat all sounds alike. Adults do so,[27,28] and so do young infants.[29,30] Even if different *p* sounds are not identical (the *p*s in the English words *pit* and *spit* differ systematically, and people can certainly perceive this difference[31]), at the level of phonology, this difference is ignored. This means phonological patterns are made of abstract discrete objects (the "p" category), not the sounds themselves.[32-36] To use a metaphor, we can liken phonological patterns to a ball. When you construct the ball, you don't mold it directly from the plastic stuff. Rather, you first extract individual Lego pieces from the plastic, and then you combine them together.

There are several such abstract categories of speech sounds, defined by their manner of articulation. Consonants like *b* are produced by fully obstructing the air stream, so they are called stops (other stops are *p, t, d, g,* and *k*); consonants like *l* (produced by partially obstructing the airflow with the tongue) are liquids (and so is *r*). And to reiterate, these classes are abstract: a stop is a stop is a stop, no matter how it is produced (softly or loudly), and irrespective of whether it is presented aurally or in print.

Categories such as stops and liquids help explain why we *blog.* Linguists have long suspected that the language system includes rules that restrict the combination of stops and liquids. These rules require syllables to begin with stop–liquid syllables, as in *blog.* While all rules can be violated (recall that syllables like *lbog* are fine in Russian), violations are nonetheless costly, so rule violators like *lbog* are relatively ill-formed and, for this reason, are systematically avoided. These rules are universal and innate[36,37]; they are present in the brain of each and every speaker, irrespective of whether these syllables are present in their language or not.

So, do languages universally like *bloggers*? In the case of English, it's hard to tell. English has plenty of sequences like *bl* (they appear in *block, blame*), as well as *br, gl,* and *kr* (in *breath, glow,* and *crave*). To the extent that English speakers prefer *blog,* this could be simply due to its familiarity, rather than its abstract structure.

But there are reasons to doubt that syllable preferences result from experience alone. And to explain why, I need to tell you some more about the anatomy of syllables.

So far, we have discussed only sequences like *blif* and *lbif* (or more precisely, the stop–liquid sequence vs. the liquid–stop sequence). But these two examples are merely the extreme endpoints of a broader hierarchy of syllables. Best formed on this hierarchy (that is, the structure that is most consistent with the rules of grammar, hence, easiest for the language system to compute) are syllables like *blif,* followed by *bnif* (stop–nasal combinations); worse are *bdif* (stop–stop). and worst of all are *lbif* (liquid–stops). The entire hierarchy is illustrated in (1).

$$blif > bnif > bdif > lbif \qquad (1)$$

$$\text{well - formed} \longleftrightarrow \text{ill - formed}$$

There are reasons to believe that this hierarchy is universal. If you tally the frequency of these syllable types across languages, you find that, as you descend the hierarchy, the syllable becomes less frequent, as fewer languages allow it. What's more, languages that tend to have the worse-formed syllables (on the right) tend to also have better-formed ones (on the left).[26,35] So while Russian tolerates *lbif*, it also allows the remainder of the hierarchy, whereas English (with *blif*) does not allow any of the worse types. But, of course, the regularities across languages could occur for strictly historic reasons that have nothing to do with the brain. The interesting question is whether they do. Could the syllable hierarchy reflect universal linguistic principles that are active in every brain—yours and mine?

To find out, we can turn back to English. English, of course, allows sequences like *blif*, but the remaining types (*bnif, bdif* and *lbif*) are structures that English speakers have never heard before. In a series of experiments, my colleagues and I examined whether English speakers will nonetheless consider *bnif*, for instance, as better formed than *lbif*.

We reasoned that if *lbif* is ill-formed (that is, it violates the universal restrictions on syllable structure), then this sequence will be harder for the language system to compute, and consequently, it will be encoded less faithfully. We know from past research that when people hear syllables that are illicit in their language, they tend to "repair" them by inserting an illusory vowel in between the illicit consonants.[38] These repairs explain why English speakers pronounce *B'nei Israel* (Hebrew for "sons of Israel") as *Benei Israel*. So, we expected English speakers to likewise repair novel forms like *bnif*. The critical question, however, is not whether *bnif* will be repaired, but how often it is relative to *bdif* and *lbif*.

If people are sensitive to the syllable hierarchy, then as you go "south" on the syllable hierarchy, repair should likewise increase. *Lbif* (the worst of the worst) should be repaired the most (as *lebif*); the next-worst offender *bdif* should be repaired less often, and the least repaired should be *bnif*. And this is exactly what we found.

In the experiments, participants (English speakers) merely heard those words (pronounced by a Russian speaker; remember, these sequences are all fine in Russian), along with matched disyllables (*benif, bedif,* and *lebif*). And, of course, each such type was represented not by this single stimulus but by 30 words of the same type. In one set of experiments, they heard one word at a time (say, *lbif*), and were asked to indicate how many syllable it includes (one or two?); in another experiment, people hard a pair of stimuli (say, *lbif–lebif*) and indicated whether they were identical or not.

Results showed that, as the syllable becomes worse formed (going right in (1)), it becomes harder for English speakers to perceive it accurately. Rather than encoding *lbif* faithfully, they tend to represent it as a disyllable (*lebif*), and the worse formed the syllable, the more likely its distortion. So, when asked how many syllables are in *lbif*, they erroneously say "two," and when asked to compare *lbif* and *lebif*, they incorrectly say that these distinct forms are identical.[26,39–41]

It is not only English speakers that are so inclined. French[42] and Spanish[43] speakers do the same, and so do even speakers of Mandarin[44] and Korean[45]— languages whose syllables never begin with consonant clusters of any kind. Polish, on the other hand, is quite promiscuous with stop–stop combinations, like *ptak* (Polish for "bird"). In fact, in Polish, such combinations are far more frequent than stop–liquid combinations like *pl*.[46] But when Polish children acquire their language, children (age 19–38 months) produce well-formed syllables more accurately than ill-formed syllables.[46] This confirms that preferences concerning syllable structure are not solely the consequences of experiences with those syllable types. Syllables like *bdif* are disliked whether your language bans them or tolerates them.

At this point, you might agree that that the syllable hierarchy is not the product of experience alone. But you might seriously wonder whether this has anything to do with abstract rules. After all, the experiments only show that people misidentify novel sound sequences. The simplest explanation for these errors is not linguistic rules but auditory perception. Perhaps *lbif* presents greater demands on auditory processing. So, when you misidentify *lbif*, you aren't really repairing it (first encoding it as *lbif* and then transforming it to *lebif* to abide by the rules of language); your auditory system is directly encoding the stimulus as *lebif*.

This concern has certainly crossed our minds as well. To address this possibility, my colleagues and I showed that when Russian speakers heard the same stimuli, they could correctly identify the same words as having one syllable, so clearly, these stimuli are well within the capacity of the human ear. In another set of experiments, we showed that the errors of English speakers are not only oral. To do so, we repeated the original experiments when the materials were presented in print, free of any auditory demands. A large literature shows that reading and phonology are closely linked. When you read printed words (even silently), you automatically extract their abstract phonological structure—this is precisely why spelling mistakes such as *roze* (for *rose*) are so hard for us to detect when we attempt to proofread our work[47–49] (more on this in Chapter 13). If the difficulties with *lbif* are linguistic (rather than auditory), the abstract syllable preferences should be maintained even when the words are presented in print. And this is exactly what we observed with English speakers.[1] [39,44,50,51]

Very clever, you might reply, but I'm still not convinced. Perhaps articulation is the source of people's troubles. When you perceive *lbif*, you might try to silently repeat this sequence to yourself. In fact, there is a large body of research to suggest that your brain's motor system is automatically engaged when you hear speech sounds. Merely hearing *ba* engages the motor area that controls the lips; hearing *da* activates the area controlling the tongue[52–54]; we will return to this in Chapter 9. The difficulties, then, occur not in perception, but rather because articulation is hard.

Taking this possibility to heart, my colleagues and I repeated the same syllable count experiment (e.g., does *lbif* have one syllable or two?) while suppressing the articulatory motor systems in multiple ways. One set of experiments disrupted the participants' motor systems using transcranial magnetic stimulation (a method that temporarily disrupts activity in specific brain areas by generating electromagnetic stimulation on the scalp)[55]; another set of experiments disrupted articulation mechanically by having people immobilize their lips and tongues.[44] If the syllable hierarchy is due to articulatory demands, then once we disrupted articulation, people's sensitivity to the hierarchy (evident in their difficulties with bad syllables) should disappear. But both sets of experiments showed that people remained fully sensitive to syllable structure. In line with this possibility, an fMRI experiment showed that the processing of "bad" syllables engages not the motor areas of the brain, but rather parts of Broca's area in the left hemisphere—one of the brain's principal language hubs.[56]

To take stock of the results so far, we saw that adult speakers of different languages (English, Spanish, Korean, Mandarin, French) converged on similar preferences for syllables that they had never heard before. It is unlikely that this preference is only induced from experience (because we find it even in languages like Korean and Mandarin, which have no syllables that are even remotely similar to the ones we had used, as well as in Polish, a language in which ill-formed clusters are more frequent than well-formed ones). It is also not solely due to auditory difficulties (recall that printed words elicit similar effects) or articulatory challenges (they persist even when the articulatory

---

[1] In this task, people were asked to determine whether two items (e.g., *lbif* vs. *lebif*) were identical. To render the discrimination harder, the two words were presented in different case types (e.g., *lbif–LEBIF*), separated by a delay of 2.5 seconds. Results showed that worse-formed syllables elicited slower responses than better formed ones.

motor system is disrupted). So, could the abstract restrictions on syllable structure be innate? Would they be present even in newborns?

A final set of experiments turned to newborn infants—one- to three-day-olds in the maternity ward. In the experiment, newborns heard blocks of auditory syllables of one particular type, either the "good" stop–liquid combinations (e.g., *blif, brop, crog*) or the opposite "bad" sequence (e.g., *lbif, rbop, rcog*), while their brain activity was monitored using near infrared spectroscopy (a method that examines blood flow in the brain by measuring their scalps' absorption of infrared light). If *lbif* is challenging solely because of its unfamiliarity or its excessive motor demands, then no such effects should be observed with newborns. But our results suggest that, like the brains of adult English speakers, newborn brains had to "work overtime" when presented with "bad" syllables like *lbif*.[57]

But the skeptic in you may still be wondering. You might recall our previous discussion of the early auditory capacities of human fetuses and wonder whether they could offer an alternative explanation for these facts. We know that fetuses can hear their mothers' voices in utero.[58] Couldn't newborns' preferences for *brop* result from overhearing their (Italian) mothers exclaiming *bravo*! (but never *rbavo*)? Unlikely. And to explain why, we need to go back to the building blocks of phonology—the buckets for *b* and *p* and *r* and *l*.

As I mentioned earlier, infants make these distinctions practically from birth. In fact, they can do so better than their parents. For example, Japanese infants can contrast *rain* and *lain,* a distinction that their parents struggle to maintain.[59,60] But as the infants grow up, they lose many of the contrasts that are absent in their language and maintain the ones that are functional—this is known as "perceptual narrowing." Critically, this narrowing occurs only after the initial six months of life. And here's the rub. If newborns prefer *blif* because they overheard similar sequences in utero, then once they are born, their sound discrimination (of *l* and *r*) should also mirror their parents'. Japanese newborns, for instance, should treat *l* like *r*. But we know this is *not* the case. Moreover, by the best estimates, the mother's abdomen attenuates these distinctions. While it transmits the general rhythmical pattern of the language (akin to a distant drumming of consonants and vowels) finer-grained distinctions between consonants (which are critical for the contrast between *blif* and *lbif*) probably don't get through.[61,62]

To conclude, we see that, newborn infants show a preference for well-formed syllables like *blif,* which they have never heard before. These results do not tell us directly how newborns encode syllables like *blif* or whether their behavior is governed by the same abstract principles that are evident in adults. But they do suggest that the scaffolds for abstract phonological structure are already present at birth.

These conclusions join those of the previous sections to suggest that our knowledge of language is based on principles that are innate. But the picture of "innateness" emerging from these data is nuanced. We begin our linguistic lives equipped with universal principles that favor certain syllables over others. These principles, however, are soft biases, rather than inviolable laws. While all languages dislike syllables like *lbog*, some languages nonetheless tolerate them (as is the case with Polish and Russian). And there is a good reason to do so: by diversifying its syllable inventory, a language can express a larger number of concepts in shorter words.

But one should not lose the innate linguistic forest for the trees. As we saw, syllables like *lbog* are difficult for all brains to process, irrespective of whether they are present in the language (as is the case with Polish) or absent (as with English), and all newborns apparently start their life with a dislike of such syllables. So, variation does not preclude innateness. And language is by no means the only case where innate differences can yield different outcomes. As the developmental biologist Evan Balaban reminds us,[63] genetically identical plants can differ substantially on their morphology and size. Innateness only provides a shared scaffolding, but its realization in the organism can vary, depending on the environment and chance. Finding similar interactions between genes and experience in complex cognitive traits such as language should come as no surprise.

***

This chapter has examined the case for innate knowledge of language by focusing for the most part on a single case study from the phonology of spoken language. This was a deliberate choice, designed to allow us to delve into the thick of the evidence. But in closing, I would like to briefly mention a few other reasons to suspect that knowledge of language is abstract and innate. The evidence, this time, comes from an entirely different class of languages— ones that rely on our hands and eyes, rather than our ears and mouths.

Sign languages—the primary forms of communication of deaf individuals—are languages like all others. Different sign languages are mutually unintelligible, much like English and French, and each such language relies on rules and duality of patterning, just like spoken languages.

So without exposure to American Sign Language (ASL), for instance, a deaf child will not spontaneously sign ASL, just as an isolated hearing child will not spontaneously commence forming English sentences. Many deaf children, however, are born to families that don't speak a sign language, so because of their sensory deprivation, these children effectively live on a linguistic "desert island" so to speak—they have had no access to the language of their community.

Remarkably, such children spontaneously develop complex systems of signs. These systems (called "home signs") are not conventional sign languages like ASL, but they are nonetheless language-like, inasmuch as they show some resemblance to existing sign languages, and they also differ from the rudimentary gestures used by the parents.[64,65] Moreover, when deaf children are assembled in a community, a new sign language gradually emerges, complete with abstract rules and duality of patterning.[66–70] The spontaneous emergence of grammar, on the one hand, and its resemblance to the grammar of existing (spoken) languages, on the other, suggests that some knowledge of language relies on principles that are innate and abstract.

Further support for this claim is presented by deaf individuals who acquire English as a second language. Second-language acquisition for these children is a double challenge. Not only does the oral language present them with a sensory hurdle, but all this happens relatively late in life, and it is well known that language acquisition becomes harder with age (the thick accent of late second-language learners is a painful reminder of this fact). Interestingly, these children stand a better chance to master English if they have had previously acquired ASL (compared to children who have had no language experience). In fact, the "savings" incurred by the early exposure of deaf children to ASL were just as pronounced as those incurred by hearing English learners who were exposed to another spoken language, such as French or Urdu.[71]

One explanation for this finding is that children can transfer their knowledge of language from one modality (e.g., manual signs) to another (speech). Recent results from my lab directly support this possibility.[72]

In this research, we asked an audacious question: If you, an English speaker, were to encounter ASL for the first time, how would your brain register those stimuli. Would it treat them like dance, or would it seek to encode them just like any other unfamiliar language, akin to Hebrew or Urdu?

Surprisingly, our results support the latter possibility. First, we found that when naïve speakers first see ASL signs, they represent those signs by applying the same set of putatively innate rules that they also project to their spoken languages. This projection is particularly noteworthy given that the rules in question concern phonology (defined as patterns of meaningless linguistic elements). Second, when speakers had to choose between conflicting rules, their decision was informed by the structure of their spoken language. English speakers, for example, represented signs distinctly from Hebrew speakers, and these differences were predictable from the different morphologies of those two languages.[72] If speakers can spontaneously project principles from their spoken language to ASL, then those rules cannot be "about" either speech or signs, specifically. Rather, those results suggest that some of our linguistic principles are quite abstract.

***

Summarizing the discussion, in the past three chapters, we have seen that humans are born possessing a number of innate abstract concepts concerning the physical world, the social world, and language. Human newborns know that objects are cohesive entities that move continuously upon contact; they can represent the numbers of objects and events, distinguish between objects and agents, and show a preference for well-formed syllables over ill-formed ones. As infants mature, these social and linguistic scaffolds are enriched. They show an understanding of the goals of others, and they exhibit a rudimentary preference for "good" over "bad," rewarding agents accordingly. And just as infants eventually grow taller and heavier, in the domain of language, people eventually "grow" an abstract system of rules that govern syllable structure based on principles that are present at birth.

In each of the three domains, the relevant knowledge is demonstrably abstract, distinct from sensory pressures. We have seen that the newborn's notion of an occluded object is quite distinct from the sensory impression that the object leaves on her retina, and that the notion of an approximate number extends to sound and sight. Similarly, our understanding of "good" and "bad" goal-motivated agents has no sensory correlates. And finally, our understanding of the "syllable" applies to different sensory stimuli (both spoken and printed words); in fact, syllables also play a role in sign languages.[73,74]

Innateness, however, does not invariably imply that the capacity is fully formed at birth. In each of the domains we reviewed, the roots of those abstract concepts are evident at birth, but their full form sometimes emerges only later in life––this was especially evident in the social and linguistic domains. Innate capacities can also give rise to some variation. While all languages dislike syllables like *lbog*, some allow them whereas others do not. But the later developmental onset of some traits and their propensity to variation does not necessarily mean that their underlying concepts are learned by cultural immersion alone. Cultural immersion cannot account for the presence of cross-cultural universals in moral and social reasoning, on the one hand, and the convergence with nonhuman primates, on the other. Similarly, in the case of language, we have seen that speakers show knowledge of abstract linguistic principles that are unattested in their own languages, whereas deaf individuals form (sign) language anew in the absence of a language model.

Now that we have had a taste of what we *actually* know from birth, we will next examine what we *think* we know—the stories we tell ourselves about the origins of our ideas. Chapter 6 shows that there is a huge gulf between these two narratives. Chapters 7 and 8 consider why, tracing the reasons to some of the principles of core knowledge that were discussed in this chapter. Like those ideas themselves, our blindness to them is also innate.

References

1. Pinker S. *The Language instinct*. New York, NY: Morrow; 1994.
2. Hauser MD. *The evolution of communication*. Cambridge, MA: MIT Press; 1996.
3. Hauser MD, Chomsky N, Fitch WT. The faculty of language: what is it, who has it, and how did it evolve? *Science*. 2002;298:1569–1579.
4. Kaminski J, Call J, Fischer J. Word learning in a domestic dog: evidence for "fast mapping." *Science*. 2004;304(5677):1682–1683.
5. Pepperberg IM. Cognitive and communicative abilities of grey parrots. *Current Directions in Psychological Science*. 2002;11(3):83.
6. Giret N, Péron F, Nagle L, Kreutzer M, Bovet D. Spontaneous categorization of vocal imitations in African grey parrots (*Psittacus erithacus*). *Behavioural Processes*. 2009;82(3):244–248.
7. Hockett CF. The origin of speech. *Scientific American*. 1960;203:89–96.
8. Suzuki R, Buck JR, Tyack PL. Information entropy of humpback whale songs. *Journal of the Acoustical Society of America* 2006;119(3):1849–1866.
9. Miksis-Olds JL, Buck JR, Noad MJ, Cato DH, Stokes MD. Information theory analysis of Australian humpback whale song. *Journal of the Acoustical Society of America* 2008;124(4):2385–2393.
10. Payne RS, McVay S. Songs of Humpback Whales. *Science*. 1971;173:585–597.
11. Balaban E. Bird song syntax: learned intraspecific variation is meaningful. *Proceedings of the National Academy of Sciences of the United States of America*. 1988;85(10):3657–3660.
12. Marler P, Pickert R. Species-universal microstructure in the learned song of the swamp sparrow (Melospiza georgiana). *Animal Behaviour*. 1984;32(3):673–689.
13. Ouattara K, Lemasson A, Zuberbühler K. Campbell's monkeys concatenate vocalizations into context-specific call sequences. *Proceedings of the National Academy of Sciences of the United States of America*. 2009;106(51):22026–22031.

14. Zuberbühler K. A syntactic rule in forest monkey communication. *Animal Behaviour.* 2002;63(2):293–299.
15. Terrace HS, Petitto LA, Sanders RJ, Bever TG. Can an ape create a sentence? *Science.* 1979;206(4421):891–902.
16. Savage-Rumbaugh ES, Murphy J, Sevcik RA, Brakke KE, Williams SL, Rumbaugh DM. Language comprehension in ape and child. *Monographs of the Society for Research in Child Development.* 1993;58(3-4):1–222.
17. Chomsky N. *Syntactic structures.* The Hague, the Netherlands: Mouton; 1957.
18. Chomsky N. *Language and mind.* New York, NY: Harcourt, Brace & World; 1968.
19. Chomsky N. *Rules and representations.* New York, NY: Columbia University Press; 1980.
20. Wright R. A review of perceptual cues and robustness. In: Steriade D, Kirchner R, Hayes B, eds. *Phonetically based phonology.* Cambridge, England: Cambridge University Press; 2004:34–57.
21. Mattingly IG. Phonetic representation and speech synthesis by rule. In: Myers T, Laver J, Anderson J, eds. *The cognitive representation of speech.* Amsterdam: the Netherlands; 1981:415–420.
22. Ohala JJ. The origin of sound patterns in vocal tract constraints. In: MacNeilage PF, ed. *The production of speech.* New York, NY: Springer-Verlag; 1983:189–216.
23. Evans N, Levinson S. The myth of language universals: language diversity and its importance for cognitive science. *Behavioral and Brain Sciences.* 2009;32:429–492.
24. Blevins J. *Evolutionary phonology.* Cambridge, England: Cambridge University Press; 2004.
25. Greenberg J, H. Some generalizations concerning initial and final consonant clusters. In: Greenberg JH, Ferguson CA, Moravcsik, EA, eds. *Universals of human language.* Vol 2. Stanford, CA: Stanford University Press; 1978:243–279.
26. Berent I, Steriade D, Lennertz T, Vaknin V. What we know about what we have never heard: evidence from perceptual illusions. *Cognition.* 2007;104:591–630.
27. Liberman AM, Harris KS, Kinney JA, Lane H. The discrimination of relative onset-time of the components of certain speech and nonspeech patterns. *Journal of Experimental Psychology.* 1961;61(5):379–388.
28. Lisker L, Abramson A. A cross-language study of voicing in initial stops: Acoustical measurements. *Word.* 1964;20:384–422.
29. Eimas PD, Siqueland ER, Jusczyk P, Vigorito J. Speech perception in infants. *Science.* 1971;171(968):303–306.
30. Werker JF, Tees RC. Cross-language speech perception: evidence for perceptual reorganization during the first year of life. *Infant Behavior and Development.* 1984;7:49–63.
31. Ladefoged P. *A Course in Phonetics.* 2nd ed. New York, NY: Harcourt Brace Jovanovich; 1975.
32. Chomsky N, Halle M. *The sound pattern of English.* New York, NY: Harper & Row; 1968.
33. Keating PA. Phonetic and phonological representation of stop consonant voicing. *Language.* 1984;60(2):286–319.
34. Pierrehumbert J. Phonological and phonetic representation. *Journal of Phonetics.* 1990;18:375–394.
35. Berent I. The phonological mind. *Trends in Cognitive Sciences.* 2013;17(7):319–327.
36. Prince A, Smolensky P. *Optimality theory: constraint interaction in generative grammar.* Malden, MA: Blackwell; 1993/2004.

37. Clements GN. The role of the sonority cycle in core syllabification. In: Kingston J, Beckman M, eds. *Papers in laboratory phonology I: Between the grammar and physics of speech.* Cambridge, England: Cambridge University Press; 1990:282–333.

38. Dupoux E, Kakehi K, Hirose Y, Pallier C, Mehler J. Epenthetic vowels in Japanese: a perceptual illusion? *Journal of Experimental Psychology: Human Perception and Performance.* 1999;25:1568–1578.

39. Berent I, Lennertz T, Smolensky P, Vaknin-Nusbaum V. Listeners' knowledge of phonological universals: evidence from nasal clusters. *Phonology* 2009;26(1):75–108.

40. Berent I, Lennertz T, Smolensky P. Markedness and misperception: it's a two-way street. In: Cairns CE, Raimy E, eds. *Handbook of the syllable* Leiden, The Netherlands: Brill; 2011:373–394.

41. Berent I, Lennertz T, Balaban E. Language universals and misidentification: A two way street. *Language and Speech.* 2012;55(3):1–20.

42. Maïonchi-Pino N, Magnan A, Écalle J. Syllable frequency effects in visual word recognition: developmental approach in French children. *Journal of Applied Developmental Psychology.* 2010;31(1):70–82.

43. Berent I, Lennertz T, Rosselli M. Universal linguistic pressures and their solutions: evidence from Spanish. *The Mental Lexicon.* 2012;13(2):275–305.

44. Zhao X, Berent I. Universal restrictions on syllable structure: evidence From Mandarin Chinese. *Journal of Psycholinguistic Research.* 2016;45:795–811.

45. Berent I, Lennertz T, Jun J, Moreno MA, Smolensky P. Language universals in human brains. *Proceedings of the National Academy of Sciences.* 2008;105(14):5321–5325.

46. Jarosz G. Defying the stimulus: acquisition of complex onsets in Polish. *Phonology.* 2017;34(2):269–298.

47. Van Orden GC. A ROWS is a ROSE: spelling, sound and reading. *Memory and Cognition.* 1987;15:181–190.

48. Van Orden GC, Pennington BF, Stone GO. Word identification in reading and the promise of subsymbolic psycholinguistics. *Psychological Review.* 1990;97:488–522.

49. Perfetti C, Zhang S, Berent I. Reading in English and Chinese: evidence for a "universal" phonological principle. In: Frost R, Katz L, eds. *Orthography, phonology, morphology, and meaning.* Amsterdam, The Netherlands: North-Holland; 1992:227–248.

50. Berent I, Lennertz T. Universal constraints on the sound structure of language: phonological or acoustic? *Journal of Experimental Psychology: Human Perception & Performance.* 2010;36(1):212–223.

51. Tamasi K, Berent I. Sensitivity to phonological universals: the case of fricatives and stops. *Journal of Psycholinguistic Research.* 2015;44(4):59–81.

52. Pulvermüller F, Huss M, Kherif F, Moscoso del Prado Martin F, Hauk O, Shtyrov Y. Motor cortex maps articulatory features of speech sounds. *Proceedings of the National Academy of Sciences of the United States of America.* 2006;103(20):7865–7870.

53. D'Ausilio A, Pulvermüller F, Salmas P, Bufalari I, Begliomini C, Fadiga L. The motor somatotopy of speech perception. *Current Biology.* 2009;19(5):381–385.

54. Möttonen R, Watkins KE. Motor representations of articulators contribute to categorical perception of speech sounds. *Journal of Neuroscience.* 2009;29(31):9819–9825.

55. Berent I, Brem A-K, Zhao X, et al. Role of the motor system in language knowledge. *Proceedings of the National Academy of Sciences of the United States of America.* 2015;112:1983–1988.

56. Berent I, Pan H, Zhao X, et al. Language universals engage Broca's area. *PLoS One.* 2014;9(4):e95155.

57. Gómez DM, Berent I, Benavides-Varela S, et al. Language universals at birth. *Proceedings of the National Academy of Sciences of the United States of America.* 2014;111(16):5837-5341.
58. Kisilevsky BS, Hains SMJ, Brown CA, et al. Fetal sensitivity to properties of maternal speech and language. *Infant Behavior and Development.* 2009;32(1):59-71.
59. Tsushima T, Takizawa O, Sasaki M, et al. *Discrimination of English /r-l/ and /w-y/ by Japanese infants at 6-12 months: Language-specific developmental changes in speech perception abilities.* Paper presented at the 3rd International Conference on Spoken Language Processing, Yokohama, Japan, September 18-22, 1994.
60. Kuhl Patricia K, Stevens E, Hayashi A, Deguchi T, Kiritani S, Iverson P. Infants show a facilitation effect for native language phonetic perception between 6 and 12 months. *Developmental Science.* 2006;9(2):F13-F21.
61. Mehler J, Jusczyk P, Lambertz G, Halsted N, Bertoncini J, Amiel-Tison C. A precursor of language acquisition in young infants. *Cognition.* 1988;29(2):143-178.
62. Ramus F, Mehler J. Language identification with suprasegmental cues: a study based on speech resynthesis. *Journal of the Acoustical Society of America* 1999;105(1):512-521.
63. Balaban E. Cognitive developmental biology: history, process and fortune's wheel. *Cognition.* 2006;101(2):298-332.
64. Goldin-Meadow S, Mylander C. Gestural communication in deaf children: noneffect of parental input on language development. *Science.* 1983;221(4608):372-374.
65. Goldin-Meadow S, Mylander C. Spontaneous sign systems created by deaf children in two cultures. *Nature.* 1998;391(6664):279-281.
66. Senghas A, Kita S, Ozyurek A. Children creating core properties of language: evidence from an emerging sign language in Nicaragua. *Science.* 2004;305(5691):1779-1782.
67. Senghas A, Coppola M. Children creating language: how Nicaraguan sign language acquired a spatial grammar. *Psychological Science.* 2001;12(4):323-328.
68. Sandler W, Meir I, Padden C, Aronoff M. The emergence of grammar: systematic structure in a new language. *Proceedings of the National Academy of Sciences of the United States of America.* 2005;102(7):2661-2665.
69. Sandler W, Aronoff M, Meir I, Padden C. The gradual emergence of phonological form in a new language. *Natural Language and Linguistic Theory.* 2011;29:505-543.
70. Kastner I, Meir I, Sandler W, Dachkovsky S. The emergence of embedded structure: insights from Kafr Qasem sign language. *Frontiers in Psychology.* 2014;5.
71. Mayberry RI, Lock E, Kazmi H. Linguistic ability and early language exposure. *Nature.* 2002;417(6884):38-38.
72. Berent I, Bat-El O, Brentari D, Dupuis A, Vaknin-Nusbaum V. The double identity of linguistic doubling. *Proceedings of the National Academy of Sciences of the United States of America.* 2016;113(48):13702-13707.
73. Sandler W, Lillo-Martin DC. *Sign language and linguistic universals.* Cambridge, England: Cambridge University Press; 2006.
74. Brentari D. *A prosodic model of sign language phonology.* Cambridge, MA: MIT Press; 1998.

C. Our Blindness to Innate Ideas

6

Nativist Intuitions

Blindness is easy to recognize in others, but far harder to detect in ourselves. Just before I got my first pair of glasses, my husband had developed the strange habit of pointing out imaginary distant objects to me; it took time for me to realize that those objects were actually there. Self-blindness is even harder to detect, and congenital self-blindness is the most opaque of all. Now that we have established that innate ideas could plausibly exist, we are in a better position to ask whether we can spot them.

In this chapter, we will submit our psychological vision to a series of tests that measure our ability to look within ourselves and reason about the origins of our own ideas. The symptoms of "nativism blindness" that we are watching for are simple. The blind person fails to see what's in front of her and maintains that obliviousness even when prompted to attend to it. When we are blind to innate ideas, we consistently fail to recognize them as potential sources of our knowledge, and we persist in our position even when prompted. Some forms of blindness are selective—we are oblivious to some things, but not others. For example, people with prosopagnosia fail to recognize familiar faces, but they have no trouble telling faces from objects.[1] I suggest that our blindness to innate ideas has a similar clinical profile. So, to make the diagnosis, we should further demonstrate that our blindness is narrowly defined—we readily believe that some of our abilities are innate, but are blind to the possibility that our ideas might be. One of the questions that we will consider in this chapter is whether people are especially prone to psychic blindness when they reason about innate ideas.

To get at these issues, my lab invited participants to reason about various hypothetical "desert island" scenarios, in which a group of individuals (adults, infants, or nonhuman creatures—animals or even aliens) are raised in isolation (we have briefly mentioned some of these tests in Chapter 2). These "islanders" are fully cared for, but they are devoid of regular contact with other members of their species, so they are unable to observe their behaviors and capabilities or otherwise learn from them. If certain psychological traits

The Blind Storyteller. Iris Berent, Oxford University Press (2020). © Iris Berent, 2020.
DOI: 10.1093/oso/9780190061920.001.0001

are innate in the species, then those behaviors should emerge spontaneously in the group. The spontaneous emergence of a trait demonstrates its innateness. Of interest is which traits—cognitive or noncognitive—are innate.

My lab has presented people with several such scenarios.[2] In one experiment, we asked participants to reason about 80 traits of adult humans—half of them cognitive, half of them noncognitive. We carefully chose the cognitive traits to correspond to behaviors that have been broadly documented by ethnographers in many human communities, so they could plausibly be considered innate.[3] These include such behaviors as "forming sentences," "reflecting on one's past and future," "recognizing taboos," "keeping track of time," and "having classifications of body parts." The matched noncognitive behaviors were emotions (e.g., "anger in response to hostility," "love for one's family," "fear of danger") and motor traits ("walking to move around," "sitting to relax," "lifting an object with hands").

Since any given trait can often be classified in multiple ways—for example, people can conceive of "forming sentences" as either a cognitive activity that relies on ideas or as a motor act of "talking"—we asked two other groups of participants to classify the traits. One group sorted them into three bins—"thinking," "action," and "emotions," while yet another group contrasted "processes" and "ideas." The results confirmed that cognitive traits were reliably more likely to be classified as both "thinking" and "ideas" compared to the noncognitive traits.

Our main question was whether people believe that cognitive traits are less likely to be innate. To find out, we asked a third group of participants to rate all of the traits for their propensity to emerge spontaneously on our desert island. The results suggested that people were less likely to state that adult cognitive traits will emerge spontaneously compared to noncognitive (motor and emotional) traits. Moreover, the rating of the trait for innateness correlated with its association with "ideas"—the more likely people were to classify a given trait as an "idea," the less likely they were to classify it as "innate" (as likely to emerge spontaneously).

Innateness, however, is difficult for people to gauge in the behavior of adults. First, adults have plenty of opportunities to learn things, and they exhibit considerable individual differences in their linguistic and social behaviors. So it is no wonder that participants believe that traits such as "forming sentences" are learned rather than innate.

Another obstacle to discerning the innateness of adult traits is presented by the role of "triggers." As we saw in previous chapters, some innate traits are present at birth, but others emerge only later in development. Such late-emerging traits often depend on certain minimal experiences, called "triggers." Language, for example, is arguably an innate human trait, yet feral children who are raised in isolation do not develop language spontaneously.[4] The trigger for language is likely social interactions. Indeed, when deaf individuals are raised in a group (along with other deaf children), sign language emerges spontaneously, akin in structure and complexity to all other languages. This has been documented in Nicaragua[5,6] and Israel.[7] To be clear, "triggers" are not the same thing as "learning"—the children in these cases did not have an opportunity to learn sign language from the hearing adults in their environment, because they did not use a sign language. But this social experience is apparently necessary to trigger the innate linguistic capacities that are present in the child. And these triggers might have complicated the reasoning of some of the participants in our desert island situation. Perhaps some stated that the islanders failed to develop complex cognitive traits because they knew they lacked the necessary triggers for them, not because they believed that cognitive traits are not innate.

Positing the existence of infant islanders allows us to counter this possibility. Since the behavior of newborn infants is far less dependent on both learning from experience and triggers, infants present a more sensitive test of innateness. So, are people more likely to credit infants with having innate ideas?

Not really. When we presented people with numerous cognitive traits that have been observed in early infancy (e.g., "Expecting stationary objects to move only if contacted by other moving objects"; "Understanding that objects still exist when occluded";[8] and "Preferring human faces to non-human figures"[9]), people still rated them as less likely to be innate (that is, as less likely to emerge spontaneously among the islanders) compared to non-cognitive traits, both motor (e.g., "Sucking on their thumb")[10]) and sensory ("Contrasting low musical tones and high tones"[11]). And once again, the innateness of a trait was negatively associated with "ideas" (as determined by another group of participants)—the more strongly a trait was classified as an "idea," the less likely it was to be viewed as "innate."

To further clarify whether people only view ideas as *less* likely to be innate (relative to noncognitive traits) or whether they really think that ideas *aren't* innate, in another set of experiments, we asked participants to explicitly indicate whether or not each trait is inborn using a simple yes/no response. The results were quite clear-cut: people responded that noncognitive traits are innate, and this was the case for both adult and infant traits, but ideas are not (i.e., the proportion of "inborn" responses was lower than chance). And as in previous experiments, the "innateness" responses were strongly and negatively associated with the perception of these traits as "thinking" or "ideas."

But does this really show that they are *blind* to innate ideas? Not necessarily. Perhaps people fail to see how cognitive traits emerge in infants because they cannot fathom the idea of testing the cognitive capacities of newborns. After all, few people are aware of the sophisticated infant research that I discussed in the previous chapter. So perhaps people would prove to be more open to the existence of innate ideas if they were given an opportunity to learn how infant research works.

With these thoughts in mind, we presented yet another group of participants with four detailed scenarios of infant research. Three described experiments with number, language and moral preference (all of them were discussed in Chapters 3–5). The number experiment examined whether newborn infants can detect the congruence between a number of sounds and lights[12]; the language case concerned newborns' preference for well-formed syllables like *blog* compared to ill-formed ones such as *lbog*.[13] The moral case was the experiment, carried out on three-month-old infants, that showed their preference for "helpers" (a character helping another climb up a hill) over "hinderers" (a character who pushes the climber in the opposite direction).[14] For comparison, we also presented this group with a description of an emotional trait—infants' preferences for happy over angry faces.[15] With just a few slight modifications for simplicity and clarity, we explained the design of each experiment (complete with a pictures) and provided a detailed description of the expected outcomes (e.g., if infants have moral preferences, then they should prefer to look longer at the helper figure than the hinderer). Then we asked them to provide a clear yes/no response as to whether infants will exhibit the relevant trait.

The results were unambiguous. People overwhelmingly predicted that newborns will show emotional preferences, but they did not believe that newborns will exhibit cognitive traits. For number and moral preference, people explicitly stated that these behaviors will be absent in newborns; for the language preference, they were at chance.

These conclusions have now been confirmed by another lab. When the psychologists Jenny Wang and Lisa Feigenson[16] asked people to reason about the origin of cognitive traits that are present in young infants ("thinking an unsupported object will fall"), participants responded that these traits are learned, much like we learn how to read, and unlike sensory capacities, such as seeing and hearing, which were correctly viewed as innate. Moreover, Wang and Feigenson obtained these results with adult participants in the US and India, with six-year old children, with educated academics, and even with academics whose area of expertise is in the mind sciences. These scientists should have known better, but they incorrectly asserted that core knowledge is learned, not innate.

Taking stock of the results thus far, we've seen that people explicitly state that cognitive traits are unlikely to emerge spontaneously in newborns, and they also rate cognitive traits as less likely to emerge spontaneously in older infants and adults. Furthermore, when asked to clearly indicate whether or not these ideas are innate, their response was "no", and correspondingly, they asserted that such traits are learned. It is unlikely that they think so only because they don't understand how cognition can be tested, as people maintain the same conclusions even after being presented with detailed descriptions of such experiments. And it also doesn't look like people simply show a generalized aversion to all forms of nativism; people have no trouble accepting that emotions, for instance, are innate. So, it appears that people *selectively* maintain that cognitive traits are not innate. The strong association between innateness and "ideas" explains why—cognitive traits reflect ideas, and people think that ideas aren't innate (for reasons that will be discussed at length in the following chapters). Indeed, the more likely a trait is to be associated with "ideas," the less likely it is to be thought innate.

But what does this behavior really mean: are we merely oblivious to innateness, or are we actually blind? Obliviousness can be remedied by steering one's attention in the right direction, but blindness will persist. And obliviousness to innate ideas could emerge for a good reason. All of the cases examined thus far concern humans—a topic on which we all possess considerable expertise. Too much knowledge can be problematic. Perhaps people believe that cognitive human traits cannot be innate because many of them exhibit variation (e.g., we all speak different languages) and involve learning (e.g., we learn the rules of grammar in school). Our previous experiences with human traits can render us oblivious to their innateness. So, which one is it—obliviousness or blindness—that underlies our underestimation of innate ideas?

To find out, a final series of experiments from my lab sought to minimize the "curse of knowledge" by having participants reason about traits that they know very little about—those of nonhuman animals and space aliens. To overcome their obliviousness, we redirected the participants' attention by telling them explicitly that all of the traits considered are innate, in the sense that they emerge early in development in all member of the species and that they are evolutionarily adaptive; some of these experiments further stated that scientists believe these capacities are inborn.

Each experiment presented participants with detailed descriptions of cognitive and noncognitive traits. One experiment concerned birds. Cognitive traits were behaviors that heavily rely on a specific information structure. For the quail, this was the unique three-part structure of its songs ("They always begin with two short parts and end with a long acoustic trill"). The matched noncognitive behaviors were motor, such as the head motions of the quail ("The males rapidly bob their heads up and down at a specific range of frequencies"). Another experiment featured a pair of alien traits—the specific structure of their communication and their locomotion behavior. In each case, people rated the likelihood of the trait to emerge spontaneously in a "desert island" situation.

The results of the two experiments fully agreed with the human traits. People stated that cognitive traits are less likely to be innate (that is, emerge spontaneously) compared to motor traits. And people maintained this opinion even when they were explicitly told that both traits—cognitive and motor—are in fact innate.

People thus evince a systematic tendency to disregard the innateness of cognitive traits. They do so across multiple traits of both adults and infants, humans and nonhumans, and despite explicit information to the contrary (that the traits *are* in fact innate). And the tendency is quite selective—people are all too willing to consider emotions and motor traits as innate. But when it comes to ideas, they believe innateness is unlikely: the stronger the association of a trait with "ideas," or "thinking," the less likely they are to consider innateness. This does not look like a harmless case of inattention in a person that otherwise has 20/20 vision. When it comes to nativism and ideas, people are systematically blind.

References

1. Rapcsak SZ. Face Recognition. *Current Neurology And Neuroscience Reports*. 2019;19(7):41–41.
2. Berent I, Platt M, Sandoboe GM. People's intuitions about innateness. *Open Mind: Discoveries in Cognitive Science*. 2019;3. doi:10.1162/opmi_a_00029

3. Pinker S. *The blank slate: The modern denial of human nature.* New York, NY: Viking; 2002.
4. Curtiss S, Fromkin V, Krashen S, Rigler D, Rigler M. The linguistic development of Genie. *Language.* 1974;50(3):528–554.
5. Senghas A, Kita S, Ozyurek A. Children creating core properties of language: evidence from an emerging sign language in Nicaragua. *Science.* 2004;305(5691):1779–1782.
6. Pyers JE, Senghas A. Language promotes false-belief understanding: evidence from learners of a new sign language. *Psychological Science.* 2009;20(7):805–812.
7. Sandler W, Meir I, Padden C, Aronoff M. The emergence of grammar: systematic structure in a new language. *Proceedings of the National Academy of Sciences of the United States of America.* 2005;102(7):2661–2665.
8. Spelke ES, Kinzler KD. Core knowledge. *Developmental Science.* 2007;10(1):89–96.
9. Reid VM, Dunn K, Young RJ, Amu J, Donovan T, Reissland N. The human fetus preferentially engages with face-like visual stimuli. *Current Biology.* 2017;27(12):1825–1828.e1823.
10. Wurth CW. Apgar test for the neurological assessment of newborns. *Cerebral Palsy Journal.* 1966;27(1):5–7.
11. Háden GP, Németh R, Török M, Winkler I. Predictive processing of pitch trends in newborn infants. *Brain Research.* 2015;1626:14–20.
12. Izard V, Sann C, Spelke ES, Streri A. Newborn infants perceive abstract numbers. *Proceedings of the National Academy of Sciences of the United States of America.* 2009;106(25):10382–10385.
13. Gómez DM, Berent I, Benavides-Varela S, et al. Language universals at birth. *Proceedings of the National Academy of Sciences of the United States of America.* 2014;111(16):5837–5341.
14. Hamlin JK, Wynn K, Bloom P. Three-month-olds show a negativity bias in their social evaluations. *Developmental Science.* 2010;13(6):923–929.
15. Datyner A, Henry JD, Richmond JL. Rapid facial reactions in response to happy and angry expressions in 7-month-old infants. *Developmental Psychobiology.* 2017;59(8):1046–1050.
16. Wang JJ, Feigenson L. Is Empiricism Innate? Preference for Nurture over Nature in People's Beliefs about the Origins of Human Knowledge. *Open Mind.* 2019;3:89–100.

7

The Tempest Is Brewing

Remember Remy, the Humanities cat (from Chapter 1)? Remy passes his days amidst Harvard's academic towers in leisure, utterly oblivious to the grave scholarly problems that preoccupy his human admirers. Remy, is, no doubt, blind to such notions, and the reason is quite clear: Remy was born a cat, and being a cat entails a distinct personality style along with certain cognitive limitations. It now turns out that we humans are not so different from Remy. Our limitations are, of course, distinct, but blind we nonetheless are, and as we will shortly see, our condition, too, is likewise congenital. We now turn to consider the reasons for our predicament. Why are we so blind to the workings of our own minds? What forces render it so difficult for us to look within ourselves and recognize the origins of our ideas?

In Chapter 2, we considered several explanations for our nativism blindness, our profound resistance to the notion that some of our ideas are innate. Maybe we are blissfully ignorant. Perhaps our frequent engagement with learning makes us believe that *all* knowledge must be learned. A related proposal by the philosopher Peter Carruthers[1,2] is that we are overly confident that we understand how knowledge is obtained (from experience, communication, and inference), so we dismiss the possibility of a fourth route—that knowledge could be innate. Or maybe we lose track of our innate instincts in the same way that we might look for our eyeglasses, forgetting that they are still on our noses—perhaps those ideas are so deeply engrained in us that we no longer notice that they mediate our view of things.[3] Or to draw an analogy from another one of our senses, consider how strange our own voices sound to us when we hear them on tape. We are so used to hearing them distorted by the vibrations of our skulls that we fail to recognize what they really sound like. The same holds for nativism blindness. It's not that we are opposed to innate ideas; it's that our experiences and our cognitive architecture render them invisible to us, even though they shape our reasoning.

Another explanation asserts that people are actively averse to innate ideas.[4] Innateness does carry a steep philosophical and social price tag. Recognizing

The Blind Storyteller. Iris Berent, Oxford University Press (2020). © Iris Berent, 2020.
DOI: 10.1093/oso/9780190061920.001.0001

that some of our mental capacities and ideas are inborn opens up the possibility that we are not all created equal. This notion would seem to shake our core view of ourselves as free agents, threaten our deeply held principles of human equality, and open the door to prejudice, discrimination, and other injustices. That's a higher price than many of us would care to pay.

But none of these proposals explains the experimental results outlined in Chapter 6. Blissful ignorance and mind opacity fail to explain why we would maintain our denial of our innate traits even after we have been explicitly informed that these capacities *are* in fact innate. Similarly, a socially/philosophically based resistance to nativism does not explain why we are averse to innate ideas specifically; this is also a challenge for the mind-opacity explanation. While it makes sense that we would be incensed about the innateness of socially relevant emotions, such as aggression, and about inequalities in cognitive capacities such as intelligence, our social and philosophical concerns should have no bearing on our resistance to abstract notions such as "number" and "syllable." While each of these previous proposals can explain some of our coarse gut reactions to innateness, none of them explains the selective nature of the aversion we have shown here—why we are especially resistant to innate *ideas*.

In what follows, I will outline a novel solution to this problem. I suggest that our resistance to innate ideas results from two principles of core cognition—Dualism and Essentialism. These two principles are likely innate, and they are quite ancient evolutionarily; as we saw (in Chapters 3 and 4), the roots of Dualism are also evident in nonhuman animals. Indeed, the principles of Dualism and Essentialism are adaptive, as they guide our understanding of the physical, social, and natural worlds; clearly they do us lots of good. But they can run amok when they are applied to problems that they were not designed to handle, and reasoning about innate ideas is such a case.

When we reason about the origins of our knowledge, we instinctively apply our innate core knowledge of Dualism and Essentialism. Unbeknownst to us, the two principles collide to form a perfect storm. Our resistance to innate ideas is a byproduct of this conflict—collateral damage, as it were. It emerges from the clash between these two titanic forces.

This chapter traces the formation of the storm. I first introduce its two engines—the intuitive principles of Dualism and Essentialism; next, I describe how the incompatibilities between these core principles give rise to our blindness to innate ideas. The next chapter puts these ideas to experimental tests.

Dualism

Thanks to advances in genetics and developmental biology, it is now possible to build replicas of human organs—ears, kidneys, and livers. Replicating a whole human being is still within the realm of science fiction, but philosophers have long been interested in such procedures. Their interest lies not in the contributions of these procedures to science and health, but in their potential to shed light on how we reason about human bodies and minds.

Consider one such imaginary procedure, inspired by the work of the British philosopher Derek Parfit.[5] The procedure concerns a hypothetical "personal replication" machine. You would enter the machine's chamber, wait a few seconds, and when the "ready" buzzer goes off and the door opens, two "you's" would emerge—your old original self and your replica (let's call him "youtoo"). Unlike cloning, which only copies your genes, replication promises to duplicate your entire adult body—the joint product of your genes and the whole array of experiences that have made you who you are. Parfit has used such scenarios to explore the notion of personal identity— whether "you" and "youtoo" are one and the same person, indeed, whether a "person" can even be said to exist. Here, however, we focus on the outcomes of the replication—specifically, which of the original's features transfer to the replica.

Does it duplicate your physical properties, such as your hairstyle and your eye color? Probably yes. But what about some of your mental states? Will youtoo recognize your spouse? Will he share your taste for art and music? Will he speak English and know your home address?

When the psychologists Matthias Forstmann and Pascal Burmer[6] asked people to consider similar scenarios, they noticed a sharp divide in reasoning about bodies and minds. People stated that the replica would faithfully preserve the physical properties of the original human's body. But when it came to mental states ("He knows exactly at what time his train to work arrives in the morning"; "He reacts to being called by his nickname"), full replication seemed less likely. And people arrived at this conclusion instinctively, without much deliberate "philosophizing." In fact, when the experiment attempted to interfere with deliberate reasoning (by having participants answer the same questions while keeping a complex alphanumeric series in memory, such as "n63#maQ"), they were even *less* likely to believe that the original's mental states would transfer to the replica. The psychologists Bruce Hood, Nathalia Gjersoe, and Paul Bloom reported similar results when they asked those questions of children.[7] For both age groups (adults and children), the mind–body divide only seemed to apply to humans; when the replication was of a nonhuman (a robot or a camera), people had no difficulty accepting that the information available to the original would transfer to the replica.

Why are we so sure that our minds are distinct from our bodies? Science tells us that minds and bodies are one and the same—our psyche *is* our brain. So, if the brain were to be replicated, then our psychological states should be perfectly replicated as well. But our gut feelings tell us otherwise. The notion of replicating mental states—thoughts and beliefs—just seems weird; it is qualitatively different from the replication of an arm or an ear.

The psychologist Paul Bloom[8] argues that this is because we are intuitively and innately Dualists. Bloom is concerned not with Descartes' philosophical stance—a product of deliberate and rational thought—but with the intuitive workings of our cognition. We view bodies and minds as two separate entities, each of which follows a distinct set of principles. Bodies are material, whereas minds are immaterial.

Dualism is already evident in early infancy. Infants, indeed, newborns, expect objects to obey the laws of physics—*contact, cohesion,* and *continuity.*[9] Recall (from Chapter 3) that newborns expect objects to behave as cohesive entities. So when they see a moving object that is partly occluded, they automatically assume it is complete, rather than a collection of independent parts.[10] Newborns also expect an object to move by contact and continuously—an impossible launching event (Ball A collides with Ball B, but B launches only after a delay, or in a different direction) elicits surprise.[11] These expectations operationally define the psychological notion of a material object.

Agents, however, are not subject to these same physical expectations. When a man approaches a woman, 7-month old infants show no surprise if the woman moves spontaneously (suspending the requirement for contact).[12] Infants are likewise willing to have agents violate the continuity requirement. When five-month-olds see an object moving continuously in between two screens (see Figure 7.1A), they will assume that the event features a single object, whereas a discontinuous motion (the object appears and disappears behind each screen without ever moving in between them) suggests that there are two different objects.

How do we know what an infant assumes? We can infer the infants' interpretation of the original event by next presenting them with a movie featuring either one or two objects. Since infants are novelty seekers, we would

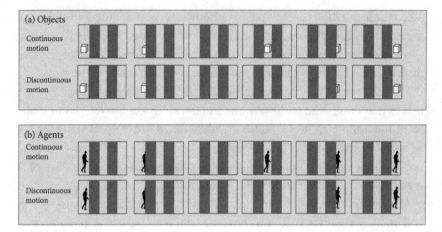

Figure 7.1. Continuous vs. discontinuous motion for objects and humans.
Redrawn, from Kuhlmeier et al. (2004);[13] person image licensed under CC BY-SA.

expect them to be more interested (that is, to look longer) at a novel event. For example, if they originally assumed that there was one object, they should now look longer at two objects. The psychologists Valerie Kuhlmeier, Paul Bloom, and Karen Wynn found that infants in the continuous motion experiment preferred looking at two objects (as they had inferred that there was only one), whereas infants in the discontinuous motion experiment preferred looking at one object (as they had expected there to be two). These results confirm that infants believe that physical objects must move continuously. Remarkably, infants are willing to suspend this belief for agents. So when the same motion scenario depicted two tiny people (matched in size to the objects, see Figure 7.1B), the infants' preference did not differ in the continuous and discontinuous conditions.[13] Agents, then, are free of the physical constraints that we apply to material objects.

Agents, on the other hand, are subject to other requirements that apply to them alone. For example, infants expect agents to follow their goals. When they see a hand attempting to reach one of two objects, they expect the hand to continue reaching toward that same object, even when its position is changed. Infants, however, do not expect the same thing to happen when the hand is replaced by a rod. Similarly, infants witnessing the helper/hinderer scenario (where a character attempts to either help or hinder another from climbing up a hill; see Chapter 4) prefer the "helper" over the hinderer when those characters are equipped with eyes (suggesting an animate agent).

Infants showed no such preferences when the eyes were removed (suggesting an inanimate object).[14,15]

The finding that agents are exempt from the material requirements that apply to objects and that (in the mind of infants), they must obey psychological mental states that apply to them alone, are in line with the idea that mental states are immaterial, and thus distinct from the materiality that defines objects.

Additional evidence that people perceive mental states as immaterial is presented by experiments that asked children to reason about the transfer of traits from one individual to another. Earlier, we saw that, when children reason about the replication of the body, they believe that physical properties are more likely to transfer than psychological ones (as do adults[67]). But when children consider what happens after we die (after the demise of the body), it is now psychological traits that they consider most likely to persist, and psychological traits that concern abstract ideas, even more so.[16] Similar results obtain when children imagine a situation that invokes the reincarnation of one creature in another[17]: children spontaneously presume that the mind can spontaneously leave the body; we will consider the evidence in detail in Chapter 14.

Once we grow up, we don't seem to simply shed our Dualism along with our baby teeth. We've already seen that people draw a sharp mind–body divide when they reason about human replicas. A conversation with Tammi, my hairdresser, further drives this home.

Heads are obviously Tammi's area of expertise, and like all successful hairdressers, she is also a good psychologist, albeit one with a decidedly Dualist take. Tammi and I were discussing a common acquaintance—a sickly, elderly lady.

Me: She is a difficult woman. But she is very sick, and the disease has probably wrecked her brain . . .
Tammi: Well, I have seen some sick women rise above their illness.
Me: Yes, but her brain is impaired . . .
Tammi: It doesn't matter! If she only had the will power, she would have risen above her predicament.

Paul Bloom[8,18] agrees that Dualism continues to shape our reasoning as adults. Our propensity to project purpose and intentionality onto nonmaterial agents can explain a large array of phenomena, ranging from our religious beliefs (God and souls are immaterial intentional beings, after all) to our willingness to invest millions in a piece of art, which we see as a direct product of its creator's intentions, but not in its seemingly identical replica (which we don't). We will return to some of these consequences in subsequent chapters.

Dualism can even shape your health. If, in your mind, "you" includes only your immaterial self, then you might be less inclined to protect the well-being of your physical body. Research suggests that it's possible to change participants' health attitudes merely by highlighting their Dualist beliefs. In a series of studies, the psychologist Matthias Forstmann and colleagues compared the health behaviors of two groups of participants.[19] One group was primed for Dualism by having them read a passage stating that minds and bodies are distinct; another group read passages stating that "minds and bodies are both rooted in the same physical substance," priming them toward Physicalism. Results showed that participants in the Physicalism condition were more likely to state that they typically engage in healthy behaviors ("I limit the amount of fats"). Strikingly, when offered the choice of a meal, participants in the Physicalism condition were more likely to make a healthier choice.

So, we are intuitive Dualists. From early infancy, we contrast our immaterial minds and our material bodies, and this belief continues to shape many of our attitudes and behaviors into adulthood. As we will see, our beliefs about the origins of our knowledge are another casualty of Dualism. But before we can explore innate ideas, we need to consider the second engine of the perfect storm—our notion of Essentialism.

Essentialism

Let us return to our replication machine for another thought experiment. Now we will suppose that the science of replication has moved from the stage of pure research on humans to the commercial reproduction of people's beloved pets. In fact, things are going so well that the facility is booming and buzzing with activity. The lab has two replication chambers that operate in parallel, and a fresh new lab assistant takes charge.

The assistant enters the waiting room and greets two excited pet owners— the owner of a dog, Lassie, and the owner of Lia, a cat. He leads each of the animals into its designated chamber and closes the doors behind them. He then turns on the two machines and waits patiently until the lights stop blinking and the "ready" buzzers sound. But when he opens up their doors, he is greeted by a horrible surprise. Somehow the wires in the two machines had been crossed. Instead of two cute dogs and two cute cats, there are four "half baked" creatures that look like both. What's worse, the assistant has neglected to record his notes of the procedure, and he can't remember which pet went into which machine, and hence which of these monsters corresponds to Lia the cat and which to the dog Lassie. At this point, he is no longer sure whether the pet owners are even interested in collecting the replicas (for which they paid heftily), but surely they will want their originals back. What is the assistant to do?

Most people would probably advise the assistant to not rely on mere appearances. Given the machine's malfunction, it would be entirely possible that the color of the cat and dog's original fur was changed. But most people would not accept that the essence of the original living thing was lost, no matter how much it physically changed. Maybe it looks like a cat/dog now, but one of those chimeras is still Lassie and one of them is still Lia. After all, your dog can get a haircut, and your black cat can be stained by fresh white paint, but they are still your dog and cat. We may not know the precise genetics that defines the dog and cat as such, but we nonetheless expect that the animal still possesses some unique material aspect in its insides. So, the material insides of two of those half-baked creatures hold the best promise to reveal their true essence. *Essentialism*, the intuitive belief that every living thing possesses an immutable material essence, is a second principle of core knowledge.

And once again, it is not only adults who hold this belief. The psychologist Frank Keil has shown that elementary school children know that painting white stripes on the back of a raccoon will not turn it into a skunk, whereas a coffee pot (an artifact) can readily be converted into a bird feeder. This finding suggests that the essence of living things is immutable—neither a superficial nor a radical physical transformation can erase it. Further, this biological essence resides in the material "insides" of living things. So, when the children are informed that, upon careful inspection, researchers have discovered that an animal that looks just like a raccoon actually possesses the insides of a skunk, the children conclude that the animal must be a skunk, not a raccoon (as suggested by its appearance). On the other hand, a similar discovery about an artifact (that the insides of a bird feeder are really those of a coffee pot) makes no difference for its classification.[20]

The psychologists Susan Gelman and Henry Wellman have documented that beliefs about the essence of living things are even held by three-year-olds. These young children know, for instance, that the insides of a pig are more similar to the insides of a cow than the insides of a piggy bank (which looks just like a pig on the outside). Moreover, children state that the removal of a dog's insides (its blood and bones) is more likely to alter its identity than the removal of its fur.[21] Unlike artifacts, natural kinds possess an immutable essence that defines them as such and that depends on their material "insides," the three-year-olds they spoke to affirmed.

Other evidence suggesting that this biological essence is material is provided by its physical localization. When kindergarteners were asked to advise a scientist on how to determine what kind of animal was found frozen within a block of ice, they suggested that a sample must be taken from the animal's insides. They did not, however, believe that this method of sampling was necessary when the scientist was testing an inanimate substance (a rock or a metal).[22] Biological essence, they insisted, is localized at the center of animals, whereas the physical properties of nonliving things are distributed. Moreover, that tiny material piece is understood to play a role in biological inheritance.

Children indeed seem to have a rudimentary notion of inheritance. Preschoolers know, for example, that horse parents are more likely to transmit novel physical traits (e.g., hairy ears) to their own babies than to other horses, yet acquired traits (e.g., a scratch on a leg, acquired from walking through the bushes) are not transmitted.[23] Children also know that adoptees (a kangaroo raised by goats) will maintain the physical properties of their biological parents (having a pouch, hopping). Critically, when asked to reason about the mechanism of inheritance, they describe it in terms of the transmission of a tiny piece of matter. For example, they state that a brown puppy acquires its color by receiving a "tiny little piece" from its parents.[24] So, children know that living things (but not artifacts) are defined by physical properties that are localized in a tiny piece of matter that they inherit from their biological parents.

But how do children acquire this belief? Unlike intuitive physics (which has been documented in newborns), naïve Essentialism is typically observed only in childhood, so one might wonder whether this notion is learned from experience. Indeed, younger children sometimes fail to show an understanding of essence and biological inheritance. For example, kindergarteners (as opposed to elementary school children) do believe that a racoon that is painted to look like a skunk is a skunk,[20] and preschoolers believe that an adopted child can preserve the knowledge of its biological parents (red light signals "stop").[25] These observations are potentially problematic because they seem to suggest that the children's judgments are not based on a notion of biological inheritance at all.

Children, in this view, know too well that traffic conventions are learned. So if they insist that offspring maintain the beliefs of their biological parents, then their reasoning must be based not on inheritance but on the fact that parents and offspring belong to the same category.[25] Categories, indeed, provide a rich source of predictions. If you know that John and Jack are members of the Eagle soccer team and that they both like pizza, then you might well assume that Joe the goalie is a pizza lover as well. This inference is based on the notion that members of the same category share common traits. And family is certainly a salient category. Since parents and their offspring belong to that same category, young children in the experiment might conclude that family members share traits simply by virtue of their category membership, rather than by inheritance. Granted, children must possess some understanding of biology, as they assume a stronger link between biological parent and child relative to adoptees. Beyond this basic fact, however, trait transmission may not be due to inheritance.

But these results do not necessarily show that these children are devoid of Essentialist beliefs. For one, some children might assume that conventional beliefs are innate, in the sense that the potential to acquire those beliefs is inherited from biological parents. Another possibility is that some of these children do know that conventional beliefs are learned, but they incorrectly state that offspring acquire the beliefs of their biological parents for methodological reasons—because the experimenter had previously probed them about the biological inheritance of physical traits and, in so doing, she inadvertently biased their responses to subsequent questions.[26] Similar methodological considerations could explain the failure of young children to recognize the identity of a painted raccoon—those children might be confused by the incongruence between the raccoon's insides and its outsides.[21]

There are also other reasons to doubt that our Essentialist beliefs are solely acquired by learning. First, Susan Gelman[26] notes that the Essentialist beliefs of young children are often stronger than those of older children and adults. For example, 4-year-old children state that stereotypical gender behavior (girls play with dolls; boys want to be firefighters) will develop irrespective of environment (whether an infant boy is raised with boys or girls), whereas 9-year old children and adults are acutely sensitive to the social environment.[27] Young children, however, do not attribute the same behavioral stereotypes to infants. This is significant, because it suggests that children's predictions concerning gender are based on their beliefs about latent biological potential (infant boys are born with the biological potential to exhibit certain behaviors once they mature), rather than similarity to members of the same gender category (the behavior of infant boys is determined by their similarity to other infant boys).

Similar results were obtained cross-culturally. In one such study, the Vezo people of Madagascar were invited to reason about differences between distinct racial groups. Children tended to appeal to biology (that is, they expected children to acquire those traits from their biological, rather than their adoptive parents), whereas most adults underscored the role of socialization.[28cited in26] The results challenge the notion that children only learn about biological essence from their elders, and they show that Essentialism is a general phenomenon that is not specific to Western culture. Other cross-cultural demonstrations of innate Essentialism include those with children of the Yukatek Maya,[29] the Menominee (rural native Americans), and Brazilians.[30]

Another challenge to the empiricist view of Essentialism is presented by the fact that some precursors of Essentialism are found in infancy. Earlier (in Chapter 4), we saw that newborns can differentiate at least one type of living thing—human agents—from artifacts.[31-35] Six-month-olds also differentiate artifacts from plants: they are more likely to believe that a novel object is edible when it comes from a plant than from a group of similar manmade artifacts.[36] Finally, infants spontaneously assume that animals have insides. In a series of experiments, eight-month-old infants were first presented with a novel object that appeared to be animate—either because it was self-propelled and agentive (it engaged in a "quacking" conversation with the experimenter) or self-propelled and furry. The inanimate control was either not self-propelled, not agentive/furry, or both (neither self-propelled nor agentive/furry). The infants were subsequently surprised to discover that the seemingly animate object didn't have insides (it was hollow and it rattled), but they showed no surprise when the inanimate object was shown to be hollow.[37] This finding is in line with the possibility that young infants expect agents to possess a material biological essence.

In summary, there are several challenges to the notion that Essentialism is solely learned from experience. First, infants show early sensitivity to biological kinds (plants and agents) and they possess knowledge regarding the physical constitution of agents. Second, the Essentialist beliefs of children differ from those of their parents. Third, Essentialist beliefs are observed across several cultures. These observations are all consistent with the possibility that Essentialism is an innate principle of core knowledge.

An Inevitable Collision

Let us take stock of our conclusions so far. We have seen that people are intuitive Dualists and Essentialists, and that it is not unreasonable to suppose that these notions could be innate. Indeed, the roots of Dualism and Essentialism are found in early infancy, they are evident across cultures, and (in the case of Dualism), they have parallels in the cognition of nonhuman animals. Furthermore, both principles have strong adaptive value—Dualism defines our understanding of the physical and social world, whereas Essentialism determines our understanding of biological kinds.

Clearly, these principles are in place for reasons that are utterly unrelated to our understanding the origins of knowledge; they are not there for "philosophizing." But they nonetheless form part of our cognitive endowment. And when applied toward reasoning about the origins of our own knowledge, they could very well combine to create a perfect storm of distortion.

Per Dualism, we think of the mind as immaterial, distinct from the material body. Ideas (mental states) must therefore be immaterial as well. Per Essentialism, however, we know that innate traits *must* be material, as the biological essence of living things is linked to material properties that are housed in their "insides" and transmitted from parents to offspring. So, if ideas are immaterial (Premise 1) and innate traits must be material (Premise 2), it therefore follows that (in our minds, anyway) ideas cannot be innate!

Premise 1 (Dualism):	*Ideas are immaterial.*
Premise 2 (Essentialism):	*Innate traits must be material.*
Consequence (Antinativism):	*Ideas cannot be innate.*

We have indeed seen (in Chapter 6) that people have serious difficulties in even entertaining the possibility that ideas could be innate. They resist the notion of innate ideas in reasoning about adult humans, infants, and even animals and Martians—creatures of which they know relatively little. In fact, people resist this notion even when they are explicitly informed that the relevant behaviors are in fact innate (that they are universal to all members of the species, they emerge early in development, etc.). The persistent reluctance to consider innate knowledge, despite clear evidence to the contrary, sounds quite suspicious.

But suspicion is not conviction. Before we can demonstrate that people are guilty as charged, we need a motive. And previous explanations—the proposal that people are blind to innateness generally or that they are concerned about the implications of innateness for social justice—don't sufficiently explain why we are selectively resistant to innate *ideas*.

The clash between Dualism and Essentialism is the smoking gun. Each of these principles of core knowledge is independently motivated for reasons that are unrelated to reasoning about knowledge—they likely evolved to guide our understanding of the physical, social, and biological world. But when we use them to reason about the question of nativism, they conspire to lead us to precisely the wrong conclusion, rendering us blind to the truth about our own nature.

What remains to be seen is whether people do in fact apply the two biases—that ideas are immaterial and that innate traits must be material—in this fashion. The next chapter evaluates this question experimentally.

References

1. Carruthers P. *The opacity of mind: an integrative theory of self-knowledge.* New York, NY: Oxford University Press; 2011.
2. Carruthers P. How mindreading might mislead cognitive science. *Journal of Consciousness Studies.* 2020.
3. Cosmides L, Tooby J. Beyond intuition and instinct blindness: toward an evolutionarily rigorous cognitive science. *Cognition.* 1994;50(1):41–77.
4. Pinker S. *The blank slate: the modern denial of human nature.* New York, NY: Viking; 2002.
5. Parfit DA. Divided minds and the nature of persons. In: Blakemore C, Greenfield SA, eds. *Mindwaves.* New York, NY: Blackwell; 1987:19–26.
6. Forstmann M, Burgmer P. Adults are intuitive mind–body dualists. *Journal of Experimental Psychology: General.* 2015;144(1):222–235.
7. Hood B, Gjersoe NL, Bloom P. Do children think that duplicating the body also duplicates the mind? *Cognition.* 2012;125(3):466–474.
8. Bloom P. *Descartes' baby: how the science of child development explains what makes us human.* New York, NY: Basic Books; 2004.
9. Spelke ES, Kinzler KD. Core knowledge. *Developmental Science.* 2007;10(1):89–96.

10. Valenza E, Leo I, Gava L, Simion F. Perceptual completion in newborn human infants. *Child Development*. 2006;77(6):1810–1821.
11. Mascalzoni E, Regolin L, Vallortigara G, Simion F. The cradle of causal reasoning: newborns' preference for physical causality. *Developmental Science*. 2013;16(3):327–335.
12. Spelke ES, Phillips A, Woodward AL. Infants' knowledge of object motion and human action. In: Sperber D, Premack D, Premack AJ, Sperber D, Premack D, Premack AJ, eds. *Causal cognition: A multidisciplinary debate*. New York, NY, US: Clarendon Press/Oxford University Press; 1995:44–78.
13. Kuhlmeier VA, Bloom P, Wynn K. Do 5-month-old infants see humans as material objects? *Cognition*. 2004;94(1):95–103.
14. Hamlin JK, Wynn K, Bloom P. Social evaluation by preverbal infants. *Nature*. 2007;450(7169):557–559.
15. Hamlin JK, Wynn K, Bloom P. Three-month-olds show a negativity bias in their social evaluations. *Developmental Science*. 2010;13(6):923–929.
16. Bering JM, Bjorklund DF. The natural emergence of reasoning about the afterlife as a developmental regularity. *Developmental Psychology*. 2004;40(2):217–233.
17. Chudek M, McNamara RA, Birch S, Bloom P, Henrich J. Do minds switch bodies? Dualist interpretations across ages and societies. *Religion, Brain & Behavior*. 2018;8(4):354–368.
18. Bloom P. Religion is natural. *Developmental Science*. 2007;10(1):147–151.
19. Forstmann M, Burgmer P, Mussweiler T. "The mind is willing, but the flesh is weak": the effects of mind–body dualism on health behavior. *Psychological Science*. 2012;23(10):1239–1245.
20. Keil FC. The acquisition of natural kind and artifact term. In: Demopoulos W, Marras A, eds. *Language learning and concept acquisition*. Norwood, NJ: Ablex; 1986:133–153.
21. Gelman SA, Wellman HM. Insides and essence: early understandings of the nonobvious. *Cognition*. 1991;38(3):213–244.
22. Newman GE, Keil FC. Where is the essence? Developmental shifts in children's beliefs about internal features. *Child Development*. 2008;79(5):1344–1356.
23. Springer K. Children's awareness of the biological implications of kinship. *Child Development*. 1992;63(4):950–959.
24. Springer K, Keil FC. Early differentiation of causal mechanisms appropriate to biological and nonbiological kinds. *Child Development*. 1991;62(4):767.
25. Solomon GE, Johnson SC, Zaitchik D, Carey S. Like father, like son: young children's understanding of how and why offspring resemble their parents. *Child Development*. 1996;67(1):151–171.
26. Gelman SA. *The essential child: origins of essentialism in everyday thought*. New York, NY: Oxford University Press; 2003.
27. Taylor MG. The development of children's beliefs about social and biological aspects of gender differences. *Child Development*. 1996;67(4):1555–1571.
28. Astuti R. Are we all natural dualists? A cognitive developmental approach. *Journal of the Royal Anthropological Institute*. 2001;7(3):429–447.
29. Atran S, Medin D, Lynch E, Vapnarsky V, Ucan Ek E, Sousa P. Folkbiology doesn't come from folkpsychology: evidence from Yukatek Maya in cross-cultural perspective. *Journal of Cognition & Culture*. 2001;1(1):3–42.

30. Sousa P, Atran S, Medin D. Essentialism and folkbiology: evidence from Brazil. *Journal of Cognition and Culture.* 2002;2(3):195–223.
31. Meltzoff AN, Moore MK. Imitation of facial and manual gestures by human neonates. *Science.* 1977;198(4312):75–78.
32. Meltzoff AN, Murray L, Simpson E, et al. Re-examination of Oostenbroek et al. (2016): evidence for neonatal imitation of tongue protrusion. *Developmental Science.* 2017;21(4):e12609.
33. Nagy E, Pilling K, Orvos H, Molnar P. Imitation of tongue protrusion in human neonates: specificity of the response in a large sample. *Developmental Psychology.* 2013;49(9):1628–1638.
34. Farroni T, Csibra G, Simion F, Johnson MH. Eye contact detection in humans from birth. *Proceedings of the National Academy of Sciences of the United States Of America.* 2002;99(14):9602–9605.
35. Rönnqvist L, von Hofsten C. Neonatal finger and arm movements as determined by a social and an object context. *Early Development and Parenting.* 1994;3(2):81–94.
36. Wertz AE, Wynn K. Selective social learning of plant edibility in 6- and 18-month-old infants. *Psychological Science.* 2014;25(4):874–882.
37. Setoh P, Wu D, Baillargeon R, Gelman R. Young infants have biological expectations about animals. *Proceedings of the National Academy of Sciences of the United States of America.* 2013;110(40):15937–15942.

8

A Perfect Storm

> Look, look at this. We got Hurricane Grace moving north off the
> Atlantic seaboard. Huge . . . getting massive. Two, this low south
> of Sable Island, ready to explode. . . . What if Hurricane Grace runs
> smack into it? You could be a meteorologist all your life . . . and never
> see something like this. It would be a disaster of epic proportions. It
> would be . . . the perfect storm.
>
> —Sebastian Junger, *The Perfect Storm* (2000)[1]

In previous chapters, we have seen that people are systematically biased
against innate ideas. This bias, I suggest, is not the product of innocent ignorance (they are not simply unaware of the possibility that ideas could be
innate), the salience of learning, the opacity of their own psyches (people
cannot gauge their own mental faculties and instincts), or worries about the
ethical implications of nativism. Instead, antinativism is in our nature. It's an
unintended byproduct of the collision between two ancient cognitive principles that guide our reasoning about the physical, psychological, and biological worlds. And that collision is unavoidable. It's a perfect storm.

Chapter 7 named the storm makers—the twin principles of Dualism and
Essentialism—and described their destructive potential. If we believe that
ideas are immaterial (as required by Dualism) and if we simultaneously require innate traits (those that define the biological essence of an organism) to
be material (as mandated by Essentialism), then it is easy to see why people
think that ideas cannot be innate.

This chapter moves to track these forces in action by exposing them in
laboratory settings. The first set of experiments tests the effects of Dualism,
showing that people do, in fact, believe that traits that are considered "ideas"
must be immaterial. The second examines whether they believe that immaterial traits cannot be innate, as would be required by Essentialism.

Next, we chase the storm itself. As a proof of our forecasting skills, we demonstrate that it is possible to change the storm's course (people's intuitions
about nativism) by tweaking its ingredients. The antinativist bias can be

The Blind Storyteller. Iris Berent, Oxford University Press (2020). © Iris Berent, 2020.
DOI: 10.1093/oso/9780190061920.001.0001

heightened in a laboratory setting by increasing the perceived distance be-tween mind and body (as in Dualism) and it can be lessened by suggesting that innate biological traits have a material basis in the human body (as in Essentialism). Together, these experiments demonstrate that anti-nativism is an inevitable byproduct of the clash between these two principles.

A word of caution before we embark: storm chasing is a demanding en-deavor, so our tools (psychological experiments) are complex. We will pro-ceed slowly and carefully, but please buckle up and bear with me. The storm will soon come into full view.

Ideas Are Immaterial

Cognitive neuroscience tells us that all mental activities are material: they correspond to the electrophysiology of our brain. But how do laypeople intu-itively reason about the origins of their mental activities? Do they follow the material scientific account, or do they go immaterial, in line with Dualism?

To find out, we asked a group of people to reason about the materiality of a large number of human attributes, half of them cognitive, half of them noncognitive (the same as those described in Chapter 6).[2] The cognitive traits included such behaviors as "forming sentences," "reflecting on one's past and future," "recognizing taboos," "keeping track of time," and "having classifications of body parts." The matched noncognitive behaviors were emotions (e.g., "anger in response to hostility," "love for one's family," "fear of danger") and motor capabilities ("walking to move around," "sitting to relax," "lifting an object with hands").

To evaluate the materiality of these traits, we asked participants to con-sider a replication scenario, similar to the one discussed in Chapter 7. The instructions invited them to suppose it was possible to grow a replica of an adult human body. The replica, they were told, would preserve every as-pect of the human original, including its brain. People were next presented with that same list of traits and asked to evaluate (on a 1–7 scale) how likely it was that each of them would emerge in the replica. We reasoned that if people viewed a trait as material—one that is "in the body"—then repli-cating the body should automatically replicate the trait (for easy reference, I summarize the rationale and prediction in Box 8.1. Our main question was whether ideas would be viewed as relatively immaterial, that is, less likely to replicate.

Box 8.1 Dualism~Materiality

- *Premise 1:* The mind is immaterial and thus distinct from the material body.
- *Premise 2:* Cognitive traits (ideas) are mental states, whereas noncognitive traits (sensory, motor and emotive traits) are linked to states of the material body.
- *Consequence:* Cognitive traits (ideas) are relatively immaterial (compared to noncognitive traits).
- *Predictions*:
  - Cognitive traits should be rated as relatively immaterial (e.g., less likely to have a specific localization in the brain; less likely to transfer to a replica).
  - Materiality (as defined above) should correlate negatively with the classification of traits as "ideas."

Our results lined up with our predictions. People stated that cognitive traits such as "forming sentences" were less likely to transfer to the replica than noncognitive traits such as emotions and actions (e.g., "love for one's family"; "lifting an object with hands"). These differences, however, were not a matter of "all" or "none"—people did not outright state that cognitive traits could *never* emerge in the replica. This is not surprising; biases are often subtle—they slightly skew our judgment in a certain direction rather than blatantly determine it. A gender bias in a corporate hiring office, for example, would not necessarily result in the elimination of all women managers, but would likely reduce their proportion relative to men. And in the case of Dualism, there is good reason for the bias to be slight. After all, people are not ignorant of neuroscience; they know too well that it is the material brain that executes thinking, so every fiber of their rational being should scream that knowledge *is* material. And yet, when they reason about ideas, they veer towards the utterly irrational notion that ideas are immaterial. Slight as it may be, this irrationality is remarkable. Dualism explains why people are irrational when they reason about ideas.

Moving forward, you will indeed see that none of the biases considered in this chapter are a matter of "all" or "none," so when we come to test them in experiments, we will define them in terms that are always relative. When compared to non-cognitive traits, cognitive traits were rated as less material, but this small difference was highly reliable across individuals and across the various traits comprising each category. This difference suggests that people do not treat these two categories alike. Overall, cognitive traits are rated as less material than noncognitive traits.

To determine whether the perceived immateriality of a trait was specifically linked to "ideas," we asked another group of participants to classify the traits into two bins, one for ideas and one for processes. Next, we correlated the classification of the trait (the proportionality of "idea" responses) and its perceived materiality (as judged by its propensity for transplant). The correlation between "ideas" and "materiality" was strong, negative, and highly significant: the more likely a trait was to be classified as "idea," the less "material" it was considered to be. So not only are cognitive traits rated as less material overall, but when each trait is considered individually, its perceived materiality is linked to its perception as an "idea." These results strongly suggest that people view the cognitive traits of adults as relatively immaterial.

A second experiment examined the perceived materiality of infant traits. These traits (also described in Chapter 6) were all documented in young infants. Cognitive traits included "expecting stationary objects to move only if contacted by other moving objects," and "understanding that objects still exist when occluded"; noncognitive traits were motor actions such as "sucking on their thumbs" and sensory attributes, such as the ability to "contrast low musical tones and high tones." People were asked to determine how likely each trait was to emerge in a replica of a human infant. Once again, people thought that cognitive traits were reliably less likely to be material, and their tendency to do so strongly correlated with the classification of the traits as "ideas" (as judged by a second group of participants). The stronger the association of the trait with "ideas," the less likely it was to be seen as transferable.

The link between the perceived materiality of a trait—of adults or infants—and its perceived transferability is exactly what is predicted by Dualism. But it's still possible that this result could emerge for reasons that are entirely unrelated to the presumed immateriality of ideas. For example, participants could believe that ideas are more complex or more abstract than the noncognitive traits and that their abstraction/complexity prevents them from transplanting. The results of a control experiment counter this explanation.

The experiment made one simple change to the questions about the replicas. Instead of asking people to imagine the replication of the body, now we asked participants to consider the transfer of the same traits to the afterlife, after the body's demise. We reason that if cognitive traits are less likely the transfer in the body-replication scenario simply because these traits are complex or abstract, then the same results should obtain in the afterlife scenario. On the other hand, if cognitive traits are less prone to replication because of their immateriality, then once the scenario invokes the replication of the mind or soul in the afterlife, then cognitive traits should now be *more* likely to transfer. This is exactly what we found. And as before, the transfer correlated with the status of the traits as "ideas," except that the correlation was now positive: the stronger the association of a trait with an "idea," the more likely it was to transfer to the afterlife, in people's views. Ideas, then, are not inherently untransferable because they are too complex or abstract. Rather, people believe that ideas will fail to transfer between human and human because they lack a physical manifestation in a human body.

In subsequent experiments, we gauged materiality in another way. Here, participants were invited to advise a neuroscientist on a brain imaging experiment. The neuroscientist, they were told, has just obtained funding for a research grant to study how human traits are represented in the brain. But funding is limited, so the scientist must choose which traits to investigate. And this is a difficult question, as not all traits are amenable for study. While some traits are associated with a specific brain region, others simply don't have a clear manifestation in the human brain, so if the scientist were to target those, his study would yield no results. With this in mind, participants were invited to consider the same list of cognitive and noncognitive traits described in the previous experiment and advise the scientist which traits are likely to have a specific localization in the human brain. The logic is simple: traits that are material ought to be "in the brain"; immaterial traits are devoid of specific brain localization. Results indeed showed that people thought that cognitive traits were perceived to be less likely to have a brain localization. Moreover, the stronger the association of the trait with "ideas," the less likely was its localization in the material brain.

Again, this bias is relative, not absolute. That is, participants in our experiments did not state that ideas can *never* transfer to humans or be localized in the brain, and this is hardly surprising. As noted, most adults learn enough about science to know that thinking happens "in the brain," so they should have stated that cognitive traits reside in the material body, akin to actions, senses, and emotions. Full and equal materiality of *all* traits—cognitive or not—is the expected state of things. But this is not what people do. When we reason about ideas, we occasionally stop listening to the voice of material scientific rationality and, instead, slip into the erroneous presumption that ideas are immaterial. This bias is slight, but it highly systematic, and it requires an explanation. I suggest that it is a product of Dualism and these experiments appear to bear that out.

Innate Traits Are Material

The presumption that ideas must be immaterial explains why people would believe that ideas are less likely to transfer to replicas than physical attributes and why they are less likely to be localized in the brain. But why do people also believe that ideas cannot be innate? Here, Dualism alone cannot provide the answer. The fact that ideas seem immaterial, distinct from the body, does not logically prevent them from being innate. Essentialism presents the missing link. If people are Essentialists, then they should instinctively believe that all innate traits of living organisms must be material. But if (per Dualism) cognitive traits are immaterial, then cognitive traits cannot be innate. So, we now examine whether people are indeed intuitive Essentialists— do they believe that traits that define the essence of living organisms must be material?

To evaluate this question, we face a two-step challenge. First, we need to find out what people think about the materiality of traits. Second, we need to gauge whether a trait's perceived materiality depends on its origin. Essentialism, recall, governs our intuitive understanding of biology, so it specifically concerns traits that innately define our essence as living organisms. To test for the hallmarks of Essentialism, we must therefore gauge whether reasoning about materiality further depends on whether traits are innate or acquired.

To probe for materiality, we used the same methods described in the previous section. One set of experiments asked participants to reason about the localization of specific traits in the brain; other experiments asked people to imagine which traits would transfer if the body were replicated; the traits were the same cognitive and noncognitive traits of adults and infants described in the previous section. But this time we added a second layer to the puzzle: is reasoning about materiality shaped by Essentialism? That is, do people believe that if a trait is innate, then it *must* be material?

To test the effect of Essentialism, we asked people to evaluate the materiality of these traits under two different conditions. In the first, we explicitly informed participants that each and every one of the traits in question is *innate*, that is, inborn in humans. To be certain that there could be no misunderstanding, we explained exactly what we meant by "inborn," and provided additional examples (which did not form part of the trait list). "Inborn traits," we said, "are ones that develop in humans spontaneously. Some of these traits (e.g., having five fingers) are present at birth, but others (e.g., facial hair in men) can appear later in development. All innate traits, however, emerge in the typical course of development, even if an individual has never had the opportunity to witness these behaviors in other people."

In the second condition, we presented the same list of traits but told people that researchers believe that all of them are learned from experience (i.e., *acquired*). Lest there be no misunderstandings, we specified that "learned traits include behaviors such as reading and driving a car. Learned traits are often acquired from other members of the community, such as parents or peers. These traits typically develop over time, and they only emerge if an individual has had the opportunity to witness these traits in the behavior of other people."

We reasoned that if people believe that innate (i.e., essentialist) traits must be material, then they should consider innate traits as more likely to be controlled by a specific brain region and more likely to transfer when the body is replicated (relative to acquired traits). Of course, a priori, not all traits are equally material; we just saw (in the previous section) that people view ideas as immaterial relative to actions, for instance. But when considering actions, sensations, and emotions—traits that *are* plausibly material—innate origins should enhance the perceived materiality of the trait (for ease of reference, I summarize the rationale of the Essentialism experiments in Box 8.2).

Box 8.2 Essentialism~Materiality

- *Rationale:* Innate traits of living organisms are material
- *Prediction:*
  - A given trait should be more likely to be perceived as material (e.g., more likely to have a specific brain localization, and more likely to transfer with the body) when it is presented as innate compared to when it is presented as acquired.

This is exactly what happened for some representative results with adult and infant traits. The adult experiment gauged materiality using the brain-imaging scenario; the infant experiments employed the body-replication scenario. But the results in both cases were essentially the same. First, people thought the noncognitive traits are more material—they are more likely to correspond to a specific localization in the brain (for the adult imaging experiment), and they are also more likely to transfer to the replica (in the infant replication scenario). This confirms that noncognitive traits are perceived as more material, in line with the results discussed in the previous section. Second, people viewed these traits as more material when the traits were presented as innate compared to when the same traits were presented as acquired.[1] This suggests that people believe that innate traits are more material than acquired traits and that noncognitive traits are more material than cognitive ones.

Admittedly, however, reasoning about human traits (adult or infant) could be influenced by prior knowledge concerning the origins of cognitive traits. Perhaps people read somewhere that acquired human traits like knowledge of chess are not encoded in a single region of the brain. To secure this last escape hatch, we also asked people similar questions about traits of animals and aliens—either innate or acquired. The results turned out the same. People thought that a trait was more likely to transfer to a nonhuman replica when it was presented as innate than when the same trait was presented as acquired.

So, regardless of whether people are reasoning about adults, infants, animals, or aliens—and regardless of how materiality is assessed (via brain imaging, or replication and transfer), people view innate traits as more material than acquired traits. Another way to put this is to say that innate traits are *super material*; just by virtue of their being innate, these traits are all of a sudden seen as being more material. The superlative is deserving, because this is not the ordinary effect of materiality, seen in the previous section. There, we contrasted different traits, say, motor and cognitive, so the differences in materiality were likely grounded in their perceived link to the material body (in line with Dualism). For example, "running" was perceived as more material than "forming sentences," because running is more

---

[1] For infant traits, this was the case across the board, for both cognitive and noncognitive traits. In the adult imaging scenario, this was the case only for noncognitive traits: people thought that emotions, for instance, are more likely to be localized in the brain when they were told that emotions are innate compared to when emotions were presented as acquired. Cognitive traits, by contrast, were not reliably affected by the innateness manipulation, possibly because people thought that cognitive traits are overall unlikely to be material in the first place.

closely linked to the actions of the body. But when we consider the effect of innateness, here, the trait is utterly unchanged. People suddenly say that "running" is more material just because it is innate. Supermateriality, then, emanates not from any inherent properties of these behaviors, but from our perception of them as innate. When people are presented with biological traits, they believe these traits are more material when they are innate and thus define the essence of a natural kind. This conclusion is in line with Essentialism.

Correlation or Causation?

The results of all these experiments are consistent with the possibility that reasoning about innateness is shaped by core knowledge of Dualism and Essentialism. Dualism renders mental states immaterial, distinct from the material body, and participants indeed considered cognitive traits (i.e., "ideas") as relatively immaterial and hence less likely to be localized in the brain and thus less likely to be transferred to a replica. Essentialism, on the other hand, predicts that innate traits of living organisms must be material, and participants indeed considered a trait to be more material when they were informed that it was innate compared to when they were told that the same trait was acquired.

The conjunction of these two principles predicts that cognitive traits cannot be innate. And indeed, we saw (in Chapter 6) that people systematically resist the notion of innate ideas. We also saw (earlier in this chapter) that the status of a trait as "idea" (or "thinking") negatively correlates with its perceived materiality. Likewise, adult traits considered as ideas (or thinking) fail to show the effect of "super-materiality"—they show no boost in materiality when presented as innate compared to when the same trait is presented as acquired. Figure 8.1 summarizes these conclusions graphically.

The robust correlations between innateness, on the one hand, and the status of traits as "ideas" and "material," on the other, strongly suggests a causal link: the possibility that ideas cannot be, innate *because* they are immaterial (per Dualism) and *because* innateness requires materiality (per Essentialism). Our aversion to innate ideas is the inevitable consequence of the collision between these two principles of core cognition. But as we know too well, correlation is not causation. The fact that the alarm on my clock always goes off just after the one on my iPhone does not prove that my iPhone

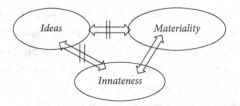

Figure 8.1. The links between ideas, materiality, and innateness. Positive associations are indicated by a continuous arrow; the broken arrow indicates negative associations.

controls my clock. Rather, the correlation could well be due to some third factor (my alarm clock runs a little slower than my iPhone).

So in a final set of experiments, we sought to secure the causal connections between the perfect storm (our aversion to innate ideas) and its presumed ingredients—Dualism and Essentialism. The storm forecast is quite clear: if Dualism and Essentialism are the generators of the antinativist tempest, then we should be able to prevent the storm by tinkering with its ingredients.

We first manipulated the effect of Dualism. To this end, we presented participants with a list of infant traits (the same traits described earlier in this chapter) and asked them to rate the likelihood that each would emerge spontaneously in a desert island situation; this is a measure of our attitude toward innateness. To determine whether our perception of innateness can be changed by manipulating Dualism, we had the participants read an essay concerning the mind–body divide prior to making their ratings. One group of participants read a passage asserting that body and mind are one and the same (in line with physicalism); another group read a narrative stating that the two are distinct (in line with Dualism). Note that the text only considered the mind–body link generally; it presented no information about the materiality of the traits in question, and it certainly said nothing about their innate origins.

If our reasoning about innateness is shaped by Dualism, then people should be more likely to rate those traits as innate when they are primed to consider body and mind as one and the same (in the physicalist condition) compared to distinct (in Dualism). The premises of the experiment are summarized in Box 8.3.

And this is exactly what we found. Regardless of trait type (cognitive or noncognitive), people who were primed for physicalism were more likely to view all traits as innate. When we further probed their perceptions of their

---

Box 8.3 Dualism → Innateness

- *Rationale*: Dualism interferes with our perception of ideas as innate by suggesting that mental states are distinct from the material body.
- *Prediction*: Attenuating the mind/body divide should prime us toward innateness.

---

own bodies and minds, we found that people who had been primed for physicalism did indeed report closer associations between their own bodies and minds. These results demonstrate that the Dualist divide between the material body and the immaterial mind shapes our reasoning about innateness.

Another experiment examined the link between innateness and Essentialism. Essentialism predicts that essentialist traits—those that innately define the essence of living things—must be material. If people are Essentialists, then rendering a trait as material should prime them to view it as innate (for a summary of this reasoning, see Box 8.4).

As in the previous experiment, we gauged innateness by having participants reason about the emergence of traits on a desert island (this time, these were adult traits; they were the same traits discussed in previous sections). But prior to making this judgment, participants were presented with information about the materiality of those traits. One condition implied that the traits are all material; participants were informed that previous research has shown that they each correspond to a specific region in the brain. In another condition, people were told that the traits do not correspond to any specific brain region and that, "in fact, scientists are wondering whether these traits even have a material basis in the human body." Each participant took part in both conditions (half of the participants first got the "material"

Box 8.4 Essentialism → Innateness

- *Rationale*: Essentialism interferes with our perception of innate traits by requiring essentialist traits (those that innately define the essence of living organisms) to be material.
- *Prediction*: Presenting putative biological traits as material should enhance their perception as innate.

---

condition; others first got the "immaterial" manipulation), and each trait was equally likely to be acquired or innate.

In case you are wondering how this experiment differs from the previous manipulation of physicalism, you are on the right track; these two conditions are indeed similar, inasmuch as Essentialism and Physicalism are both expected to increase innateness by calling attention to materiality. But the mechanisms are different. Physicalism enhances innateness by attenuating our sense of the mind/body divide generally (as opposed to the materiality of a specific trait under consideration). Essentialism, on the other hand, concerns *specific* traits that define the essence of living organisms—those that are innate.

So, Essentialism predicts that (i) materiality should primarily increase the innateness of biological traits[2] and (ii) that the perception of innateness should vary on a case by case basis, depending on the materiality of individual traits (rather than on participants' physicalist state of mind generally). Traits that are presented as material should be viewed as innate; those traits that are acquired shouldn't.

If participants' reasoning about innateness is determined by the Essentialism, then people should be more likely to view any given trait as innate when it is presented as material compared to when the *same* trait is presented as immaterial. Moreover, this effect should be evident in the same individual participants: people should *shift* their innateness rating depending on whether the traits are presented to them as material or immaterial.

This is exactly what we observed. In line with our previous experiments, people also considered cognitive traits as overall less likely to be innate. So not only do people believe that innateness renders a trait more material (as we saw in the second section of this chapter), but we now see that they also apply the converse: if a trait is material ("in the body"), then they automatically conclude that this trait is more likely to be innate.

Together, these results demonstrate that the link between innateness and core knowledge is causal, as opposed to mere association. Reasoning about

---

[2] I say "primarily" (rather than "only") because people are known to project Essentialism more broadly. For example, although Essentialism originates from core knowledge of living things, Paul Bloom and his colleagues[3-5] suggest that Essentialism is responsible for a wide range of obsessions with the inherent essence, ranging from the essence of the self (the immaterial soul) to the essence of a creation, whether it's a work of art or the universe (in both cases, essence lies in the intention of its creator). Our present experiments cannot directly evaluate the role of biology, since all the traits that we asked people to reason about putatively define humans biologically (e.g., we included no traits that are obviously acquired, like driving). But the design of our experiment can determine whether the effect of materiality is specific to the trait.

innateness is caused by the Dualist distinction between body and mind, on the one hand, and the Essentialist belief that innate biological traits are material on the other.

Conclusions

In previous chapters, we saw that people consider cognitive traits that capture ideas as less likely to be innate than actions, sensations, and emotions, rendering them systematically blind to the origins of their knowledge. Here, we presented a series of experiments that help elucidate the source of that blindness.

Not only do the results show that thinking about innateness correlates with Dualism and Essentialism, but that the link is causal. People are reluctant to believe in innate ideas because Essentialism requires innate traits to be material and Dualism suggests that ideas are immaterial. Since our experimental subjects were Western adults who'd had plenty of opportunities to learn about mind, body, and innateness from immersion in their culture, our results cannot tell us whether their biases are innate or universal. But since they reflect principles of core knowledge that are evident in young infants, the possibility that our aversion to innate ideas is innate rather than learned remains a likely possibility.

What does this all mean? Viewed narrowly, not much. Innate ideas are not a notion that we consider on a daily basis. And even if our reasoning about such matters is biased by innate core knowledge, it does not put us in any particular danger. The biases we confirmed in each of these experiments sway our reasoning only slightly; they are certainly not absolute. Moreover, intuitive core knowledge is only one feature of our minds; we don't have to acknowledge it to have it, and we have other mental tools and capacities as well. Our capacity for deliberate logical thinking and analysis, for example, can certainly allow us to keep many of our cognitive biases at bay (as I have done, in the writing of this book). But to do this requires awareness and effort. Left unchecked, the twin principles of Dualism and Essentialism constantly "whisper in our ears." And when they do, they can seriously hijack the thinking of laypeople and scientists alike. So, our innate biases can potentially sway our scientific understanding of the origins of knowledge.

But it is not only our reasoning about *what we know* (specifically, cognitive nativism) that is at risk. The preoccupation with the mind–body distinction (courtesy of Dualism) and our biological nature (understood through the lenses of Essentialism) colors our very account of *who we are*, and its implications are evident in a broad array of topics that are of direct personal and social relevance. It shapes our understanding of our basic concepts (such as our notion of a "cup") and deepest emotions (can you "read off" love and anger in people's faces?). It tampers with our understanding of our brain and its role in both health and disease, and taints our understanding of our very notion of the self and its free will. In fact, the effects of Dualism and Essentialism even extend to our views of the afterlife. The next chapters unveil these various potential casualties of the perfect storm that is the collision of Dualism and Essentialism.

References

1. Junger S. *The perfect storm: a true story of men against the sea.* 1st ed. ed. New York, NY: Norton; 1997.
2. Berent I, Platt M, Sandoboe GM. How we reason about innateness: the role of Dualism and Essentialism. Retrieved from https://doi.org/10.31234/osf.io/vy6j5. September 10, 2019.
3. Bloom P. *Descartes' baby: how the science of child development explains what makes us human.* New York, NY: Basic Books; 2004.
4. Hood BM, Bloom P. Children prefer certain individuals over perfect duplicates. *Cognition.* 2008;106(1):455–462.
5. Bloom P, Gelman SA. Psychological essentialism in selecting the 14th Dalai Lama. *Trends in Cognitive Sciences.* 2008;12(7):243–243.

PART II

WHO WE THINK WE ARE

A. Overview of Part II

Like it or not, it appears that human nature is here to stay. And "like it" we don't. "Human nature" is a notion that is difficult for us to stomach, especially when it concerns what we know. We prefer to think of our minds as utterly free to conceive of any notion and that our free mind—our proudest possession—distinguishes us from nonhuman animals like Remy the cat. Remy is a slave of nature, destined to blindly follow his innate feline instincts. We humans, by contrast, are free thinkers. Granted, there are limits on our memory, attention, and sensory acuity—our ear does not register the same frequencies as a dog or a bat. But these are mere nuisances, not fundamental shackles on our rationality. Thinking itself, we believe, is unbounded.

Our conclusions thus far, however, challenge this notion. It appears we go about our business wearing a pair of colored lenses—Dualism and Essentialism, and those prisms systematically taint our view of our reality. I say "taint" rather than "utterly obscure" because core knowledge is only one of the rich sets of capacities that comprise human cognition. We see our reality through multiple sets of lenses, some apparently clearer than others. This is why I can write this book, and why you and I can discuss such topics. But that "core knowledge" exists is undeniable, and core knowledge matters. It is the first to emerge in development, and it remains with us throughout our lives. So these lenses can wreak havoc on our self-understanding. In the first part of the book, we saw how the twin forces of Dualism and Essentialism distort our view of *what we know*. We now turn to examine their effects on our perception of *who we think we are*.

Chapters 9 and 10 start with the basics—thoughts and feelings. Chapter 9 considers simple concepts, like "cup" or "running." Where do these notions come from? Could our understanding of these ideas be related to our physical body? If I were born with no limbs and never had the opportunity to feel the shape of a cup in my hands or the contact between my feet and the ground, would I be able to fully appreciate the meaning of these notions?

Another illustration of the tense relationship between mind, body, and innateness is found in our reasoning about our emotions. We tend to believe like father, like son: happy parents beget happy babies, and angry parents beget angry offspring. Moreover, we think that emotions like "happiness" and "anger" are imprinted on the body—you can tell what I feel just by looking at my face. So while we view our cognitions as "unnatural" inasmuch as they are neither grounded in the material body nor innate, emotions, for us, are their mirror image—we believe that our emotions are naturally embodied and innate. Chapter 10 explores our fascination with innate emotions and shows how the conflict between Dualism and Essentialism can explain not only our aversion to the innateness of ideas but also our attraction to it when it comes to our emotions.

Chapters 11 and 12 move to consider how our complex relationship with our brain shapes our thinking about health and disease. The advent of neuroscience and neuroimaging presents us with vivid images of thinking brains, and people stare at them as if they were looking at a ghost. The notion that a chunk of meat in their skull is doing "their thinking" is incomprehensible. So strong is our astonishment that we assign brain studies an almost mystical significance, even when their results are plainly bogus. Chapter 11 shows how Dualism (and, to some extent, Essentialism) implants these irrational beliefs about neuroscience.

The two forces that shape our understanding of our immaterial mind and material brain further mold our reasoning about brain disorders. When we experience an irregular heartbeat, we look to mend our material body with drugs or surgery. But when we suffer from a broken heart, it's the mind, rather than the body, that we seek to heal. In fact, people shun psychotropic drugs even when their efficacy is clearly proven. They also incorrectly believe that mental disorders that are "in your brain" are in your destiny. So, tragically, the scientific progress in neuropsychiatry has not improved society's attitudes toward its patients. The realization that mental disorders are brain disorders engenders not greater compassion and hope but rather pessimism and further distancing from psychiatric patients. Chapter 12 explains how the multiple misconceptions that are associated with affective psychiatric disorders arise from the conflict between Dualism and Essentialism.

Cognitive brain disorders, such as dyslexia, also come in for their fair share of misconceptions, and this is the case among laypeople, policymakers and even teachers. But oddly, the misconceptions surrounding disorders affecting "cold" cognition are the mirror images of our errors in reasoning about psychiatric disorders that we associate with our "warm" emotions (just as we hold opposite misconceptions about typical cognition and affect, as discussed in Chapters 9 and 10). We are all too eager to assume that major depression is innate, controlled by the material brain and out of the patients' hands; for dyslexia, we incorrectly assume the opposite—that it is "just" "in your mind" (not in your brain and genes). Chapter 13 explains what dyslexia really is and shows how our misconceptions about it arise from Dualism and Essentialism.

Woody Allen has famously said he is not afraid of dying; he just doesn't want to be there when it happens. It's no wonder his words struck a chord— "not being" is a scary proposition. Yet many Americans believe that their psyches will persist after the demise of their bodies. And it's not only religious devotees who believe in the afterlife; young children say the same, and so do adults and children in other societies, including even those who are self-described "extinctivists." Our afterlife beliefs, however, are remarkably inconsistent. On the one hand, we state that some aspects of our minds are immaterial, inasmuch as they survive our bodies. But on the other hand, we believe that some of these seemingly immaterial properties of the dead act like matter; for example, they are contagious, much like germs or excrement. Chapter 14 considers our views of what happens once we are no more. We'll see that the collision between Dualism and Essentialism—the twin forces that stir up our misconceptions about our origins—are also responsible for these mistaken beliefs about our demise.

Having seen how Dualism and Essentialism toy with our understanding of our beginning and end, health and disease, Chapter 15 turns to examine how these colored lenses distort our view of our free will and the self. Whether free will truly exists is not a matter I will decide here, but whether we *think* it does is entirely within our purview. When you believe you had freely chosen to lift your finger, you essentially believe in three things: first, that you can tell whether I *did it*; second, that you can tell whether I *consciously willed the act*; and third, that there is a single, unitary, willing *"me."* All three beliefs are demonstrably wrong. Who's to blame? You guessed it—Dualism and Essentialism.

It appears that the Ancient Greeks were right in their fear of blindness, caves, and shadows. We are indeed blind or, at the very least, seriously near-sighted. Blindness, moreover, shapes our numerous stories of what we know and who we are. And all these errors in our understanding of our human nature emerge from a single source—human nature itself.

B. Thoughts and Feelings

9

It's in My Bones

Many of us follow the same daily ritual. It begins with the rich aroma of freshly brewed coffee, its darkness shimmering in the early morning sun. As you lift the cup to your mouth, you sense its weight, see its bright color, and feel the even smoothness of its curves against your palms. Last comes the rich taste and the slight rush of blood to your head. With the coffee in your veins, you are now awake and thinking.

But when you first entered the kitchen, you must have had some notion of "cup" and "coffee" that directed you toward the coffee maker. What are they, precisely? Do you hold some abstract mental notion of "cup" in your brain? Or is your understanding of such concepts constructed solely from your memories of bodily actions and sensations, like lifting and handling, tasting and smelling?

Think about it. Over the course of your life you have experienced countless daily coffee episodes, and each was slightly different—your Monday coffee was bitter; on Tuesday the cup almost slipped through your hands. Each is rich with sensory experiences (sights, smells, and tastes) and with detailed bodily interactions (the precise weight of the cup, its shape and smoothness in your hands). All of these episodes are sealed in your memory, and they surely inform your understanding of cups and coffee; this is entirely uncontroversial. Our question here is not whether your sensorimotor interactions with cups have enriched your concepts; they have. Rather, we are asking whether they *are* your concepts. Simply put, does our understanding of things depend on the bodies we have? If I were born blind and I had never seen the shiny bright redness of a coffee mug, would you and I still hold a common notion of a cup? If I was born without hands, could I still know the full meaning of "cup" without ever having held one? Are concepts only "*in our bones*"?

In this chapter, we ask what concepts are and whether they are shaped by our bodies (beyond the brain)—our limbs, torso, and the five senses. To keep things simple, I consider only how our minds encode concepts such as cups;

The Blind Storyteller. Iris Berent, Oxford University Press (2020). © Iris Berent, 2020.
DOI: 10.1093/oso/9780190061920.001.0001

Figure 9.1. Cup or bowl?
From Labov (2004)[1]. With permission from OUP.

whether cups indeed form a unique class of objects "out there in the world" is not discussed.

The topic of embodied cognition is unusually controversial. A Google Scholar search for "embodied cognition" yields over 35,000 publications, with many back-and-forth exchanges between supporters of "Abstraction" and "Embodiment." Emotions in those exchanges can run quite high. With all that heat, we might wonder whether our old friends Dualism and Essentialism aren't getting in the way of our self-understanding again. But before we look at our biases, we must first consider the two competing accounts of concepts proposed by "Abstraction" and "Embodiment."

Thinking With Abstract Representations

If I asked you to explain your concept of a "cup," you would probably point toward an actual cup; it's natural to link such concepts with objects "out there." But objects and concepts are not one and the same.

Objects can vary simultaneously across multiple physical dimensions; just look at the illustration in Figure 9.1. Our minds, however, sort these objects into one of two categories—cups or bowls. The choice of category surely has something to do with the physical properties of the object in question; cups are typically taller than bowls, while bowls have larger circumferences. But the physical properties of objects "out there" cannot fully capture our internal notion of CUP. This becomes apparent when we consider the ambiguous "in between" cases, like the third exemplar. Some of us might say it's a cup; for others, it's a bowl. But remarkably, people shift their classification of the same object depending upon its context. The linguist William Labov found that people are more likely to classify the ambiguous object as a bowl when they imagine it contains a solid food like mashed potatoes.[1] Since the stimulus is unchanged, the shift in classification must be guided by some internal principles of the mind. So concepts are not objects—they are "in your head." To understand "cup," we therefore have to consider how our minds represent such concepts.

One influential approach views these representations as abstract symbols. Jerry Fodor[2,3] and Zenon Pylyshyn[4] dubbed their proposal the computational theory of the mind (CTTM); a related theory by Herbert Simon and Alan Newell[5] is known as the physical symbol system hypothesis (PSSH). We all encounter and use "symbols" in our everyday communications: a red light signifies "stop"; a nod of the head signifies "yes." In each case, there is a physical signifier (the red light or the nod of the head) and a meaning, or what is being signified ("stop" and "yes"). Symbols convey information by linking form and meaning.

Mental symbols have similar properties. To represent meaning (e.g., CUP), the cup symbol requires a form. What this form is precisely remains unknown—we don't know how the brain encodes concepts. But in the symbolic view, the precise substance of the signifier—whether it is amino acids, silicon, paper, or stone—doesn't really matter. What does matter is the formal arrangement of symbols. The mathematician Alan Turing,[6] one of the founding fathers of computer science, has shown that thinking can be captured as symbol manipulation, a process that depends on the form of symbols and on their structural relations.

To make this a bit more concrete, consider a simple symbol manipulation process that forms complex concepts out of simple (atomic) ones. Let's assume three atomic symbols—a triangle for CUP, a circle for COFFEE, and, for good measure, a third symbol (rectangle) for BLACK. To form the complex concept COFFE CUP, we simply combine the relevant atomic symbols together (the triangle and the circle), and by the same process, we can form BLACK COFFEE from a rectangle and a circle (see Figure 9.2).

Several points are noteworthy here. First, the format of each atomic symbol is entirely arbitrary. There is no inherent link between CUP and triangles. It is precisely because the substance of the signifier doesn't matter that I illustrate symbol manipulation using geometrical shapes; I'm obviously not suggesting that this is how CUP is represented by your brain. Second, complex symbols are *structured*. The meaning of the complex symbol COFFEE CUP is determined by its form, and this form, in turn, is systematically linked to the meaning of the atomic elements. As noted, the meanings of atomic elements (triangle = CUP) are entirely arbitrary. But the forms and meanings of complex forms are not. The complex meaning COFFEE CUP is conveyed by a complex form (a circle + a triangle) whose form corresponds precisely

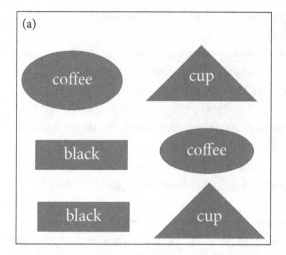

Figure 9.2. Forming complex concepts by (a) systematically combining atomic symbols or (b) coining arbitrary novel forms.

to the forms of its two semantic constituents (COFFEE, CUP). By the same token, BLACK COFFEE predictably includes the symbols for BLACK and COFFEE.

You might want to stop here and think for a moment. It all looks trivially self-evident, but it isn't. One could have certainly envisioned systems in which combinations like BLACK COFFEE are expressed by forms that are utterly unrelated to COFFEE, for example, by coining a new atomic form, a pentagon (see Figure 9.2b). This form offers no hints to its meaning, but there is nothing inherently wrong with this approach—we are perfectly capable of memorizing that a pentagon stands for BLACK COFFEE. But this is not how real cognition works. According to the CTTM, complex symbols are *compositional*: the symbol for BLACK COFFEE literally includes the symbol for BLACK and COFFEE. Moreover, the meaning of that complex form is *systematically* linked to the meaning of its atomic parts.

According to this CTTM, mental processes are guided by structure. When you think, you literally manipulate the forms of symbols, and this manipulation only "sees" forms; it is entirely blind to their meaning "on the other side." In fact, form *determines* thinking. For example, you can't think COFFEE CUP without thinking CUP. Why? Because the form of the simple CUP (a triangle) is a physical component of the complex form COFFEE CUP (triangle and circle). Similarly, if you know about COFFEE CUP and BLACK

COFFEE, you can reliably predict the meaning of BLACK CUP from its constituents. In this view, the compositionality and systematicity of thought isn't just a possibility; it's a necessity.

The hypothesis of structured symbols and structure-sensitive processes also explains a third critical property of thinking—its productivity. Productivity is our ability to understand novel concept combinations that we have never encountered before, such as BLACK BLIX. While you might not know what BLIX means, you can still categorize it as a member of a larger concept, such as OBJECT, thanks to its form. All members of the OBJECT category (cups, saucers, planets, or galaxies) share form; for example, they can each be marked by a subscript like a triangle. Once you have recognized BLIX as an OBJECT (i.e., once you have encoded it as $BLIX_\triangle$), everything that you know about objects will automatically extend to this novel instance of one, and it all follows mechanically from the physical form of the symbol. The form of symbol literally *causes* such novel thoughts to occur.

The productivity of inference, its compositionality and systematicity, are the bedrock foundations of human rational thinking. The hypothesis that thinking manipulates physical symbols provides a principled explanation of how thinking happens in a material physical system like our brain.

The Embodiment Challenge

The symbolic hypothesis, however, has been challenged by proponents of embodied cognition. The scope of the challenge varies. Some researchers outright reject the hypothesis that cognition manipulates mental representations of any kind;[7] others accept that some types of representations exist.[8,9] All proponents of Embodiment, however, assert that that the key to explaining our mental life lies not in the structure of abstract symbols but rather in our bodies and their five senses.

In this view, our body is literally the gauge for our cognition. To evaluate our understanding (*Is it a cup?*) we imagine acting on it with our hands—we *simulate* the act of touching, holding, lifting. And to interpret our perception of our surroundings (*How far away is the exit?*), we measure the distance relative to our bodily capacity to act (e.g., to walk or run). Embodiment thus determines every aspect of cognition, from perceptual encoding of a sensory stimulus to its categorization as an instance of a concept and its expression in language.[10]

The historic rise of embodied cognition can be traced to a number of theoretical developments in cognitive psychology, developmental psychology, speech perception, linguistics, and neuroscience. The ecological psychologist James J. Gibson[11] suggested that our perception of visual objects directly evaluates the opportunities they provide for action (their affordance). An enticing candy on a shelf would thus be perceived differently by an adult viewer (who can reach for the candy) and an infant (who cannot). The developmental psychologists Esther Thelen and Linda Smith further argued that the cognitive development of infants is shaped by their motor interactions with their surroundings.[12] Similar links between perception and action have been proposed with respect to speech and language. The psychologist Alvin Liberman and his colleagues suggested that humans perceive speech by enacting its articulation,[13] whereas the linguists George Lakoff and Mark Johnson suggested that linguistic metaphors are grounded in human action and space. For example, statements such as *he is consumed by love* or *you are in high spirits* link love and happiness to eating and the "up" spatial trajectory, respectively. Our understandings of such events (in perception) are linked to action.

Perception and action, however, are apples and oranges of sorts; how do we link one dimension to the other? Advances in neuroscience offer a solution to this conundrum. The breakthrough came with the discovery of a group of neurons in the brains of Macaque monkeys that respond to both action (e.g., when the monkey picks up a piece of food) as well as a perception of an action (e.g., when the monkey watches a human reach for the food). These so-called mirror neurons promised to provide the neural basis for the integration of perception and action.[14,15] Whether the hype surrounding mirror neurons is justified is a matter of controversy,[16,17] but they have provided the impetus for countless studies. Literally thousands of papers suggest that our concepts and percepts depend on the capacity of our bodies to act, and these perception–action links have been seen in studies of both behavior and the brain. Some of these demonstrations are plainly wild.

One set of results shows that the properties of our bodies shape our estimates of our visual space. Wondering how far away the glasses you are trying to reach on the table are? Whether you can fit through a narrow doorway? Whether you can jump over a gap? Or how steep the hill you are about to climb is? Your answers will depend on the action potential of your body. If you have a tool in your hand (a stick), the glasses appear closer;[18] jumpable gaps appear wider when you wear heavy weights around your ankles;[19] people with broader shoulders (or with outspread arms) perceive the doorway to be narrower;[20] and hills appear steeper to people who are wearing heavy backpacks, are fatigued, have poor physical fitness, or are elderly.[21] The converse is true for the sportsmen around us: good swimmers judge their swimming targets as closer than bad swimmers do (as do people who are wearing flippers),[22] and skilled golfers perceive holes to be bigger than duffers do.[23]

Action also colors our understandings of concepts, words, and sentences. In one study, participants read a story that was presented incrementally. To move to the next sentence, they had to rotate a knob either clockwise or counterclockwise. Unbeknownst to them, the story referenced actions involving rotation. Results showed that people read the action sentence faster when the direction of their manual response matched the direction of motion implied by the sentence (*he turned the key in the ignition*, a clockwise motion).[24] In another study, people matched pictures to sentences faster when their potentials for action matched. For example, people were quicker to match a picture of an eagle with its wings outspread to the sentence "the ranger saw the eagle in the sky" than to "the ranger saw the eagle in the nest."[25] What's the difference? An eagle in the sky must have its wings open, whereas the one in the nest does not. The findings suggest that our understanding of the sentence corresponds to details concerning the action potential of the body.

Moreover, implied action activates relevant motor areas in the brain. Here, we should note that our brain motor system (in the primary motor cortex) includes distinct areas that control different parts of the body (arms, legs, lips, tongue). Strikingly, these brain areas are launched in a selective fashion by verbs that imply distinct actions. When people read verbs like "kick," they activate the leg motor area more than the arm motor area; when they read verbs like "pick," they activate the arm motor area more than the area that controls the legs.[26] Perception seems to trigger action. Conversely, when the relevant motor areas in the brain are stimulated (using transcranial magnetic stimulation [TMS], a technique that temporarily alters brain activity using electromagnetic pulses delivered to the scalp), people recognize related words faster. For example, stimulation of the arm motor area elicited faster responses for "pick" relative to "kick," whereas the stimulation of the leg motor area yielded the opposite (a faster response for "kick" relative to "pick").[27] (I should note that "motor" areas of the brain could also mediate non-motoric functions, so the fact that reading "kick," for example, activates the leg motor area does not prove that people simulate kicking. Nonetheless, the selectivity of these responses [e.g., the activation of the "leg" motor area for "kick," not "pick"] and the convergence with the behavioral findings [reviewed earlier] is striking).[28-29]

If motor action supports the recognition of action verbs, then one would expect individuals with motor impairments to show deficits in their understandings of action. In line with this possibility, paraplegic individuals exhibit difficulties in motion perception (but not in contrast sensitivity).[30] Other results suggest patients whose motor cortexes are damaged show impaired understanding of verbs denoting actions, whereas those with lesions to visual areas show impaired comprehension of nouns with strong visual associations.[31]

Together, these results (which are just a small sample of the literature) suggest strong bidirectional links between our understanding of concepts and actions, links that are evident in both behavior and the brain. Perceptual abilities are modulated by action potential, whereas changes in action potential alter thinking. This seems to turn the tables on the debate. Rather than asking whether cognition is embodied, one ought to be asking what evidence there is to suggest Abstraction.

Arthur Glenberg, one of the most prominent researchers on embodied cognition, puts it this way:

> Given that embodied constructs can explain cognition and action, there is no need to invoke abstract symbols. In the early days of embodiment research, cognitive scientists were skeptical: At one conference, a prominent cognitive scientist publicly suggested that notions of embodiment were the equivalent of "fairy dust" and challenged researchers to demonstrate the validity of the ideas. Using the methods of science, the field rose to that challenge. Now the onus is on traditional cognitive scientists.[10p169]

In Defense of Abstraction

Glenberg believes that the evidence for Embodiment pulls the rug out from under the Abstraction hypothesis. I don't believe that necessarily follows. Abstraction and Embodiment are not mutually exclusive. Cognition could well encompass multiple distinct mechanisms that run according to different computational principles. The conclusion that one mechanism exists does not automatically preclude the other.

In fact, people could conceivably hold two competing representations— embodied and abstract—of the same event. For example, consider again the representation of action verbs such as *kick*. As we saw, reading the word *kick* activates the leg motor areas,[26] whereas stimulating the leg motor area facilitates the response to the same word[27]—the empirical evidence for this is indisputable. But as the psychologist Alfonso Caramazza and his colleagues point out,[32,33] these results do not preclude an abstract notion of "kicking." First, brain motor areas can serve multiple (non-motoric) functions, so the activation of the leg motor area presents no proof that a person is contemplating motor action. Even if we grant that the word *kick* triggers motor activity, this doesn't show that the concept of "kicking" *is* motor action.

To use an analogy, lightning often goes with thunder, so it's natural to associate the two: when you think "lightning," thunder comes to mind. Similarly, since you always show up to parties with your spouse, your friends form a strong association between you and your spouse. Does it mean that "lightning" *is* thunder? Or that people confuse you and your spouse? Not at all. What things *are* and what they are *associated* with are two different notions. Your association with your spouse doesn't erase your own identity, nor is lightning eliminated by thunder. By the same token, the association between the word "kicking" and leg activity does not necessary mean that the concept of "kicking" *is* a leg action. In other words, it does not show that people *only* encode kicking in an "embodied" motor format.

Moreover, there is strong empirical evidence to suggest that *some* cognitive capacities *are* abstract. I will not burden you with an exhaustive review. Instead, I will show that Embodiment is neither necessary nor sufficient for thinking. It's perfectly possible to engage in some forms of abstract thinking when embodied support is unavailable (as is seen with people with disabilities); conversely, typical individuals (for whom embodied cognition is wide open) do not invariably deploy it. Clearly, Embodiment is not required for thinking. Neither is it sufficient for thinking in and of itself. Embodied cognition is obviously challenged by abstract concepts such as "time" and "justice." Moreover, without abstract symbols, embodied cognition cannot capture the systematicity and productivity of thought.

Embodiment Isn't Necessary for Thinking

If our understanding of *kicking* is mediated by leg movement, then it stands to reason that individuals with motor disabilities should experience difficulties in action perception, and such difficulties have indeed been reported.[30] Brain lesions, however, rarely impair *only* motor areas, so it's possible that the difficulties of these patients might result from impairment to non-motor (e.g., language) functions.[34] And even if the results were indeed due to motor impairment, they still cannot determine whether motor action is *necessary* for our understanding, or whether it merely enriches such concepts by providing the conceptual "icing on the cake."

To get at this empirically, the psychologists Gilles Vannuscorpsa and Alfonso Caramazza[35] explored action concepts in individuals who were born either without upper limbs or with severely shortened ones. Remarkably, these participants were as at least as efficient as controls (and, in some cases, more efficient) in identifying actions, naming actions presented by point-light displays, memorizing novel actions, and interpreting goal-oriented actions. These results suggest that a conceptual understanding of action does not require motor simulation.

Similar results have been reported for individuals who are congenitally blind. Congenitally blind individuals exhibited intact understandings of action verbs, and they did so by relying on the same brain areas that sighted individuals use.[36] In another study, a congenitally blind child was able to spontaneously interpret the geometry of space. For example, she was able to predict novel paths to connection between four objects.[37] And, as discussed in Chapter 3, newly sighted individuals show at least a partial ability to spontaneously recognize objects from sight.[38,39] Thus, sensory and motor disabilities do not necessarily lead to conceptual deprivation.

Other results suggest that, despite their intact sensory and motor capacities, typical individuals do not necessarily deploy them in thinking. For example, when people interpret sentences describing a "bouncing" action, they do not activate the same visual brain area they use to perceive that action.[40] Results from my own lab suggest that people can extract the structure of spoken language without relying on articulation. In particular, people maintain their preference for well-formed syllables (e.g., *blif*) over ill-formed ones (e.g., *lbif*), when articulation is disrupted, either by stimulating the lip motor area in the brain (using TMS)[41] or by preventing motor action (having people bite on their lips or tongues).[42] The brains of newborns show the same preference, well before these infants have uttered their first word (and despite no experience with either).[43] Taken together, these results suggest that at least some aspects of cognition do not require sensation and action.

Embodiment Is Not Sufficient to Explain Thinking

It's one thing to show that we understand the concept of *kicking* by moving our legs. But what about *time, object,* and *justice?* How does Embodied cognition deal with these notions? One proposal suggests that such concepts are really not abstract at all; all concepts, in this view, could ultimately be boiled down to sensations and actions.[7] Another theory suggests that abstract concepts can be captured by an appeal to the "perception" of one's own internal states.[9] I don't find these proposals convincing. The first suggestion, that abstract concepts *are* embodied, conflates concepts with their (remote) sensorimotor associations. The second does not specify how one could encode the internal state of "time" if one lacks that abstract concept. In short, the problem of abstract concepts remains wide open. Here, however, I'd like to focus on a still deeper challenge for Embodiment—the problem of thinking itself.

The whole point about thinking is that it's lawful. Thinking is *compositional*—the thought *Socrates is a man* implies the concept of *man.* It's *systematic*—you lawfully move from premises such as *Socrates is a man* and *All men are mortal* to the inference that *Socrates is mortal.* Finally, it's *productive*—you would reach the same conclusions for *Blix is a man.* Compositionality, systematicity, and productivity are the foundations of human cognition. So, if you are in the business of proposing a novel account of how the mind works, it is these three problems that you have to tackle.

The CTTM meets that challenge, thanks to its reliance on structured symbols and structure-sensitive processes. Symbols can define categories (Man) whose instances, actual (John) and potential (Blix), are all treated alike, so knowledge about Man automatically extends to Blix. Structure sensitivity also allows us to form relations between symbols. For example, we can discover that *Men* is a constituent of *Mortal Men,* and more generally that A is a constituent of AB. Identity (*a rose is a rose,* and, generally, an X is an X) is another critical formal relation. The capacity to encode symbols and to operate on structure are "hardwired" in the system. This doesn't necessarily mean that specific symbols (OBJECT) or relations (XX) are innate, but it does mean that the computational mechanisms that encode them do not need to be learned. To use an analogy, think about knowledge (concepts and propositions) and computational mechanisms as cookies and baking utensils. In this baking analogy, cookies may not be inborn, but the tools that you use to bake them—rolling pins, cookie-cutters, mixers, and so on—might be.

Embodiment, recall, rejects the notion of abstract symbols, so for proponents of embodied cognition, these facts present a formidable challenge: you have to somehow "bootstrap" these abstract categories and relations from specific *episodes* that encode one's sensorimotor experiences. Your notion of a "hill" will depend on how much energy you expended climbing one with your heavy backpack, the weather (a warm day will make you sweat; humidity makes things worse), and your physical state (have you gotten enough sleep?). And if you wish to reason about the mortality of John, you will need to consult your encounter at Starbucks on Thursday at 4:31 PM, when it was really cold outside. How do you move from such sensorimotor episodes to "universals"—knowledge about John, and Men in general? And how do you draw systematic inferences that depend on structure (e.g., a blix is a blix)?

The psychologist Larry Barsalou,[8,9,44,45] one of the major theoreticians in the field of embodied cognition, is hopeful that the structure will spontaneously "emerge." Although the brain can only encode specific embodied episodes at the onset of learning, he says, it eventually develops the capacity to encode symbols and relations. But detailed computational work suggests that this optimism is ill-founded.

When the psychologist Gary Marcus[46–48] carefully examined artificial "neural networks" of the kind envisioned by Barsalou, he found that they failed spectacularly, even on simple relations such as identity (a rose is a rose). The networks were able to learn and generalize, but what they learned was not abstract relations (e.g., an X is an X) but the associations between specific instances (e.g., between this rose and that rose). The computer scientists Brenden Lake and his colleagues obtained similar results for other logical relations and computational models.[49,50] And notice that these failures occurred despite a huge discount—the networks were already given an abstract representation of concepts (e.g., "rose") to work with, saving the need to extract it from the details provided by distinct bodily inputs like smell, touch, and motor effort, which is a formidable problem in its own right (e.g., how is one to integrate scales like "distance" with motor scales like "physical exertion" in order to compute the size of visual percepts?).[51]

This should be really bad news for those who believe that human cognition can be solely captured by embodied cognition. But the emphasis is on *solely*. Nothing in this discussion questions the possibility that cognition encodes some forms of embodied representations alongside other representations that are abstract. So, at last, we are in a position to ask why: Why are we so taken by the notion that cognition lies *solely* in our bodies? Why are we reluctant to consider the strong evidence for abstraction?

Who's Afraid of Abstract Ideas?

To understand our attitudes toward Abstraction, we need to revisit our complex relationship with Dualism and, possibly, Essentialism. This suggestion is not entirely original. The psychologist Arthur Glenberg and his colleagues have already named Dualism as a prime suspect, but, ironically, they evoke it to support the opposite claim. They believe that Dualism is responsible for our dissatisfaction with Embodiment. Abstraction, they assert, is inherently committed to Dualism, so it precludes Embodiment. I reject that accusation categorically. First, I will explain why. Then I will examine whether our discomfort with Abstraction arises not from Abstraction per se but from the biases of our core cognition.

Abstraction Isn't Committed to Dualism

Glenberg and colleagues believe that Abstraction subscribes to Cartesian Dualism. In their words:

> The PSSH makes a Cartesian distinction between thought and action, treating mind as disembodied. That is, according to PSSH, the exact same thoughts occur when a computer is manipulating symbols by using rules and when a person is manipulating the same symbols by using the same rules. The particulars of the body housing the symbol manipulation were thought to be irrelevant.[52p575]

Glenberg and colleagues are right to state that thinking, in the PSSH, depends only on the structural arrangement of symbols, not on their substance (neurons or silicon). And they are also right to state that the constitution of the rest of the body—whether we have limbs or wings—doesn't matter either. Where they fail, in my opinion, is in concluding that PSSH implies Cartesian Dualism. Not in the least!

Cartesian Dualism, to reiterate, is the claim that the mind is immaterial, distinct from the material body. The CTTM and PSSH, on the other hand, assert that symbol manipulation depends on the structures of physical symbols. Recall our squares, triangles, and circles in the previous section. In this view, thinking of BLACK COFFE implies thinking COFFEE, because the symbol for BLACK COFFEE *physically contains* the symbol for COFFEE. Physical symbols are the *cause* of thinking. It's only the arrangement of *physical* symbols that is "seen" by the thinking device, not their meanings, and it is those arrangements that make the machine "tick." The P in "physical symbol hypothesis" is there for a reason; it stands for "physical." Physical *is* material.

It's tempting to think otherwise for two reasons. First, in everyday language, "abstraction" in frequently associated with "ethereal" or "immaterial," so it's easy to confuse the quotidian sense of abstraction with the scientific notion of Abstraction. Doing so would be akin to conflating the quotidian sense of relativity with Einstein's theory; it's obviously inappropriate when we are reasoning about science.

A second confusion might arise from the assumption that symbol manipulation does not depend on the substance of the signifier (e.g., neurons, silicon, paper). But being substance-independent and being immaterial are *not* the same things. Rather, the CTTM asserts that for the purpose of explaining certain key aspects of thinking (such as how you form complex propositions like "large coffee"), one can consider *general* computational principles of symbol manipulation that are independent of how those symbols are implemented in the brain. This approach, called *functionalism*, is quite ubiquitous in science, and it has nothing to do with the mind-body distinction specifically. To explain why patients with sickle cell anemia suffer from excruciating pain, it might be sufficient to note that their red blood cells are clumping together and, consequently, interfering with the circulation of blood in their body; the biophysical mechanisms that cause those cells to congregate and their genetic regulation is not directly relevant to this immediate anatomical question. Does it mean that the anatomical explanation is "immaterial," just because it doesn't go all the way down to the level of DNA? Of course not! Rather, each biological phenomenon can simultaneously be explained at different levels, and you choose the level of explanation depending on the question at hand. By the same token, cognitive scientists choose to explain some aspects of thinking at the level of symbols because they believe that this level of analysis provides the most transparent account of the phenomenon they wish to study. The choice of "symbols" does not negate the material brain, any more than the choice of an anatomical explanation for a symptom of a disease negates genetics.

The Magical Spells of Core Knowledge:
Dualism and Essentialism

So, if Abstraction does not necessitate Dualism, if it does not presume that cognition is immaterial, distinct from the body, then why do scholars assume it does? Why do they dismiss the support for Abstraction and insist that concepts are *only* "in our bones"?

This question is not one we can settle definitively. Scholars disagree for multiple reasons, scientific and otherwise, and I'd be remiss if I reduced a scientific dispute to just one cause. Additionally, there is no hard scientific evidence documenting laypeople's infatuation with Embodiment, so we don't know whether these attitudes are widely shared. For these reasons, we have to tread lightly. All that being said, allow me to suggest a possibility.

Perhaps Dualism is indeed to blame for our troubles with Abstraction, because people erroneously believe that thinking—the representation and manipulation of abstract ideas—lacks a material basis in the body. Perhaps it is this mistaken belief (and not Abstraction per se), that paradoxically entices them to view Abstraction as unlikely. Previous chapters have documented this bias in great detail. People, as we have seen, believe that ideas cannot be identified in the brain or transferred from donors in hypothetical brain transplants. Moreover, this bias, as we saw, is directly linked to Dualism. For example, the bias against ideas is diminished once a person is primed to think of body and mind as one and the same (as suggested by Physicalism).

Our intuitive Dualist view of ideas as immaterial poses multiple challenges for our understanding of thinking. First, if ideas are immaterial, then it's hard for us to see how thinking can be captured by the manipulation of physical material symbols, as proposed by the Abstraction hypothesis. Dualism also gets in our way when we try to explain how immaterial thinking occurs in our material brains and how it can effect changes in our material bodies—for example, compelling us to move our legs as we contemplate the concept of *kicking*.

Essentialism further exacerbates our troubles. We intuit that some of our concepts are universally shared; people all over the world can relate to the notion of "kicking." It is likely the same for other concepts, such as "mother" and "child." But the prospect of universal concepts raises an irreconcilable dilemma. Essentialism—the belief that innate traits must be material—implies that innate concepts are material; Dualism, on the other hand, tells us that concepts must be immaterial. For our blind mind, the notion of *innate immaterial concepts that are encoded in the material human body* is an oxymoron—a dissonance that requires a resolution.

There are three logical solutions to this problem, each dealing with one of the components of this three-legged conceptual monster: innateness, material body, and thinking. One solution is to reject *innateness*; that is the solution we had considered in previous chapters. Another solution maintains that concepts are immaterial but denies that they are encoded in our material *bodies*. Going that route could indeed promote discomfort with Embodiment, just as Glenberg feared, but this bias originates from core knowledge, not Abstraction itself. In fact, Dualism may well interfere with our capacity to fully grasp the notion of Abstraction as the manipulation of physical symbols; another side-effect will become evident when we consider our irrational love affair with neuroscience (in Chapter 11).

The third and final solution resolves the mind–body tension by getting rid of *cognition*. It rejects the notion that thinking consists of the manipulation of mental representations and instead situates thinking in the material body. This solution requires that we overcome our natural tendency to view thinking as immaterial, so it is unclear whether laypeople will spontaneously go that route. But once thinking is reframed as action, the three-legged monster immediately dissolves. If "kick" is encoded by the movement of my limbs, then the problem of how the cognitive state of thinking about kicking results in the physical activity of my leg is eliminated: thinking and action are one and the same. And if my understanding of CUP solely consists of the interactions of my material body with real cups—and not of some immaterial idea—then it is clear how those material experiences can be encoded in my material brain, and how those material forces can cause the series of material acts that make up my morning coffee ritual—it's all completely "in my bones." *That* is the lure of Embodied cognition.

References

1. Labov W. The Boundaries of Words and Their Meanings. In: Aarts B, Denison D, Keizer E, Popova G, eds. *Fuzzy grammar a reader*. Washington, DC: Oxford University Press; 2004:67–89.
2. Fodor JA. *The language of thought*. Cambridge, MA: Harvard University Press; 1975.
3. Fodor J, Pylyshyn Z. Connectionism and cognitive architecture: a critical analysis. *Cognition*. 1988;28:3–71.
4. Pylyshyn Z. *Computation and cognition: Towards a foundation for cognitive science*. Cambridge, England: MIT Press; 1984.

5. Newell A, Simon HA. Computer simulation of human thinking. *Science.* 1961;134(3495):2011–2017.

6. Turing AM. Computing machinery and intelligence. *Mind: A Quarterly Review of Philosophy.* 1950;59:433–460.

7. Wilson A, D, Egolonka S. Embodied cognition is not what you think it is. *Frontiers in Psychology.* 2013;4.

8. Barsalou LW, Kyle Simmons W, Barbey AK, Wilson CD. Grounding conceptual knowledge in modality-specific systems. *Trends in Cognitive Sciences.* 2003;7(2):84–91.

9. Barsalou LW. Grounded cognition. *Annual Review of Psychology.* 2008;59:617–645.

10. Glenberg AM. Few believe the world is flat: how embodiment is changing the scientific understanding of cognition. *Canadian Journal of Experimental Psychology/Revue canadienne de psychologie expérimentale.* 2015;69(2):165–171.

11. Gibson JJ. *The ecological approach to visual perception.* Boston, MA: Houghton Mifflin; 1979.

12. Thelen E, Smith LB. *A dynamic systems approach to the development of cognition and action.* Cambridge, MA: MIT Press; 1994.

13. Liberman AM, Cooper FS, Shankweiler DP, Studdert-Kennedy M. Perception of the speech code. *Psychological Review.* 1967;74(6):431–461.

14. Gallese V, Fadiga L, Fogassi L, Rizzolatti G. Action recognition in the premotor cortex. *Brain.* 1996;119:593–609.

15. Rizzolatti G, Fogassi L. The mirror mechanism: recent findings and perspectives. *Philosophical Transactions of the Royal Society of London Series B, Biological Sciences.* 2014;369(1644):20130420–20130420.

16. Hickok G. *The myth of mirror neurons: the real neuroscience of communication and cognition.* 1st ed. New York, NY: W. W. Norton; 2014.

17. Hickok G. Eight problems for the mirror neuron theory of action understanding in monkeys and humans. *Journal of Cognitive Neuroscience.* 2009;21(7):1229–1243.

18. Witt JK, Proffitt DR, Epstein W. Tool use affects perceived distance, but only when you intend to use it. *Journal of Experimental Psychology Human Perception and Performance.* 2005;31(5):880–888.

19. Lessard DA, Linkenauger SA, Proffitt DR. Look before you leap: jumping ability affects distance perception. *Perception.* 2009;38(12):1863–1866.

20. Stefanucci JK, Geuss MN. Big people, little world: the body influences size perception. *Perception.* 2009;38(12):1782–1795.

21. Bhalla M, Proffitt DR. Visual-motor recalibration in geographical slant perception. *Journal of Experimental Psychology Human Perception and Performance.* 1999;25(4):1076–1096.

22. Witt JK, Schuck DM, Taylor JET. Action-specific effects underwater. *Perception.* 2011;40(5):530–537.

23. Witt JK, Linkenauger SA, Bakdash JZ, Proffitt DR. Putting to a bigger hole: golf performance relates to perceived size. *Psychonomic Bulletin & Review.* 2008;15(3):581–585.

24. Zwaan RA, Taylor LJ, de Boer M. Motor resonance as a function of narrative time: further tests of the linguistic focus hypothesis. *Brain and Language.* 2010;112(3):143–149.

25. Zwaan RA, Stanfield RA, Yaxley RH. Language comprehenders mentally represent the shapes of objects. *Psychological Science.* 2002;13(2):168–171.

26. Hauk O, Johnsrude I, Pulvermüller F. Somatotopic representation of action words in human motor and premotor cortex. *Neuron.* 2004;41(2):301–307.

27. Pulvermüller F, Hauk O, Nikulin VV, Ilmoniemi RJ. Functional links between motor and language systems. *The European Journal of Neuroscience*. 2005;21(3):793–797.

28. Martino J, Velasquez C, Vázquez-Bourgon J, de Lucas EM, Gomez E. Cross-modal recruitment of auditory and orofacial areas during sign language in a deaf subject. *World Neurosurgery*. 2017;105:1033.e1031–1033.e1035.

29. Schomers MR, Kirilina E, Weigand A, Bajbouj M, Pulvermüller F. Causal influence of articulatory motor cortex on comprehending single spoken words: TMS evidence. *Cerebral Cortex*. 2015;25(10):3894–3902.

30. Arrighi R, Cartocci G, Burr D. Reduced perceptual sensitivity for biological motion in paraplegia patients. *Current Biology*. 2011;21(22):R910–R911.

31. Neininger B, Pulvermüller F. Word-category specific deficits after lesions in the right hemisphere. *Neuropsychologia*. 2003;41(1):53–70.

32. Mahon BZ, Caramazza A. A critical look at the embodied cognition hypothesis and a new proposal for grounding conceptual content. *Journal of Physiology*. 2008;102(1–3):59–70.

33. Leshinskaya A, Caramazza A. For a cognitive neuroscience of concepts: moving beyond the grounding issue. *Psychonomic Bulletin & Review*. 2016;23(4):991–1001.

34. Bedny M, Caramazza A. Perception, action, and word meanings in the human brain: the case from action verbs. *Annals of the New York Academy of Sciences*. 2011;1224:81–95.

35. Vannuscorps G, Caramazza A. Typical action perception and interpretation without motor simulation. *Proceedings of the National Academy of Sciences of the United States of America*. 2016;113(1):86–91.

36. Bedny M, Caramazza A, Pascual-Leone A, Saxe R. Typical neural representations of action verbs develop without vision. *Cerebral Cortex*. 2012;22(2):286–293.

37. Landau B, Gleitman H, Spelke E. Spatial knowledge and geometric representation in a child blind from birth. *Science*. 1981;213:1275.

38. Held R, Ostrovsky Y, de Gelder B, et al. The newly sighted fail to match seen with felt. *Nature Neuroscience*. 2011;14:551.

39. Chen J, Wu E-D, Chen X, et al. Rapid integration of tactile and visual information by a newly sighted child. *Current Biology: CB*. 2016;26(8):1069–1074.

40. Dravida S, Saxe R, Bedny M. People can understand descriptions of motion without activating visual motion brain regions. *Frontiers in Psychology*. 2013;4:537.

41. Berent I, Brem A-K, Zhao X, et al. Role of the motor system in language knowledge. *Proceedings of the National Academy of Sciences of the United States of America*. 2015;112:1983–1988.

42. Zhao X, Berent I. The basis of the syllable hierarchy: articulatory pressures or universal phonological constraints? *Journal of Psycholinguistic Research*. 2018;47(1):29–64.

43. Gómez DM, Berent I, Benavides-Varela S, et al. Language universals at birth. *Proceedings of the National Academy of Sciences of the United States of America*. 2014;111(16):5837–5341.

44. Pezzulo G, Barsalou L, Cangelosi A, Fischer M, McRae K, Spivey M. Computational grounded cognition: a new alliance between grounded cognition and computational modeling. *Frontiers in Psychology*. 2013;3(612).

45. Barsalou LW. Abstraction in perceptual symbol systems. *Philosophical Transactions: Biological Sciences*. 2003;358(1435):1177–1187.

46. Marcus GF. Rethinking eliminative connectionism. *Cognitive Psychology*. 1998;37(3):243–282.

47. Marcus G. *The algebraic mind: Integrating connectionism and cognitive science.* Cambridge: MIT Press; 2001.
48. Marcus G. *Deep learning: a critical appraisal.* 2018. Retrieved from arXiv:1801.00631
49. Lake BM, Baroni M. *Generalization without systematicity: on the compositional skills of sequence-to-sequence recurrent networks.* 2017. Retrieved from arXiv:1711.00350
50. Loula J, Baroni M, Lake BM. *Rearranging the familiar: testing compositional generalization in recurrent networks.* 2018. Retrieved from arXiv:1807.07545
51. Firestone C. How "paternalistic" is spatial perception? Why wearing a heavy backpack doesn't-and couldn't-make hills look steeper. *Perspectives on Psychological Science.* 2013;8(4):455–473.
52. Glenberg AM, Witt JK, Metcalfe J. From the revolution to embodiment: 25 years of cognitive psychology. *Perspectives on Psychological Science.* 2013;8(5):573–585.

10

Our Big Hearts

My first days with my newborn son unfolded under a thick cloud of blue haze: the sheer physical exhaustion after a difficult delivery; the long, sleepless nights; the guessing game of his loud wails. But a brief random encounter amidst the chaos changed my whole outlook on life.

It was a precious moment of quiet. My son was finally fast asleep in the car's backseat, and I was looking out the window. We were in Mexico City at the time, and in that gigantic metropolis, red traffic lights give the "go" signal for a sprint of micro-commerce. Sellers launch into the line of cars, chanting and waving their goods—food, toys, and household items. At that particular intersection, the seller was an indigenous woman, humbly offering a variety of chewing gums. She was walking barefoot in a traditional dress, her baby snuggled in a shawl strapped to her back. She seemed as foreign to the city as I was. We did not exchange a word. We had no language in common, no shared past or future. But at that moment, a new realization hit me with the force of lightning: we are one and the same. Ten days ago, before the arrival of the sleeping eight-pound creature behind me, we had absolutely nothing in common, but in my mind, we were now alike. —She, I, and every one of the millions of other women with infants in that vast valley. We were mother and child.

Emotions such as motherly love define who we are. They are celebrated in works of art and literature and untangled on the therapist's couch. Michelangelo's Pieta conveys the maternal grief of a saint; Harry Potter is protected by the love of his wizard mother; whereas in *Oedipus Wrecks*, Woody Allen's character is afflicted by a Jewish Mother—a chronic condition from which no mortal has ever recovered.

Emotions are the gauge of our well-being. They focus the spotlight of our attention and set our actions and goals. If you have had a baby, you have probably found yourself lying in bed awake, listening to every one of her breaths and, at the onset of a silence, rushing to the crib. Emotions also leave their fingerprints on our bodies—maternal love is associated with specific neural

The Blind Storyteller. Iris Berent, Oxford University Press (2020). © Iris Berent, 2020.
DOI: 10.1093/oso/9780190061920.001.0001

circuits, distinct from romantic love, and it is linked to the expression of do-
pamine (a neurotransmitter), oxytocin, and vasopressin (neurohormones)
in the brains of humans as well as nonhuman animals.[1-3] When mother and
infant are engaged in face-to-face interactions, their heart rhythms are literally synchronized.[4]

But are our emotions truly ingrained in us? In my own mind, the notion
of universal maternal love seemed as clear as the light of day. But this assumption is based on an enormous leap of faith; in fact, my presumption
could appear offensive in its audacity. I presumed to know the emotions of
a stranger—an indigenous woman from an entirely different culture, social
reality, and economic universe. Could she and I have possibly felt the same
about our babies? Are emotions universally shared?

In this chapter, we turn our attention to matters of the heart. We begin
by examining how we—laypeople—think about our emotions. We next contrast our intuitive beliefs with the findings emerging from science. As in our
previous discussion of concepts (matters of the mind), we will see that our
beliefs about our affective lives are also systematically biased. While our
blindness to emotions and ideas take opposite paths (we are averse to innate
ideas but all too cozy with innate emotions), the origin of these biases is one
and the same—our core knowledge of Dualism and Essentialism. We will
see how our intuitive cognition derails our understanding of our psyches;
Chapter 12 next shows how it sabotages our science and clouds our understanding of clinical matters, ranging from psychotherapy to mental disorders
and psychotropic drugs.

Naïve Psychology of Emotions

In naïve psychology, emotions are innate affective states that we wear "on our
sleeves"—they readily manifest in our facial expressions and physical bodies.

Kristen Lindquist and her colleagues[5] were the first to unveil these
convictions. In their study, American college students rated nouns from multiple categories. Some named psychological states, such as emotions (anger,
disgust) and cognitive states (decisions, memories, morality); others denoted
biological concepts, such as natural kinds (e.g., snakes, water) and bodily
states (hunger, sight), or concepts unrelated to biology, such as abstract nominal kinds (e.g., courting, marriage). Results showed that emotions were rated
high on biological attributes (e.g., inherence, naturalness, and pre-existence),

akin to bodily states (hunger, pain) and natural kinds (snakes, water) and distinct from abstract nominal kinds (courting, marriage) and cognitive states (ideas, morality). Lindquist and her colleagues concluded that emotional categories (e.g., anger) are viewed as essentialist natural kinds.

But do people believe that emotions are innate and material, akin to the physical design of our bodies? Subsequent results from my own lab suggest that they do. You might recall (from Chapter 6) that when asked to predict the behavior of newborn infants, participants asserted that newborns would spontaneously prefer a "happy" to an "angry" face (but show no knowledge of number or morality). Another experiment presented people with a large list of adult human traits and asked them to rate the likelihood that a trait would emerge spontaneously in a desert island situation. For emotions, participants responded positively (i.e., they rated the emotions significantly higher than the scale's "neutral" midpoint value). And when asked to reason about a futuristic scenario in which a donor's body is replicated, people reckoned that the donor's emotions would transfer to the replica (unlike his or her ideas). Together, these results suggest that people view emotions as innate, material, and embodied.

Do people, then, really believe that emotions can be deciphered from the face and the body? For example, do we think that there are distinct facial and physiological expressions for "anger" and "fear"? And do they believe that these emotional facial expressions are universal?

To find out, we presented people with a list of 20 terms denoting emotions and asked them to respond to three questions.[6] One question was how likely it is that each would "show" on the face. Specifically, we asked, "How likely is it that you could tell that a person is experiencing this particular emotion from their facial expression?" A second question was whether each emotion would elicit a physical bodily response (e.g., a change in blood pressure, heart rate, perspiration). To evaluate the universality of these expressions, the third question invited people to take part in a thought experiment, modeled after the procedures employed in actual research in affective science (described next). In the thought experiment, a group of indigenous hunter-gatherers who have had no previous interactions with Westerners would be asked (with the help of an interpreter) to recognize 20 different emotions. They would be presented with an event (e.g., "a person encounters a threatening animal in the jungle and he is afraid for his life") along with pictures of two distinct facial expressions ("horror" vs. "euphoria") and asked to pick the picture that corresponds to the person depicted in the story. How likely is it that the indigenous people would recognize those 20 facial emotions?

Results indicated that people thought emotions are imprinted in our bodies and that those marks are universal. The 20 emotions were not all treated alike—the so-called basic emotions (surprise, anger, fear, happiness, sadness, and disgust)[7] were rated highest. But on average, people rated all emotions significantly higher than the "neutral" midpoint, and this was the case with each of the three questions. In other words, people asserted that emotions leave their mark on our physiology and that they can be read "in the face," even in the faces of people who have never seen a Westerner. Moreover, responses to the three questions were strongly correlated. The more likely an emotion is to leave its imprint on the body—either externally (in the face), or internally (by changing blood pressure, heart rate, or perspiration), the more likely people are to view this emotion as recognizable universally (across the 20 emotion terms, the correlations were 0.94 and 0.81, respectively). The propensity of emotions to leave their marks on the body and face showed high agreement as well (a correlation of 0.83).

How good are we as psychologists? Does our naïve theory of emotion correspond to reality? One potentially incriminating clue is presented by the association we form between the imprint of emotions on the body and their universality. Logically speaking, these two variables need not be linked. Motherly love, for instance, could certainly be universal without leaving any noticeable marks on the face, though there are good reasons for it to be imprinted internally—by changing blood pressure or heartrate. But in our intuitive minds, universality and embodiment are intimately tied together.

For the naïve psychologist, the body–universality link is not merely an association: it's a causal chain. In a second experiment, we asked people to make the same judgment about the universality of emotions, except that now, participants were explicitly informed about the materiality or nonmateriality of these traits. One group was told that each emotion corresponds to a discrete brain region (i.e., material). Another was told that these emotions are not associated with specific brain regions; in fact, the scientist tells them, she isn't sure that these emotions even have a material basis in the human body (i.e., immaterial). To be clear, the information about the brain is not logically related to innateness—while language, for instance, typically engages a certain brain network, no known brain area is solely dedicated to language. But the participants who were told that emotions are "in the brain" (material) rated emotions as more likely to be innate. So, for our participants, traits that are in the body are innate. That's red flag number one.

Here is another warning sign. In a third experiment, we informed still another group of participants that certain emotions are not universally recognized by all cultures, so scientists believe they are acquired from experience. With this information in mind, we asked them how likely it is that those emotions would be recognized by the hunter-gatherers. People didn't budge. They still overwhelming thought that the so-called basic emotions (fear, anger, disgust, surprise, sadness, and happiness) would be universally recognized. They did not simply ignore what we told them—when compared to a previous "neutral" group (who was not provided with any information about innateness), the confidence in innate emotions had demonstrably decreased. But the belief in innate emotions was hardly eliminated—people still asserted that emotions would emerge in the body universally. So, our conviction that emotions are innate and embodied is not merely a belief; it's a *bias* that is maintained despite explicit evidence to the contrary.

Sound familiar? It certainly should! Our beliefs in innate emotions are the exact mirror image of our intuitive aversion to innate ideas. As we saw in previous chapters, people irrationally maintain that ideas cannot be material or inborn, but for emotions, we assert just the opposite. I suggest this is no coincidence. These two biases emanate from a single source—our core knowledge of Dualism and Essentialism. It is Essentialism, specifically, that irrationally compels us to assume that traits that leave their signatures on our body are innate. It is precisely because we believe we can "read" emotions off of people's faces, and sense them physically—in our digestive tracts and the racing of blood in our veins—that we are led to presume that emotions are innate and hence universal.

Biased as these beliefs might be, however, are they necessarily wrong? Aren't emotions really imprinted in our bodies? And aren't these fingerprints universally shared?

Affective Science: Are Emotions Innately Engraved in Our Bodies?

To put our naïve psychology in perspective, we now embark on an excursion into affective science. As we will see, the facts are far more complex than what our intuitive understanding suggests. While innate emotions are a slam dunk in our naïve psychology, in real affective science, this question is extremely controversial. The vast literature on the topic resembles the piles of evidence collected in a decades-old murder investigation; we cannot do justice to all of it here. But a few illustrations will suffice to make the point. My goal, after all, is not to offer the definitive verdict. It is not the murderer we are after, but the detectives.

A Case for Innateness

Much of the research on the origins of emotions explores their manifestations in the body—both externally (in the face, voice, and posture) and internally (in the brain and muscles). To determine whether these physical manifestations are universal, researchers asked whether facial and vocal expression of emotions can be recognized cross-culturally, especially by the members of small-scale societies that have had little contact with the Western world. If they identify them as we Westerners do, then these expressions are likely innate.

A landmark paper by the psychologist Paul Ekman and his colleagues[8] examined the recognition of facial emotions by members of five cultures—both literate groups (from the United States, Brazil, and Japan) as well as groups from remote villages in New Guinea and Borneo who had limited contact with Westerners. Participants were shown a still photograph of a Caucasian person along with six affective terms (presented in the participants' native language); their task was to select the word that best goes with the picture. Results showed similar recognition of happiness, anger, and fear in all groups. Other studies (using similar methods) found the same among members of the Fore[9] and Bahinemo[10] in New Guinea and the Burkinabe Faso, a small-scale society in West Africa.[11]

Remote groups also appear to recognize emotions from nonverbal vocalizations. In one study, members of the Shuar (a hunter-horticulturalist group in Amazonian Ecuador) were able to match vocal expressions of basic emotions (produced by American English speakers) with their facial expressions.[12] In another study by Disa Sauter and colleagues,[7] members of the Himba—a seminomadic group from northern Namibia—were presented with vignettes that depicted an emotion (e.g., a person was sad because their close relative had died); next they heard two vocalizations—one depicting the relevant emotion and the other a distractor. When asked to choose the vocalization that matched the story, the Himbas' overall recognition was above chance, and for basic emotions, this was the case whether the vocalizations were produced by a British or a Himba actor. These results suggest that some basic emotions can be universally recognized from both facial expressions and vocalizations.

Many studies have concurred. A 2002 analysis[13] of 97 studies from 182 cross-cultural samples and 42 nations found that in more than 96% of the studies, participants were able to "correctly" recognize emotions displayed by members of other cultural groups' facial expressions, vocalizations, or body postures. The channel of communication mattered, as did the specific emotions: Happiness, for instance, was best-recognized from faces; anger was most readily conveyed by voices. But cross-cultural recognition of emotions appears to be a reliable phenomenon.

Other results suggest that emotions can be recognized by newborn infants. But in this case, the channel of expression (face vs. voice) matters much more. Infants show no reliable preference for happy faces compared to either angry[14] or disgusted faces.[15] This is not because infants cannot *discriminate* between distinct facial expressions; results suggest that they certainly can. To test discrimination, infants were first presented with a set of identical faces (either two neutral or two fearful expressions). Once the infants lost interest, the display switched to two different expressions (neutral vs. fearful). If infants can detect the change, then they should now regain interest (that is, look longer), and results suggested that they did. But while infants discriminated between the two facial expressions, they were indifferent to their significance—for example, their reaction to the change did not vary when the original display featured two neutral or two fearful faces. Similarly, when given the opportunity to stare at two simultaneous displays—either static[14] or dynamic[15]—newborn infants showed no preference for happy faces. So, despite their capacity to tell "angry" from "happy" faces, there was no evidence that infants interpreted the "angry" faces as negative, let alone as expressions of anger specifically.

Newborns, however, *do* respond to emotional vocalizations. In these studies,[16,17] newborn infants were presented with a single nonsense word ("dada"), produced to convey anger, happiness, or fear (preliminary work confirmed that adult listeners overwhelmingly recognized the emotions as intended). The study used an oddball procedure. Infants repeatedly heard a vocalization of a single emotion (e.g., happiness), which was occasionally interrupted by another vocalization (e.g., anger); for example, happy, happy,

happy, happy, *angry*, happy, happy, happy, etc. Another group got the opposite arrangement (angry, angry, angry, *happy*, etc.). As infants heard the deviant, their brain response was monitored. Results showed that they not only detected the change (as evident from the spike in their brain response) but the magnitude of the change was larger for the "angry" vocalization relative to either the "happy"[17] or "fearful" one.[16] The stronger response to "anger" is not simply due to the sheer acoustic properties of the angry sounds. To counter that possibility, the researchers created control stimuli that superimposed the intonational contours of the original vocalizations on synthesized stimuli that did not sound like human speech. The anger "music" was thus the same, but it did not sound like a human voice. Here, no selective response to the angry intonation was observed. The consistent brain responses to anger are in line with the possibility that newborns disfavored this threatening emotion relative to nonthreatening ones—either positive (happiness) or negative (fear).

Constructivist Skepticism

The results described so far would seem to suggest that the expression of basic emotions, such as anger and fear, are universal and that they are readily recognizable from birth, at least from vocalizations. This would seem to strongly suggest that discrete emotions are innate and, moreover, that these emotions leave their distinct fingerprints on the human body. But subsequent findings have raised multiple challenges to this conclusion.

One worrisome gap in the narrative is presented by the newborn results discussed at the end of the previous section. If we truly wear emotions on our sleeves, and if newborns can decode human faces, then why do newborns differentiate between auditory vocalizations of emotions but not facial ones? While it is of course possible that different expressions would become available at different rates (either because vision is later to develop or because the innate system of vocal expressions "comes aboard" before the facial ones), there is a simpler explanation for the discrepancy that assumes no innateness at all.

Newborns, as we saw in Chapter 3, are not blank slates devoid of experiences; they have had months of in-utero residence, which allowed them to share many of their mothers' auditory experiences, including the sounds of voices. Not only can the fetuses hear those sounds, but they could conceivably learn their emotional significance by discerning their effects on their mothers (e.g., by detecting changes in her heart rate). Whether mothers do in fact produce distinct physiological reactions to distinct emotions is not entirely clear (especially when considering negative emotions like anger and fear).[18] But if such information is available to the fetus, then the link between emotional vocalizations and the mother's physiology could present the fetus with obvious opportunities to learn about the significance of emotional vocalizations, if not facial expressions.

Other results cast doubt on the view of emotions as "pancultural." Consider again the recognition of emotional vocalization. While Sauter and colleagues reported that the remote Himba can reliably recognize basic emotions, subsequent studies by Maria Gendron and her then-mentor Lisa Feldman Barrett and colleagues[19] did not find the same. When Gendron and colleagues asked the Himba to determine which of two vocalizations matched a story, their overall recognition was no better than chance. When asked to freely describe those vocalizations, the Himba did not reliably volunteer the expected emotional category; in fact, their responses consisted mostly of action terms (e.g., screaming) rather than emotions (e.g., fear).

Similar results obtained when the Himba were asked to recognize emotions from faces.[20] Participants were asked to sort the faces into piles and then label them with words. Results suggested that the sorting behavior of the Himba was markedly distinct from that of the U.S. participants, and so were the labels provided by the two groups. While U.S. participants described the faces in terms of their emotions (e.g., happiness), the Himba typically described the same faces in terms of actions (e.g., laughing).

Why did these recent findings disagree with the earlier conclusions of Sauter, Ekman, and colleagues? Researchers[21][22] blame the discrepancy on research methodology. Psychologists know too well that the answers they get from participants can vary greatly depending on how they pose the questions to them. And the questions posed by Gendron and colleagues were markedly different from those in the early study by Ekman and his colleagues. Early studies asked participants to choose among a given set of options, akin to a multiple-choice test (e.g., which of the following two faces—a smile or a frown—matches the word "happiness"?). In the subsequent studies, the questions were open-ended, as in an essay test (e.g., describe the [smiling] face). If you have ever taken a multiple-choice test, you know that many of the questions allow you to get by even if your understanding of the material is rather fuzzy—all you have to do is reason through the options. This would explain why performance dropped markedly in the open-ended sorting and labeling tasks of Gendron and colleagues. A review of the literature further suggests that there were systematic methodological differences between the earlier reports of emotion universals and the later findings by Gendron and others.[21,23-25] Gendron and colleagues thus contend that the facial expressions of emotions are not universal.

Lisa Feldman Barrett takes this argument a step further and asserts that it is impossible to read a person's emotions from their face.[26-28] In her view, discrete emotions (e.g., anger vs. fear, as opposed to "negative affect") have no invariant bodily manifestation at all. If you were to inspect the fingerprint of discrete emotions like "anger" in the body, you would find no invariant signature, even among members of a single culture. Indeed, as I am writing these words, a media scandal is raging over the facial expression of a teenager who is staring right at the face of a chanting Native American elder. Is he sneering sarcastically, or is his expression neutral? In Barrett's view, there is no way to tell. Her reading of the literature suggests that there are no consistent facial expressions of contempt (or any other emotion) and no invariant patterns of response in the automatic nervous system, such as heart rate and breathing; and there are also no brain regions or even networks that consistently express a single emotion. Although the brain state of "anger" (for instance) is demonstrably distinct from, say, "fear" across individuals, this convergence, according to Barrett, is merely a mathematical abstraction. When you inspect the manifestation of "anger," you do not necessarily find the same neural fingerprint across different expressions, even within a single individual. She concludes that "variation is the norm. Emotion fingerprints are a myth."[26p23]

These observations led Barrett to propose that emotions are not innate but made. Your mind constructs emotions such as "anger" or "fear" much as it does any other cognitive categories. Think, for example, of children, passports, photo albums, your pet, and medications—what do these things share in common? "Not much," you'd say. But if I asked you to think of things to take from your home during a fire, you would probably construct a similar list. The items on your list are not inherently similar to each other (your kids don't look like your pet), and their being grouped together is certainly not innate. Yet, when presented with a goal, your mind instantly forms such categories in an ad hoc way.[29] Emotional categories, in the constructivist account, are made in just the same way.

How do you make an emotional category? The ingredients, in Barrett's telling, are minimal. Newborns begin their lives devoid of any emotions; in fact, Barrett believes that infants "are born unable to see faces"[26p99]; all they have is affect, which is determined by two systems—valence (positive vs. negative affect) and arousal (high. vs. low). Valence and arousal are akin to two knobs on an old analog radio—one selects the frequency (the valence of affect), and the other sets the volume (arousal magnitude). The affective "music," so to speak, is conjointly set by the value of those two scales—fear and lethargy are both negative affects, but they have different levels of arousal (fear elicits higher arousal than lethargy); elation and serenity, on the other hand, are both positive affects—the former is high in arousal, whereas the latter is low.

How, then, do you move from continuous amorphic affects to discrete emotions, such as "fear" and "anger"? According to the constructivist view, you learn! Emotions are concepts—they define classes of affective experiences ("anger at an aggressor," "anger at the person who cuts ahead of you in line") as a single category, much like cognitive categories such as "object" and "living thing." And in the constructivist view, concepts aren't inborn: they are learned from experience. Emotions are constructed in the same way you construct a list of things to take from one's home during a fire. Two ingredients, according to Barrett, are necessary for construction. One is the capacity to track the associations between events in one's experience. With "fear," for instance, you might learn to associate your negative affective responses with certain fear-inducing stimuli, such as snakes, loud noises, and dark rooms. The second critical ingredient is language. The linguistic label of "fear" is what allows you to group all of these fear-inducing instances in a single class. Without language, concepts—whether they are "cold" cognitive concepts such as "object" or "hot" emotions like "fear"—would not be formed. It is for this reason that preverbal infants and nonverbal animals can show no emotions. Without language, they can only experience a negative affect. They cannot categorize it as "fear" as distinct from, say, "shame" or "anger." Linguistic social creatures that we are, adults learn emotions via the same mechanisms that allow us to learn about math, cooking, and geography. We are endowed with no special toolkit for emotions, nor are emotions inborn.

Are Innate Emotions a Myth?

So are innate emotions a myth? Are the previous reports of cross-cultural universals an illusion, prompted by a series of unfortunate methodological errors?

Not so fast, I would suggest. As a starter, let us revisit the debate on whether emotions leave universal fingerprints on our bodies. Given the previous section, this would seem utterly out of the question. How could you and the Himba possibly converge on your expressions of anger if you and I don't consistently display anger in the same way? But upon inspection, the two claims are not necessarily contradictory. Your bodily expression of "anger" after a frustrating day at work, for instance, may very well vary, depending on whether you are talking to your boss or to your spouse; this would not be a shocking discovery. This, however, is not to say that those various manifestations would be utterly unrelated to each other (or to my own various manifestations of anger). It's one thing to ask whether the manifestations of "anger" vary; it is another to ask whether, underneath all this undeniable variation, some level of invariance exists.

The invariance in those facial expressions may not necessarily be visible to the naked eye. This becomes evident when one compares the dynamic facial expressions of pain and sexual pleasure.[30] To the viewer, those two expressions are often indistinguishable. Moreover, the expressions of "pain" and "pleasure" vary across cultures. When scientists generated dynamic computer models of "pain" and "pleasure" informed by both the faces and the percepts of British and East Asian participants, the models for the two groups were distinct. All this would seem to suggest that these two emotions are devoid of any universal "fingerprints." But when the computer models were analyzed, several shared components were discovered. And indeed, these models were reliably recognized, and not only within cultures but across groups. For example, the East Asian participants were able to reliably discriminate between the British versions of "pain" and "pleasure," even though they had minimal exposure to Brits.[30] To be clear, these results do not prove that these expressions are innate, as participants were not entirely deprived of contact with the other culture. But they do open up the possibility that, despite undeniable variation, some components of facial expressions are universal.

Whether this invariance is recognized universally is yet unclear. The answer, as we saw in the previous section, is bound to vary, depending on the experimental method of choice. Proponents of open-ended procedures contend that discrimination ("multiple-choice") methods are fraught with hidden biases. Opponents state that in the absence of some constraints, participants from another culture would fail to show invariance for reasons having nothing to do with innate emotions per se.

The battle on the bodily fingerprints of emotions goes on and on. Maria Gendron and her colleagues contend that the Himbas' "success" in discriminating emotion vocalization (e.g., the negative target "angry" and the positive foil "happy") is based on affect alone (positive vs. negative), not discrete emotions. If they are right, then discrimination should vanish if the target and foil were matched for valence (e.g., by using the valence for "anger" for "fear"). But when Sauter and colleagues did so (by reanalyzing their original Himba results to match the target and foil for affect), emotion recognition was maintained.[31] Another study by Daniel Cordaro and colleagues likewise observed that villagers from Bhutan, who had arguably had no contact with Westerners, were nonetheless able to reliably recognize the vocal expressions of emotions produced by English speakers.[32]

Gendron and colleagues are not convinced. You might recall that in the vocalization recognition task, people first heard a story that described an affect, then they matched the vocalizations to the story. To make sure participants understood the story, Sauter and colleagues asked participants to describe what the protagonist was feeling. If participants were unable to volunteer the information spontaneously, the story was repeated, and there lies the second source of contention. Sauter and colleagues believe that the repetition was necessary to ensure comprehension, but in the eyes of Gendron and colleagues, this procedure provided an opportunity for people to learn about the emotions of the protagonist. Indeed, when Gendron and colleagues eliminated the repetition, the Himba's "success" with emotion vocalizations vanished.

Who is right? Was the feedback necessary to establish understanding or was it a biasing intervention? Of course, both can be true. Members of different cultures can certainly vary with respect to their ability to consciously access their emotions, and the feedback might very well have contributed to the participants' ability to verbalize their understanding of emotions. But there is a difference between verbally discussing emotions, on the one hand, and knowing about emotions and their links to facial expressions, on the other. Even if the repeated probing encouraged participants to attend to the emotion, or even helped them recognize that an emotion was expressed, it is difficult to see how the feedback allowed them to learn what the emotional category means, let alone link it to facial expressions and vocalizations. So, in my reading of the literature, the possibility that emotions could have some innate signatures on the body remains wide open.

But it's time to move on. In the heat of all this controversy about the significance of smiles and sighs, it's easy to lose track of our original question. And that question, you might recall, concerned not faces and voices but *emotions*: we asked whether emotions are innate. If we are after innate emotions, why do we obsess with their bodily fingerprints? Do emotions have to have bodily signatures to be considered innate? Must we all express innate anger in the same way? Does intense happiness really require that we smile?

Make no mistake—when I'm contrasting emotions and their bodily fingerprints, I'm not forming a Dualist divide between the mind and body, nor am I advocating the study of emotions by "telepathy." I'm not questioning whether emotions are "in the brain," or that their study requires us to pay attention to their physical responses—behavioral, physiological, and neural. What's at stake is whether innate emotions *are* these responses—that fear, for instance, is a specific facial expression, a particular vocalization, or a specific response of the autonomous nervous system. If innate emotions consist of bodily responses, then it is heart rate, facial muscle response, and brain activity that we ought to study. But if those physiological signatures are merely the fingerprints of our suspect (innate emotions), then finding the fingerprints would be helpful but not indispensable. After all, it's the suspect, not the fingerprints, that we're after.

What Are (Innate) Emotions? The Suspect and Its Fingerprints

In our naïve psychology, emotions are bodily reflexes—they exert their effects on us instantly, automatically, and unconsciously, much like an eye blink or knee jerk. It is no wonder we identify emotions with our bodies. But as we know too well, we are not always the best judges of what's really going under the hood.

Consider shame, for instance. What could be more physical than the uncontrollable blush of shame flooding your face? Think about one of your most embarrassing moments. I distinctly recall one of mine. It happened decades ago, when I was taking my first international trip. I had just landed at the airport in Zurich, and I was excited to be going to the Alps. But thanks to the carelessness of some baggage handler, when my huge orange backpack appeared on the luggage carousel, it had been ripped open, and all of its contents—shirts, pants, and underwear—were scattered around it, slowly and humiliatingly circling in plain sight for every passerby to see. It felt absolutely awful; the shame I felt seemed to arise directly from my guts. But such reactions are much more complex. My own saving grace was that I knew no one at that airport. If the same event happened again when I was on my way to a conference, with some of my esteemed colleagues standing around, I would feel even worse. On the other hand, if it were just my family watching, my distress would be far milder, and if my backpack contained only an impersonal book and a sweater, no harm would be done at all.

So emotions are not rigid bodily fingerprints, they are nuanced computations that depend on an evaluation of information. My shame response explicitly tracked the nature of the damage (exposed underwear vs. books), the viewers (family, strangers, or coworkers), and the expected effect of the display on my social status. All of this mental computation goes on entirely under the radar, but it is nonetheless there. Emotions, then, are computed, much like we use computation to determine whether we see an object or a person, or when we decipher the meaning of a sentence. While we think about emotions as "hot" reflexes, in reality, they depend on exactly the same type of thought processes that occur in "cold" cognition. The evolutionary psychologists John Tooby, Leda Cosmides, and their colleagues[33-36] further assert that these computations are universal and that they have evolved to provide adaptive solutions to specific recurrent problems in our ancient evolutionary history. Fear, for instance, is designed to protect one from predators, whereas pride and shame protect one's social "capital."

When evolutionary psychologists hypothesize that emotions are universal, what they mean is that the computational programs that give rise to emotions are universal. This hypothesis, however, says nothing about the bodily fingerprints of emotions themselves. Not only is there no reason to expect emotions to invariably and universally "show" on our faces, in some cases, it would be foolish to expect that they would.[35] You may want to display fear among kin, so that they can come to your rescue, but why should you advertise it to your antagonists? As noted by Daniel Sznycer and his colleagues, "Robotic invariance in facial expressions of emotion is not expected on an evolutionary view, nor is it necessary for emotion to be a fruitful scientific concept."[35p57]

For evolutionary psychologists, then, the critical test for emotions is not their bodily manifestations but their computational properties. If emotions such as pride or shame are innate, then one should be able to show that the principles that link these mental states to their putative triggers are universal. In line with this possibility, research in numerous small-scale societies has shown that, when asked to reason about a shameful event ("he steals from members of his community"), the magnitude of the expected shame closely matched the magnitude of the social devaluation associated with the act, with a high level of agreement between communities.[36] Pride, in contrast, tracked the increase in individual social value, both within as well as across communities.[34] These findings provide evidence for the universality of emotions while totally ignoring how people inflect their voice or lift an eyebrow.

If innate emotions are mental states, then their multiple bodily manifestations are merely the icing on the cake. They are the fingerprints of emotions, not their essence. Why should anyone then presume otherwise? To address this question, we need to move our attention from the crime to the detective.

Meet the Detective: A Psychological Profile

Let's take stock of the discussion thus far. We have seen that our intuitive reasoning about emotions is fraught with biases and that these biases are clearly evident when we contrast the reasoning of laypeople with the conclusions emerging from affective science. But scientists may not be entirely immune to these dangers themselves, and when their guard is down and their emotions are up, some of these tendencies could influence their research findings.

One bias concerns the origins of emotions. While affective scientists are still actively debating whether innate emotions exist, for laypeople, the question is squarely settled—emotions are surely inborn.

The link between emotions and the material body is another slippery slope. Laypeople believe that emotions imprint their universal signatures on the face and that distinct emotions are innately localized in distinct areas of the brain. Scientists, on the other hand, know that emotions are complex computations, not bodily reflexes. But somehow in the midst of the battle of innateness, science seems to have lost track of the distinction between emotions (mental states) and their bodily manifestations, and the search for innate emotions has been conflated with the hunt for their bodily fingerprints.

Emotions, then, present another case of blindness—blindness to matters of the heart. Our failure to know ourselves should come as no surprise—we have seen this repeatedly when we considered the origins of ideas. Our errors about emotions present the mirror image of those mistakes. We presume emotions to be innate; for ideas, we assume learning. And while we easily equate emotions with material bodily states, we struggle to situate ideas in our material brains. Yet the origin of all these errors is one and the same—our old friend, Essentialism, and to a lesser extent, Dualism.

In the last part of this chapter, I will first show how Essentialism can lead us to confuse emotions with their bodily fingerprints; next, we will see how the material manifestations of emotions lead us to assume that emotions must be innate. The third casualty of our core cognition is the erroneous presumption that "hot" emotions cannot be based on cognitive computation, courtesy of Essentialism and Dualism. These same biases also cloud our understanding of affective mechanisms. Finally, in closing, we will explore some of the implications of our blindness to our reasoning about our potential for emotional change, questions that will form the center of subsequent chapters.

Fear Is in My Material "Heart"

Let's start where we had left our review of the science—at our curious conflation of our emotional mental states and their fingerprints on the body. The fusion of mental states with bodily actions should ring a bell—we have seen it in our reasoning about "cold" cognitive concepts, such as *cup* or *kicking* (in Chapter 9). Abstract cognitive concepts like "cup" are challenging because we naturally view them as immaterial, so we struggle to fathom how mental states could affect physical changes in the material body—how my knowledge of a "coffee cup," for example, could send me to the coffee maker. This tension between the immaterial view of concepts and the material view of our body as a whole is courtesy of our intuitive Dualism. To resolve the cognitive dissonance, it is tempting to embrace the proposal that concepts are embodied—that they reside "in our bones."

For emotions, our intuitive psychological narrative is different. Although affective science firmly establishes that emotions rely on cognitive computations, our naïve psychology tells us that "fear" is squarely "in my body"—in the expressions on my face and in the rumbling of my stomach. For example, you might recall that when the participants in our experiment assert that emotions "show" externally, in the face, they are also likely to assert that they manifest internally, in our physiology. So strong is our conviction that "fear" is embodied that the role of (immaterial) mental states hardly ever arises. The Dualist tension between the material body and the immaterial mind is thus moot. In naïve cognition, emotions are squarely within our material "hearts."

Embodied Emotions Are Innate

Our naïve understanding of emotions is informed by the principles that explain all living things. And when we consider the biological world, here Essentialism plays first fiddle. Per Essentialism, living things possess an immutable material essence that is innate. So it is our belief that emotions are imprinted in our material body that leads us to expect that emotions form part of our biological essence and, hence, that they are innate and universal.

That's exactly what our participants assert. One argument for the materiality–innateness link is presented by the strong association between the rating of emotions for their propensity to manifest in the material body (either externally, in the face, or internally, in our physiology) and their potential to emerge universally, in remote indigenous groups. The stronger our confidence about the material manifestation of an emotion, the more likely we are to consider it as innate.

Our Essentialist presumption also compels us to believe that emotions reside "in the brain." When participants in studies were specifically informed that emotions are localized in the brain (the material body), they were more likely to state that emotions are universal and innate. Our bias to materiality *causes* us to perceive emotions as innate. That bias is so strong that when we specifically informed participants that emotions are *not* localized in the brain, it hardly budged.

The Bidirectional Lure of Essentialism

1. Traits that form part of the material body are innate. If emotions are embodied, emotions are innate.
2. Innate Essentialist traits form part of the material body. If emotions define our innate human essence, emotions are material.

Essentialism, then, explains much of our emotional life. Since we believe that the material traits of living things are innate, we tend to attribute the physiological manifestation of emotions to an innate essence (see 1). As you might recall from previous chapters, however, the link between materiality and innateness is bidirectional. Not only do we view material traits as innate, but we further assume that innate Essentialist traits are material (see 2). If we assume that our emotions are our human essence, then we will also be inclined to believe that emotions must form part of our material body.

"Emotional Computations" Is an Oxymoron

As noted, Essentialism usually plays the first fiddle when it comes to our naïve understanding of emotions. But when affective science (or a therapist) offers a different account, Dualism, the second fiddle, can take the center stage for a "solo." The computational account of emotions presents such an opportunity.

Affective science tells us that emotions like "shame" are computations, much like the "cold" cognition of "cup" or "noun." But our intuitive cognition screams bloody murder—*emotions aren't computations*! Dualism is the driver of this false conviction. In our intuitive minds, computation (i.e., thinking) entails the manipulation of immaterial ideas, whereas emotions are material bodily states; in fact, we see them as an innate essence of our material body. Material innate emotions cannot possibly arise from immaterial thinking. Mind and matter don't mix and match.

Innate Computational Mechanisms Are Alchemy

It is bad enough to assert that emotions are computations. Claiming that these computations are innate goes way too far. But this is precisely what evolutionary psychology asserts, and, in so doing, it challenges our core beliefs to the max. Not only does it claim that emotions are computations (rather than bodily states); it further suggests that the mechanisms that effect this reckoning are innately specialized—that there is one innate program for shame, another innate program for maternal love.

This evolutionary theory of emotions forms part of a broader hypothesis regarding the architecture of the mind/brain known as domain specificity. In this view, the mind is innately designed like a Swiss-army knife[37,38]—it comes equipped with distinct mechanisms designed specifically to support computations in specific domains. Emotions are just one of those domains; others are vision,[39] theory of mind,[40] and, famously, language.[41,42] As a scientist, I believe there are good reasons to seriously consider this possibility. But in our intuitive psychology, domain specificity must be a mistake. Not only does it postulate an innate (material) mechanism for (immaterial) computation (an oxymoron), but it further asserts that this material–immaterial Dualist chimera gives rise to material emotions. Such assertions set every fiber of our intuitive psyches on fire. They also ignite a flame in some psychologists.

Lisa Feldman Barrett is my colleague. She is also one of the most influential psychologists at work today, and her research has gained enormous traction. I have the utmost respect for her intellect, leadership, integrity, and openness to scientific debate (despite our obvious disagreements, Lisa accepted my invitation to co-author the paper described earlier; few scientists would even sit at a table with their intellectual opponents, never mind collaborate with them). But on matters of innateness, we do not see eye to eye.

Barrett claims that the "classical" accounts of emotions "are virtually nonfalsifiable. They are bolstered, despite evidence that persistently calls them into doubt."[27p22] Similar concerns, she suggests, plague Steven Pinker's book *How The Mind Works* and Paul Bloom's account of language acquisition. What do these disparate views share in common, you might wonder? And why does she insist that they fail so categorically? The fatal flaw, according to Barrett, is that they are mere tautology. They

> assume that a psychological phenomenon is caused by a dedicated mechanism of the same name (e.g., in basic emotion theories, the experience of fear is caused by a "fear" mechanism; in theories of appraisal-as-a-mechanism, the experience of novelty is caused by a "novelty" mechanism).[27p21]

As an advocate of domain-specificity in language, I am compelled to respond.[43-46]

At first blush, Barrett's argument sounds invincible. Tautological theories are the enemies of science—who wouldn't go on a crusade to defend it against such a threat? But upon a closer look, the threat is reduced to a Quixotean windmill. As we have seen, the evolutionary account of "shame," for instance, does not simply stipulate that "shame is the product of the shame system."

The theory details the principles that guide the computation of shame, and it is those principles that are carefully tested by scientists. The same holds for nativist domain-specific accounts of language: one doesn't simply state that "language is the product of an innate language system." Rather, the burden is on one to detail what innate universal principles constrain the computation of linguistic structure and to evaluate those principles empirically; I have spent years doing just that.[43]

It is of course perfectly possible that some specific proposals of domain-specific mechanisms might be wrong, just as there are some flawed domain-generalist theories. Barrett's critique, however, is directed toward domain-specific theories *as a class*. And she is certainly not alone in that position; we have seen many other examples of this stance in Chapter 2. But this generalized discomfort with domain specificity is puzzling. Why are nativist computational accounts of emotion inherently more vulnerable to such transgressions than, say, constructivist or neural theories? And why do the same dangers also plague the seemingly unrelated nativist theories of cognition and language?

If we cannot find an obvious fault in the science for our misgivings, then we scientists might do well to search within our psyches for it. If we believe that innate traits must be material, whereas cognitive (computational) programs are immaterial, then the hypothesis that innate immaterial programs give rise to our material emotions would be impossible: not science but alchemy.

Destined to Blindness?

As the Ancient Greeks knew too well, psychological blindness does not go unpunished, and emotional blindness is no exception to the rule. The ready links we form between emotions and the material body explain why we assume that emotions are embodied and innate. These same perceived links, courtesy of Dualism and Essentialism, also explain why "hot" emotions appear diametrically opposite to "cold" concepts, examined in Chapter 9. In our intuitive psychology, emotions are natural—they are physically embodied and innate. Concepts, by contrast, are ephemeral and thus must be cultural constructs that are learned from experience. Indeed, the notion of disembodied innate concepts is an oxymoron—an irreconcilable dissonance. It is no wonder, then, that we welcome with relief the hypothesis that concepts are embodied in sensations and actions.

The same tension between mind, body, and innateness is also key to our understanding of ourselves in health and disease—the topic of the next subsection. Chapter 11 explores our complex relationship with neuroscience— why we are so fascinated by the shiny images of our brain and why we are surprised to learn that thinking happens therein. Chapters 12 and 13 next move to contrast how we reason about brain disorders that affect "hot emotions" versus "cold cognition."

Our reactions to these two classes of disorders follow directly from our misconceptions about thoughts and feelings. By misconstruing our emotions, we lose sight of our capacity to control our lives by altering our cognition. If emotions are bodily states and thinking is immaterial, then it is difficult to see how "talk therapy" can change our emotions. And since we view bodily states as innate, then evidence linking affective disorders to the brain should increase, not decrease, our false belief that mental disorders are immutable. This means that the intense effort to destigmatize mental illnesses by presenting them as physical illnesses should tragically backfire.

Cognitive disorders, such as dyslexia, elicit the opposite errors. Here, we are too quick to assume that cognition is "in our mind only," so it's no wonder that our reactions to dyslexia unfold along two conflicting lines—either we misconstrue dyslexia as a sensory visual disorder (which means it must be physical and innate) or we see it for what it typically is (a cognitive disorder), and then, our only option is to assume dyslexia is not a brain disorder at all; it's just "in your head."

References

1. Bartels A, Zeki S. The neural correlates of maternal and romantic love. *Neuroimage.* 2004;21(3):1155–1166.
2. Zeki S. The neurobiology of love. *FEBS Letters.* 2007;581(14):2575–2579.
3. Feldman R. The neurobiology of human attachments. *Trends in Cognitive Sciences.* 2017;21(2):80–99.
4. Feldman R, Magori-Cohen R, Galili G, Singer M, Louzoun Y. Mother and infant coordinate heart rhythms through episodes of interaction synchrony. *Infant Behavior & Development.* 2011;34(4):569–577.
5. Lindquist KA, Gendron M, Oosterwijk S, Barrett LF. Do people essentialize emotions? Individual differences in emotion essentialism and emotional experience. *Emotion.* 2013;13(4):629–644.
6. Berent I, Feldman Barrett L, Platt M. Essentialists biases in reasoning about emotions. arXiv. September 10, 2019.

7. Sauter DA, Eisner F, Ekman P, Scott SK. Cross-cultural recognition of basic emotions through nonverbal emotional vocalizations. *Proceedings of the National Academy of Sciences of the United States of America.* 2010;107(6):2408.

8. Ekman P, Sorenson ER, Friesen WV. Pan-cultural elements in facial displays of emotion. *Science.* 1969;164(3875):86–88.

9. Ekman P, Friesen WV. Constants across cultures in the face and emotion. *Journal of Personality and Social Psychology.* 1971;17(2):124–129.

10. Sorenson ER. Culture and the expression of emotion. In: Williams TR, ed. *Psychological anthropology.* Chicago, IL: Aldine; 1975:361–372.

11. Tracy JL, Robins RW. The nonverbal expression of pride: evidence for cross-cultural recognition. *Journal of Personality and Social Psychology.* 2008;94(3):516–530.

12. Bryant GA, Barrett HC. Vocal emotion recognition across disparate cultures. *Journal of Cognition & Culture.* 2008;8(1/2):135–148.

13. Elfenbein HA, Ambady N. On the universality and cultural specificity of emotion recognition: a meta-analysis. *Psychological Bulletin.* 2002;128(2):203–235.

14. Farroni T, Menon E, Rigato S, Johnson MH. The perception of facial expressions in newborns. *The European Journal of Developmental Psychology.* 2007;4(1):2–13.

15. Addabbo M, Longhi E, Marchis IC, Tagliabue P, Turati C. Dynamic facial expressions of emotions are discriminated at birth. *PLoS ONE.* 2018;13(3):e0193868–e0193868.

16. Zhang D, Liu Y, Hou X, Sun G, Cheng Y, Luo Y. Discrimination of fearful and angry emotional voices in sleeping human neonates: a study of the mismatch brain responses. *Frontiers in Behavioral Neuroscience.* 2014;8:422–422.

17. Cheng Y, Lee S-Y, Chen H-Y, Wang P-Y, Decety J. Voice and emotion processing in the human neonatal brain. *Journal of Cognitive Neuroscience.* 2012;24(6):1411–1419.

18. Siegel EH, Sands MK, Van Den Noortgate W, et al. Emotion fingerprints or emotion populations? A meta-analytic investigation of autonomic features of emotion categories. *Psychological Bulletin.* 2018;144(4):343–393.

19. Gendron M, Roberson D, van Der Vyver JM, Barrett LF. Cultural relativity in perceiving emotion from vocalizations. *Psychological Science.* 2014;25(4):911.

20. Gendron M, Roberson D, van Der Vyver JM, Barrett LF. Perceptions of emotion from facial expressions are not culturally universal: evidence from a remote culture. *Emotion.* 2014;14(2):251.

21. Gendron M, Crivelli C, Barrett LF. Universality reconsidered: diversity in making meaning of facial expressions. *Current Directions in Psychological Science.* 2018;27(4):211–219.

22. Russell J. Forced-choice response format in the study of facial expression. *Motivation and Emotion.* 1993;17(1):41–51.

23. Crivelli C, Russell JA, Jarillo S, Fernández-Dols J-M. The fear gasping face as a threat display in a Melanesian society. *Proceedings of the National Academy of Sciences of the United States of America.* 2016;113(44):12403–12407.

24. Crivelli C, Russell JA, Jarillo S, Fernández-Dols J-M. Recognizing spontaneous facial expressions of emotion in a small-scale society of Papua New Guinea. *Emotion.* 2017;17(2):337–347.

25. Crivelli C, Jarillo S, Russell JA, Fernández-Dols J-M. Reading emotions from faces in two indigenous societies. *Journal of Experimental Psychology: General.* 2016;145(7):830–843.

26. Barrett LF. *How emotions are made: the secret life of the brain.* Boston, MA: Houghton Mifflin Harcourt; 2017.

27. Barrett LF. Categories and their role in the science of emotion. *Psychological Inquiry*. 2017;28(1):20–26.
28. Barrett LF, Gendron M. The importance of context: Three corrections to Cordaro, Keltner, Tshering, Wangchuk, and Flynn (2016). *Emotion*. 2016;16(6):803–806.
29. Barsalou L. Ad hoc categories. *Memory & Cognition*. 1983;11(3):211–227.
30. Chen C, Crivelli C, Garrod OGB, Schyns PG, Fernández-Dols J-M, Jack RE. Distinct facial expressions represent pain and pleasure across cultures. *Proceedings of the National Academy of Sciences of the United States of America*. 2018;115(43):E10013–E10021.
31. Sauter DA, Eisner F, Ekman P, Scott SK. Emotional vocalizations are recognized across cultures regardless of the valence of distractors. *Psychological Science*. 2015;26(3):354.
32. Cordaro DT, Keltner D, Tshering S, Wangchuk D, Flynn LM. The voice conveys emotion in ten globalized cultures and one remote village in Bhutan. *Emotion*. 2016;16(1):117–128.
33. Tooby J, Cosmides L. The evolutionary psychology of the emotions and their relationship to internal regulatory variables. In: Lewis M, Haviland-Jones JM, Barrett LF, eds. *Handbook of emotions*, 3rd ed. New York, NY: Guilford Press; 2008:114–137.
34. Sznycer D, Xygalatas D, Alami S, et al. Invariances in the architecture of pride across small-scale societies. *Proceedings of the National Academy of Sciences of the United States of America*. 2018;115(33):8322–8327.
35. Sznycer D, Cosmides L, Tooby J. Adaptationism carves emotions at their functional joints. *Psychological Inquiry*. 2017;28(1):56–62.
36. Sznycer D, Xygalatas D, Agey E, et al. Cross-cultural invariances in the architecture of shame. *Proceedings of the National Academy of Sciences of the United States of America*. 2018;115(39):9702–9707.
37. Cosmides L, Tooby J. Origins of domain specificity: the evolution of functional organization. In: Hirschfeld LA, Gelman SA, eds. *Mapping the mind: domain specificity in cognition and culture*. New York, NY: Cambridge University Press; 1994:85–116.
38. Fodor J. *The modularity of mind*. Cambridge, MA: MIT Press; 1983.
39. Marr D. *Vision: a computational investigation into the human representation and processing of visual information*. San Francisco, CA: W.H. Freeman; 1982.
40. Leslie AM, Friedman O, German TP. Core mechanisms in "theory of mind." *Trends in Cognitive Sciences*. 2004;8(12):528–533.
41. Chomsky N. *Language and mind*. New York, NY: Harcourt, Brace & World; 1968.
42. Pinker S. *The language instinct*. New York, NY: Morrow; 1994.
43. Berent I. *The phonological mind*. Cambridge, England: Cambridge University Press; 2013.
44. Berent I. The phonological mind. *Trends in Cognitive Sciences*. 2013;17(7):319–327.
45. Berent I, Bat-El O, Brentari D, Dupuis A, Vaknin-Nusbaum V. The double identity of linguistic doubling. *Proceedings of the National Academy of Sciences of the United States of America*. 2016;113(48):13702–13707.
46. Berent I. On the origins of phonology. *Current Directions in Psychological Science*. 2017;26:132–139.

C. In Health and Disease

11

Insane About the Brain

It is love at first sight, and as with all great love affairs, it makes us crazy. We are madly, hopelessly, irrationally besotted with our brains.

If you have ever participated in an fMRI experiment, the rush you felt when you saw your brain in action for the first time is something you will never forget. First, you had to lie absolutely still inside a claustrophobic, coffin-like enclosure while, to the nonmusical accompaniment of metallic clanks and bangs, a succession of images and words like *dog, cat, box, run, swim,* and *grab* were presented to you. Then, when it was finally over, you stepped out of the torture chamber, stretched, and made your way to the control room.

There, with the press of a button (and a lot of physics), the researcher generated an image of your thinking brain. Not only were you relieved to discover that, yes, you really do have a brain, but you were astonished to behold visible proof that this chunk of meat actually thinks. The evidence was as clear and shiny as the light of day. One area of your brain responded to the nouns you had read (*dog, cat, box*) and another to the verbs (*run, swim, grab*). You hadn't even noticed that they were nouns and verbs, but your brain did. The images are the proof.

It's not just nouns and verbs. Scientists can capture images of your emotional brain in action, your moral brain, or your brain on music. You can see your brain in contemplation of a beautiful artwork or recoiling from a disgusting image of feces. And our brains are different. There are criminal brains, addictive brains, psychotic brains, and gambling brains. Artists and mathematicians have different kinds of brains, as do poker players and poets, old people, and neonates.

As the discoveries from neuroscience pour in, the newspaper headlines capture our imagination. They announce that "Musicians' Brains Really Work Differently,"[1] marvel at how "Reading Experience May Change the Brains of Dyslexic Students,"[2] and promise to tell you "How Learning A New Language Actually Rewires the Brain."[3]

The Blind Storyteller. Iris Berent, Oxford University Press (2020). © Iris Berent, 2020.
DOI: 10.1093/oso/9780190061920.001.0001

All of this attention begets prestige. Everyone wants to be a neuroscientist these days. Back in the 1980s, graduate students were beguiled by the psyche—it was the life of the mind that they sought to unveil. But now brain science is booming, and research universities are investing heavily in neuroscience faculty, buying expensive magnets, and housing them in shiny new buildings on which the word "brain" is prominently engraved. Can neuroscience live up to all the hype?

After all, do you really need a brain scan to tell that a musician's brain is different than a nonmusician's? The difference between Yo-Yo Ma's cello playing and your next-door neighbor's is apparent from the very first note. Where else would the difference be, if not in the brain? The same holds for learning a new language and dyslexia. Now that you've studied Spanish, you can understand what people are saying on the streets of Mexico City, and when you go to a restaurant there, you can make your waiter understand that you want your taco mild. Isn't it obvious that you can read this chapter but couldn't have done so as a toddler? Why is it surprising that the acquisition of literacy or a new language would alter your brain? What else could have changed?

Make no mistake—I'm not suggesting that brain research is superfluous. Brain research has not only transformed our understanding of cognitive and mental disorders, it sheds light on typical thinking. Going back to our example of *dogs* and *cats* versus *run* and *swim*, it is actually not at all clear whether our language system categorizes these words as "nouns" and "verbs," or whether it simply encodes them according to their meanings (e.g., animals vs. actions). But if we can show that, regardless of meaning, all nouns engage the same brain region, and that this region is not engaged by verbs, then this could provide important evidence that that nouns and verbs are real and distinct, and the results suggest that they are.[4-8] So brain research can certainly help us settle important scientific debates. But that doesn't begin to account for our fascination with it.

Brain images are mesmerizing. We stare at our thinking brains as if we are looking at a ghost, and we eagerly consume brain stories. Seeing thinking occurring "in the brain" offers us the uncanny satisfaction that we finally *really* understand how thinking happens; paradoxically, our physical brains seem to provide us with a better explanation of the mysteries of cognition than cognition itself. But this conclusion is devoid of any basis, and the illusion is not always benign. In the next chapters, we will see how our fascination with the brain can distort our understanding of ourselves while tragically biasing our ideas about disease and our judgments of crime.

To understand why this is, we must revisit the same familiar suspects—the principles of Dualism and Essentialism.

***

To appreciate our special relationship with our brains, let's compare brain-based and cognitive-based explanations for a specific phenomenon. It is well known that people tend to overestimate other people's knowledge. For example, if you happen to know that Hartford is the capital of Connecticut, you would be prone to believe that most people (80%) know that as well, even when you had previously been informed that, in reality, only 50% of people know this fact. Researchers call this phenomenon the "curse of knowledge." Now consider two explanations for this fact.

One involves no neuroscience. It simply states that "researchers claim that this 'curse' happens because subjects make more mistakes when they have to judge the knowledge of others. People are much better at judging what they themselves know." A second explanation appeals to the brain. "Brain scans indicate that this 'curse' happens because of the frontal lobe brain circuitry known to be involved in self-knowledge. Subjects make more mistakes when they have to judge the knowledge of others. People are much better at judging what they themselves know." Which explanation is better?

When the psychologist Deena Skolnick Weisberg and her colleagues[9] asked people these questions, most thought the brain explanation was better. But it really isn't. In fact, both explanations are pretty bad, as neither explains why our poor judgment of others depends on what we know ourselves. The reference to the brain in the second explanation adds nothing new—it links the phenomenon to "self-knowledge," but this fact is implicitly stated in the other explanation. Yet people felt assured that the brain explanation was superior.

It is not only laypeople who go astray. When Skolnick Weisberg and her colleagues presented the answers to Yale undergraduates who were studying cognitive neuroscience, their response was the same. In fact, the Yalies fell for the brain even when the neuroscience and no-neuroscience explanations were otherwise perfectly good. These competing "good" explanations (along with the matching poor ones) are provided below.

	Good explanation	Bad explanation
Without neuroscience	The researchers claim that this "curse" happens because subjects have trouble switching their point of view to consider what someone else might know, mistakenly projecting their own knowledge onto others.	The researchers claim that this "curse" happens because subjects make more mistakes when they have to judge the knowledge of others. People are much better at judging what they themselves know.
With neuroscience	**Brain scans indicate** that this "curse" happens because **of the frontal lobe brain circuitry known to be involved in self-knowledge.** Subjects have trouble switching their point of view to consider what someone else might know, mistakenly projecting their own knowledge onto others.	**Brain scans indicate** that this "curse" happens because of **the frontal lobe brain circuitry known to be involved in self-knowledge.** Subjects make more mistakes when they have to judge the knowledge of others. People are much better at judging what they themselves know.

Both good explanations correctly attribute the curse of knowledge to our tendency to project our own knowledge onto others. As before, the brain bit adds nothing new. But regardless of whether the explanation was good or bad, the students thought the brain explanations were superior, even though they weren't. This was further confirmed by neuroscience experts, who showed no preference for the "brain" explanations; in fact, when presented with good explanations, the experts considered the neuroscience as less satisfactory. Clearly, the infatuation of laypeople and neuroscience novices with the brain is not justified. Skolnick-Weisberg and her colleagues dubbed this phenomenon the "seductive allure of neuroscience" (SANE), and subsequently other labs noted the same phenomenon.[10-12] Our question here is why people are so biased.

One possibility is that they are taken in by the technical jargon, which carries the aura of hard science. If they notice the inconsistencies in the narrative, they attribute them to their own faulty understanding, rather than to any inadequacies of the explanation itself.

Another explanation appeals to brain images. We know that a picture is worth a thousand words, so perhaps seeing is believing. Merely invoking brain images (whether they are actually presented or not) might be enough to convince people.

A third, more sophisticated explanation appeals to the notion of reductionism. When scientists seek to explain why things happen, they often go one level lower. To explain why people get Alzheimer's disease, they go down to the level of chemistry (e.g., the structure of the amyloid protein), and to explain why the structure of the amyloid protein is ill-formed in Alzheimer's patients, they go lower still, to physics (e.g., the amyloid protein loses its structure because the forces that bind its atoms together are weakened).

Each of these possibilities has some merit, but none seems sufficient to fully account for the SANE effect. Technical jargon can be misleading, but it is not necessary to produce the effect. It is enough to simply invoke the brain; once that's done, the addition of technical jargon doesn't make the effect any stronger.[13] The prestige of hard science doesn't quite cut it either. While people prefer explanations that include superfluous neuroscience (similar to the ones in the original Skolnick Weisberg study), adding other hard science content to an explanation, such as facts from genetics or computer science, does not elicit a similar increase in credulity.[10]

Similarly, the effect of neuroscience does not seem to be about "seeing." While some researchers have observed that the addition of brain images made an explanation that much more convincing,[14] others found no such effect.[10,15,16] Brain images are not necessary to produce the SANE effect; people prefer neuroscience explanations even when they are presented with no images at all.

Could the SANE effect simply reflect the general preference for reductionism? Results suggest it's unlikely. To be sure, people do prefer explanations that appeal to lower levels of analysis. But the reduction of psychology to neuroscience had a larger effect than reductions to any other levels.[11] While reductionism offers a partial answer, it fails to explain why the link between the psyche and the brain is so much stronger than the links between the psyche and any other levels of science.

Taken as a whole, the results suggest that the SANE effect is unique. While reductionism and the seductive power of jargon, technology, and shiny pictures affect scientific reasoning generally, none of these factors is sufficient to explain our fascination with the brain.

Why, then, do we go so insane?

***

I propose that the answer has much to do with our old friends Dualism and Essentialism. We have seen that Dualism can wreak havoc with our reasoning about bodies and minds, so it makes sense that it would also be implicated in this mystery. Several researchers have indeed considered this possibility. Paul Bloom, the author of *Descartes' Baby*, notes that "we intuitively think of ourselves as non-physical, and so it is a shock, and endlessly interesting, to see our brains at work in the act of thinking."[17] Indeed, seeing your immaterial mind effect changes in your physical brain is akin to seeing an immaterial ghost lift a glass of water; in both cases there is an impossible slippage from the realm of mind to the realm of matter. It is no wonder that images of thinking brains transfix us.

But shock and awe are just one component of the SANE mystery. The research we have just reviewed suggests that people are not just intrigued by brain images; they consider narratives that appeal to the brain as more *credible* than those that don't, and they do so even when no brain images are presented.

Some researchers imply that we fall for brain stories because they are so surprising. But this seems unlikely. It is certainly not the case that surprise always begets credibility; the history of science presents plenty of evidence to the contrary. For example, when the 16th-century astronomer Nicolaus Copernicus made the astonishing discovery that the earth revolves around the sun, the Catholic Church was surprised but emphatically unconvinced. Things nowadays are no different, as witnessed by the roughly one third of the U.S. population that are shocked by Darwin's theory of evolution but place no credence in it.

But our infatuation with neuroscience is not as irrational as it might first appear. I suggest that we fall for the brain not simply because it is enticing or surprising. Rather, we go (in)SANE because, given our Dualist beliefs, the brain does indeed provide a superior and more rational explanation for reality. But to see why, we need to take a closer look at the logic of Dualism.

People know that thoughts have real consequences in the physical world. If I recall leaving my car keys on the shelf at the entrance to my home, that's where I will look for them. If you were to sneak into my home and surreptitiously place them elsewhere, say, on my dining room table, you would still expect me to search for them where *I* think they are (on the shelf), even if my belief is wrong. The same holds for sensations and emotions. When my alarm clock went off, I opened my eyes because I heard its sound, and when my cat died, I cried because I loved her; these two behaviors (opening my eyes and crying) are caused by mental states—sensations and emotions—rather than physical events. If I were deaf, an alarm clock would not make me open my eyes, and if I cared nothing for my cat, her death would not have moved me.

So mental states matter—they carry real consequences with respect to behavior; that much is given to us by our intuitive psychology. The problem is that thoughts and behavior span the opposite ends of the Dualist schism— mental states are immaterial entities, and behavior concerns the physical movement of our material bodies. Naïve physics tells us that material objects can only interact through physical contact with other material objects. Remember the launching balls from Chapter 3? Young infants would expect a material ball to change its trajectory only if it is contacted by another ball, and you'd think the same; immaterial entities, including ghosts and minds, just cannot effect changes in material objects. So the power of cognition—the ability of our immaterial minds to effect changes in matter—presents a real conundrum for our Dualist thinking.

Brains solve the Dualist dilemma. Brains are no less material than our arms and legs. If our mental states are "in the brain," and the brain and our limbs are both material, then we can conceive of a simple material explanation of how one can mechanically affect the other. We may not know all of the details, but when we transfer mental activities from the realm of the immaterial mind to the realm of the body, we can now envision how a mechanistic material explanation for behavior *might* be possible. Brain explanations pave the road to this understanding.

This is not to say that people had never been told that thinking actually occurs in the brain; obviously, they knew that. But knowing about the mind–brain link is one thing, and seeing concrete evidence of it is quite another. Given our Dualist convictions, it should not be easy for us to link our minds to our bodies, but brain images provide the bridge. When we see it in living color for the first time, we are indeed in awe. But surprise is just the consequence of this process, much like light is a consequence of the electric current that forms lightning. The reason why we fall so hard for the brain is that it shows us, palpably and concretely, how immaterial mental states cause material behavior.

***

If this explanation is on the right track, then it follows that our fascination with a brain explanation might vary depending on the trait in question. In previous chapters, we saw that we naturally link sensation, motor actions, and emotions to the brain, perhaps because these mental states can be readily associated with changes in our bodies. We can link hearing and seeing and walking to distinct parts of the body, and we likewise believe that emotions are linked to specific expressions in the face and feelings in the body. So learning that sensations, actions, and feeling are "in the brain" comes as no surprise. But when we reason about ideas—mental states that correspond to specific propositions, such as *2 + 2 = 4, sentences have a subject,* or *unsupported objects fall,* we are in real trouble. Ideas seem immaterial, so we struggle to see how these states of mind could have any material manifestation at all, and that presents a real dilemma for understanding every one of our daily actions. How could an ephemeral thought of a "cup" move my hand toward my coffee mug? And how might a mere mental "decision" move my foot toward my shoe?

It is in the realm of ideas that our mind–body dissonance is greatest, and it is here where brain scans presents the most powerful relief to our Dualist misery. If it is my material brain that made my hand move toward the material cup, then I can now understand how action happens: matter effects matter. Mystery solved.

This analysis predicts that the magnitude of the SANE effect should differ for cognitive traits (specifically, ideas) and noncognitive traits, such as sensations, actions, and emotions. Since noncognitive traits are spontaneously amenable to a material explanation, seeing them manifested in the brain is neat, though hardly transformative. But seeing that ideas are material should give us a real "aha" moment: once we see that "a cup" exists materially in the body, we can finally "get it"—we understand how thinking (brain activity) can effect change in the physical body (move my arm). Now the explanation is deeply satisfying. Inserts (1) and (2) summarize the logic of the Dualist dissonance and its solution.

(1) The Dualist Dissonance and Its Resolution
    (a) Naïve physics
        (i) The body is material.
        (ii) Only matter (e.g., an object) can effect changes in matter (e.g., the trajectory of another object).
    (b) Naïve psychology
        (i) Ideas are immaterial.
        (ii) Ideas can effect changes in behavior (the trajectory of material body parts).
    (c) Dualist dissonance: Behavior is inexplicable.

(2) The SANE Solution
  (a) Ideas are material brain states.
  (b) Material brain states effect changes in the trajectory of material body parts (behavior).
  (c) Behavior is explained by naïve physics.

To evaluate the role of Dualism in our thinking about the brain, some researchers have examined whether the SANE effect depends on people's explicit judgments regarding the link between bodies and minds. The results showed no evidence that that is the case.[15] But that is hardly surprising, as self-reports are coarse measures of tacit biases, especially irrational ones like Dualism. Moreover, given the previous analysis, the effect of Dualism may depend on the perceived materiality of the trait.

A series of studies by my graduate student Gwendolyn Sandoboe and myself examined this possibility.[18] Our approach to the SANE phenomenon was slightly different from previous studies. Rather than asking people to explicitly state which explanation is better (effectively reasoning about reasoning), we simply asked them to reason about concrete problems by acting as clinicians. First, we presented them with descriptions of clinical disorders, then we asked them to diagnose them using different tests, which we provided them. These disorders were of two types—one set of disorders disrupted sensory and motor capacities; their matched counterparts were disorders that compromised cognitive capacities.

For example, consider auditory hypersensitivity—a noncognitive condition. Neurotypical people, we said, have no difficulty filtering out distracting noises like the honk of a passing car when a friend is talking, but people with autism have troubles "tuning down" the distractors because they are hypersensitive to sounds. To diagnose this disorder, patients would be presented with video clips featuring a news correspondent reporting on site; one condition featured the reporter amidst distracting noises (e.g., car honks) presented occasionally; another had silent events (e.g., people walking by). The contrast between these two conditions gauges patients' hypersensitivity to sound. Participants were invited to choose among two tests of hypersensitivity. One test, they were told, tracked people's eye movements to see whether the sound of the distractors would divert their gaze away from the reporter. The other measured the "spike" in their brains produced by the distractors. We also told people which test results are characteristic of autism (diverting of one's eyes/brain spike in the presence of a distractor) and which are characteristic of neurotypical individuals (no slowing down or spikes). The task was to determine whether the test gives an accurate diagnosis of autism.

Note that the two tests were exactly matched with respect to the information they provided. Finding that a behavior produces a "spike" in the brain provides no additional information about the nature of the disorder compared to finding that it elicits an abnormal behavioral response. In both cases, all we see is whether the person's response is typical or abnormal. So if people find the brain test more convincing, this would not be scientifically justified; it would just be the seductive allure of neuroscience. Given that the trait in question is auditory, it should be relatively easy for people to see how it could be linked to the material body, so, by our account, the SANE effect would be modest. And this is exactly what we found. For noncognitive disorders, people were only slightly more confident that a positive result on the brain test was indicative of the disorder.

The critical question was whether people would do the same for cognitive traits, those that are typically viewed as devoid of a material basis in the body. In the case of autism, the cognitive trait concerned our ability to infer what other people think; the so-called theory of mind,[19] a trait which explicitly concerns abstract ideas. We informed participants that people with autism have difficulties inferring the thoughts of others and presented them with a concrete illustration. The scenario featured a married couple, Alice and Bob. Alice returns home from work and places the car keys into a bowl, but Bob subsequently misplaces the keys in the drawer. The test features Alice as she is about to leave for work the next morning. One condition shows her looking for the keys in the bowl (where she left them); another shows her looking in the drawer (where they actually are).

If this scenario were presented to a patient with autism, we said, he or she might well expect Alice to look for the keys in the drawer, since they know where they are, and they would have trouble reasoning about what Alice does and doesn't know. But again, we gave them a choice of two tests. One test monitors people's eye movements when Alice looks at the drawer versus the bowl; the other measures spikes in their brain activity. In both tests, unexpected events should elicit a change in response—either longer looking time or a brain spike. Once again, the behavioral and the brain tests provide precisely the same information. But this time, people found the brain test much more informative than the behavior test.

Similar results obtained in a second task, in which we asked people to make a forced choice between the two tests (using the same disorders and tests in the previous experiment). People showed a stronger preference for the brain test for the cognitive disorders. For disorders with noncognitive symptoms, test choice was at chance. Cognitive disorders, by contrast, elicited a significant preference for the brain test. A third task asked participants to provide a verbal justification for their choice. Once again, people offered many more statements endorsing the brain test relative to the behavioral test in the cognitive condition, whereas for noncognitive traits, the brain preference was slight.

To further demonstrate that people considered our noncognitive symptoms (e.g., auditory hypersensitivity) more material than the cognitive symptoms (e.g., the capacity to infer the thoughts of others), we asked another group of participants to consider how likely each trait is to correspond to a specific location in the brain (akin to the procedures discussed in Chapter 8). We reasoned that if a given trait is material, then it ought to be localized in the material brain. Results indeed showed that people rated the sensory and motor traits as more material (i.e., localized in the brain) than the cognitive ones. So, in line with our previous results (in Chapter 8), people considered the cognitive symptoms of clinical disorders as less material than the auditory symptoms. Moreover, the materiality of the trait correlated negatively with its propensity to elicit the SANE effect—the less material the trait was, the stronger was the preference for the neural over the behavioral test. Together, our results suggest that the preference for the brain is quite selective and that it specifically depends on the materiality of the symptom—cognitive or noncognitive. These results shed new light on the origin of the SANE effect.

When it comes to sensations, actions, and emotions, we can spontaneously link behavior to the brain, so saying that "seeing" happens "in the brain" is interesting, but it's not shocking. Abstract ideas, however, appear immaterial, so we are at a loss to explain how these immaterial mental states can lead to material changes in the body—how having eaten 10 pieces of chocolate, I still reach for the jar because I believe that two pieces still remain from the original dozen I bought. This effect of the mind on the material body is a thorny puzzle for our Dualist thinking.

Brain images solve this dilemma. They present vivid proof that the real cause of our behavior lies not in the ephemeral mind (as we intuitively believe) but in the material body (the brain). It is my motor cortex that made my hand move to the jar, not some vague immaterial "belief." Matter moves matter.

So, paradoxically, our infatuation with the brain is actually a rational affair, in that it follows logically from the premises that are available to us. The problem lies not in the logical inference but in the premise—our irrational belief in mind–body Dualism. It is our unfounded conviction that the mind is immaterial and distinct from the body that makes us question the causal capacity of cognition to effect changes in our material bodies. By providing a proof that mental states are material, brain imaging helps us bridge the Dualist mind–body divide. So even if in the narrow context of a particular cognitive problem (e.g., the curse of knowledge) brain and cognitive explanations are comparable, in the larger scheme of things brain explanations *are* superior, because they help us transcend the schism between the immaterial mind and the material body. Of course, the schism is entirely the product of our own irrational thinking. But given this irrational premise, the appeal to the brain is quite rational. And this is why seeing our brains "think" is so illuminating.

Seeing our brains in action, however, can also engage another system of core cognition. Per our Essentialist beliefs, our essence as humans is not only material; it is further innate and immutable. So when we see our brain "on music" or "on language," we not only jump to the conclusion that these otherwise ephemeral cognitive processes must be material and real (courtesy of Dualism); per Essentialism, we also leap toward the conclusion that those "in the brain" traits form part of our deep human nature. Traits that are "in the brain" define who we are.

Whether the SANE effect is partly due to our misconceptions about innateness is yet unknown. But there are reasons to suspect they might be. Indeed, our perceptions of materiality and innateness are causally linked. As we saw in previous chapters (Chapters 8 and 10), people would rate a trait that is "in the brain" as more likely to be innate compared to one that isn't. Thus, Dualism and Essentialism may both be responsible for our love affairs with our brains. These conditions of our human nature render us blind to our human nature, distorting our reasoning about our healthy brains.

The next two chapters move to consider how the same principles distort our accounts of disease. In line with our distinct paths of reckoning about thoughts and feelings discussed in Chapters 9 and 10, we also construct two distinct tales about the role of our brains for affective psychiatric disorders and cognitive ones. Each tale is skewed, albeit in different ways. We readily accept that psychiatric disorders are "in the brain," and we immediately jump to the conclusion that disorders that are "in the brain" are inborn and immutable; for cognitive disorders, we struggle to admit their brain etiology, so we are more likely to wrongly disregard the role of the brain and genetics.

References

1. Tsioulcas A. Musicians' brains really do work differently—in a good way. *NPR*. Nov. 20, 2014.
2. Paul AM. Reading experience may change the brains of dyslexic students. *The New York Times*. May 15, 2014.
3. Smith H. How learning a new language actually rewires the brain. Fast ForWord, 2015.
4. Shapiro KA, Moo LR, Caramazza A. Cortical signatures of noun and verb production. *Proceedings of the National Academy of Sciences of the United States Of America*. 2006;103(5):1644–1649.
5. Bedny M, Caramazza A, Grossman E, Pascual-Leone A, Saxe R. Concepts are more than percepts: the case of action verbs. *The Journal of Neuroscience*. 2008;28(44):11347–11353.
6. Cappelletti M, Fregni F, Shapiro K, Pascual-Leone A, Caramazza A. Processing nouns and verbs in the left frontal cortex: a transcranial magnetic stimulation study. *Journal of Cognitive Neuroscience*. 2008;20(4):707–720.
7. Bedny M, Caramazza A, Pascual-Leone A, Saxe R. Typical neural representations of action verbs develop without vision. *Cerebral Cortex*. 2012;22(2):286–293.
8. Peelen MV, Romagno D, Caramazza A. Independent representations of verbs and actions in left lateral temporal cortex. *Journal of Cognitive Neuroscience*. 2012;24(10):2096–2107.
9. Weisberg DS, Keil FC, Goodstein J, Rawson E, Gray JR. The seductive allure of neuroscience explanations. *Journal of Cognitive Neuroscience*. 2008;20(3):470–477.
10. Fernandez-Duque D, Evans J, Christian C, Hodges SD. Superfluous neuroscience information makes explanations of psychological phenomena more appealing. *Journal of Cognitive Neuroscience*. 2015;27(5):926–944.
11. Hopkins EJ, Weisberg DS, Taylor JCV. The seductive allure is a reductive allure: people prefer scientific explanations that contain logically irrelevant reductive information. *Cognition*. 2016;155:67–76.
12. Rhodes RE, Rodriguez F, Shah P. Explaining the alluring influence of neuroscience information on scientific reasoning. *Journal of Experimental Psychology: Learning, Memory, and Cognition*. 2014;40(5):1432–1440.
13. Weisberg DS, Taylor JCV, Hopkins EJ. Deconstructing the seductive allure of neuroscience explanations. *Judgment & Decision Making*. 2015;10(5):429–441.
14. McCabe DP, Castel AD. Seeing is believing: the effect of brain images on judgments of scientific reasoning. *Cognition*. 2008;107(1):343–352.
15. Hook CJ, Farah MJ. Look again: effects of brain images and mind–brain dualism on lay evaluations of research. *Journal of Cognitive Neuroscience*. 2013;25(9):1397–1405.

16. Schweitzer NJ, Baker DA, Risko EF. Fooled by the brain: re-examining the influence of neuroimages. *Cognition*. 2013;129(3):501–511.

17. Bloom P. My brain made me do it. *Journal of Cognition and Culture*. 2006;6(1):209–214.

18. Sandoboe G. *In-SANE for the brain: dualism and the allure of neuroscience* Boston, MA: Northeastern University; 2019.

19. Baron-Cohen S, Leslie AM, Frith U. Does the autistic child have a "theory of mind"? *Cognition*. 1985;21(1):37–46.

12

Mental Disorders

Will Graham, the protagonist of the NBC TV horror series *Hannibal*, has been under a lot of stress lately. He is helping the FBI solve a series of grue-some murders by deeply empathizing with the killer: a demanding job in-deed. To add to his troubles, Will is not getting much in the way of emotional support. Will's psychiatrist, we learn, is none other than the notorious serial killer Dr. Hannibal Lecter, who is secretly trying to turn Will into a psycho-path like himself. It is no wonder that Will's psychotherapy is going nowhere.

"I can recommend a neurologist," Lecter tells him. "But if [your condition] isn't physiological, then you have to accept that what you're struggling with is mental illness."[1p14]

Will takes a brain scan, and the neurologist wrongly tells him that the results are negative. Shocked, Will exclaims in disbelief, "So . . . what I'm experiencing is *psychological*?"

Dressed in a white lab coat, the neurologist is the picture of authority. "Brain scans cannot diagnose a mental disorder," he says, nodding gravely. "They can only rule out medical illnesses, like a tumor, that can cause similar symptoms."[1p20]

Seriously? Can mental disorders really play havoc with our psyches without leaving even the faintest trace in our bodies? Are they truly "not physiological"?

Whose voice is it anyway that is making these confident assertions? Is Hannibal channeling the voice of science and reason? Or might he be hyp-notizing TV viewers with a much more primitive mantra? Could they be hearing the primal voice of Dualism?

How horrifically appropriate. Hannibal, the annihilator-in-chief, a man who uses his own digestive tract to erase the immaterial humanity of his victims, is using his TV platform to wrongly proclaim the immaterial nature of mental illness. What's worse is that his captive audience is swallowing it. Millions of viewers are glued to the screen, taking it all in without a moment of doubt or indigestion.

***

The Blind Storyteller. Iris Berent, Oxford University Press (2020). © Iris Berent, 2020.
DOI: 10.1093/oso/9780190061920.001.0001

So let us debunk Hannibal's Dualist mantra, starting with the very notion of "mental illness." Have you ever thought about what that actually means? We know that when someone suffers from heart disease, their heart is affected, and when someone suffers from a respiratory condition, their lungs are the locus of the disease. But what are diseases of the mind? What organ of the body do *they* affect?

The curious nomenclature is the first telltale sign that Dualism is meddling with our thinking. The term originates from a long-standing practice that classifies medical conditions according to postmortem pathological examinations of patients. Conditions that cause visible changes to the brain (such as tumors and subdural hematomas, the results of cancer and head injuries) are classified as biological or neurological. But for cases in which no frank changes to the brain are visible, like major depression, bipolar disorder, and schizophrenia, the classification is "mental disorders." The inference was that the disease resulted from the patient's "weak mind" and was thus evidence of a kind of moral failure. The "treatment" options were commensurate with the presumed etiology. Patients were locked up in asylums and subjected to horrific physical and emotional punishments.[2]

The German physician Emil Kraepelin (1856–1926) was the first to apply the medical model to the classification of mental disorders, sorting them according to their symptoms, the course they followed, and their outcomes, and laying out a set of psychopharmacological protocols for their treatment that still informs our understanding of mental illness today. With modern advances in brain imaging and genetics, it is now clear that all mental disorders are diseases of the brain.[2]

Major depression, for example, is associated with changes to several interconnected brain regions, including subcortical area 25 (the subcallosal cingulate cortex, an area that regulates thought and motor control and produces serotonin transporters—proteins that regulate mood), the right anterior insula (which regulates self-awareness and social experience), and the anterior cingulate gyrus (whose two regions are associated with emotions and cognitive processes).[2] We can estimate the genetic basis of the disease by comparing its prevalence in identical twins (who share all of their genes with their siblings) and fraternal twins (who share on average half of their genes). Results suggest that if a twin has major depression, the likelihood that their sibling will also suffer from it ranges from 0.23 to 0.67 if they are identical, compared to only 0.14 to 0.37 if they are fraternal. This means that shared genes increase the susceptibility for major depression.[3] Shared genes further account for 31% to 42% of the variability between individuals.[3]

Clearly, major depression is a brain disease that can be traced to genetic causes, and the same holds for other devastating conditions, such as bipolar disorder and schizophrenia.[2] In light of these conclusions, one would expect the public to treat them like any other disease. No one would shun a cancer patient because she has a tumor in her breast. Why shun the sufferer of a disorder that ravages the brain?

But mental illness still carries a significant social stigma.[4,5] Individuals with mental disorders experience discrimination that deprives them of opportunities for employment, housing, medical care, and social relationships.[6] Kay Redfield Jamison, a renowned researcher on manic depressive illness who also suffers from the condition, notes her terror of being confined in a psychiatric hospital. "I was working on a locked ward at the time, and I didn't relish the idea of not having the key. Mostly, however, I was concerned that if it became public knowledge that I had been hospitalized, my clinical work and privileges at best would be suspended; at worst, they would be revoked on a permanent basis."[7p112]

The very label "mental disorder" invites us to project our own attitudes onto patients. "Depression," says Lisa Pryor, a physician who treats mental illness, "is like a Rorschach test: People see in it whatever they like, in order to make whatever point they like, about what they perceive to be the ills of society."[8] The stigma surrounding mental illness is also internalized by patients.[9] Patients resist some diagnoses, insisting that they do not have a psychosis, for example (a diagnosis that carries extreme stigma, as it is considered dangerous) but rather depression (a diagnosis that is more socially acceptable).[8]

The stigma is not simply a matter of ignorance. In the past 10 years, the number of neuroscience-related reports on mental illnesses has nearly doubled, and nearly a third of them concern their physiological bases.[10,11] Even lay people are more likely to list biogenetic factors (e.g., abnormalities of brain structure, neurotransmitters, and genes) as the causes of mental disorders than they used to.[6,12] This increased public awareness is the product of a large public policy campaign, launched in 1999 by the U.S. Surgeon General. The hope was that "the new integrative neuroscience" of mental health would "circumvent the antiquated split between the mind and the body that historically has hampered mental health research."[13] Whether "integrative neuroscience" has ultimately fulfilled the promise is controversial.[14] But clearly, the rise of neuroscience has not yielded greater acceptance of neuropsychiatric disorders,[6] nor has it bridged the mind-body split. At best, the consequences of the campaign have been mixed.

On the positive side, biogenetic explanations make people less likely to blame patients for their conditions. But at the same time, the "medicalized" approach leads people to distance themselves from patients.[15] For example, the more likely people are to state that schizophrenia originates from bio-genetic factors, the less likely they are to accept a schizophrenia patient as a neighbor or coworker[12] and the more likely they are to view them as dangerous.[15] Similarly negative attitudes emerge in dozens of controlled psychological experiments.[16]

It is not just the social acceptance of mental patients that is at stake. When laypeople believe that a mental illness originates from the body (be it the brain or the genes), they become more pessimistic about the patient's prognosis. They wrongly believe that the symptoms are less likely to improve, that they will persist for a longer period, and that the patient is less able to control them.[4,5,16,17]

In one such study,[18] laypeople were told about Simon, a 30-year-old schizophrenia patient who thinks that people can hear his thoughts and that they are spying on him. Simon has lost his ability to work, is secluded at home, skips meals, neglects his hygiene, and suffers from insomnia. Moreover, he hears voices that tell him what to do and what to think. This description was presented to two groups of participants. One group was given an experiential explanation for the symptoms—they were told that their onset followed the death of Simon's wife. Another group was told that doctors attribute them to Simon's genetic predisposition to schizophrenia.

The results showed that participants who were given the genetic explanation were more likely than those who were given the psychological explanation to believe that Simon is dangerous (e.g., has aggressive thoughts, is likely to act on them, and should be detained in a hospital to ensure the public's safety). They also tended to project the negative stigma onto Simon's extended family (e.g., they believed that Simon's brother was also likely to develop schizophrenia and were wary about marrying any of Simon's siblings or having children with them). They were also more pessimistic about his potential for recovery and the extent to which psychotherapy could aid him. Other studies found the same results when participants were informed that a patient's mental disorder originated from a "chemical imbalance" or "brain dysfunction."[19,20]

Similar attitudes have been recorded among psychiatric patients themselves. For example, the more likely people with depression are to attribute their symptoms to biochemical and genetic causes, the more pessimistic they are about their prognoses—they believe their symptoms are likely to last longer and that their odds of recovery are lower.[21,22] When people who have struggled with depression were presented with bogus test results that attributed their symptoms to a chemical imbalance in their brains, they became more pessimistic about their prognoses and their capacity to regulate their moods.[23] Moreover, the presumption of a biogenetic cause led patients to prefer psychopharmacology to psychotherapy,[23] in line with the reasoning of the general public.[18]

Laypeople and patients, in other words, believe that the treatment for a disease ought to be commensurable with its origin—that symptoms caused by the material body should be treated medically (e.g., by psychotropic drugs), whereas symptoms that do not have a clear material basis should be treated with psychotherapy. Moreover, the two types of therapies—for the body and the mind—are perceived as mutually exclusive. If a disease originates in the body, then not only is its sufferer more likely to benefit from a medical treatment, but he or she is *less* likely to benefit from "talk therapy."

This belief is irrational. The clinical evidence with major depression, for instance, is that psychotherapy and psychopharmacology are synergetic.[2] While it is conceivable that mental disorders with biological etiologies are more susceptible than not to medical intervention, there is no reason to expect them to be unresponsive to psychotherapy.[24] Indeed, psychotherapy (like any form of learning) demonstrably rewires the brain, whereas psychopharmacology can effect changes in the mind.[2] Yet laypeople—both healthy people and patients—believe that one form of intervention precludes the other and that the intervention of choice depends on the origin of the disorder.

Remarkably, so do trained clinicians.[5,24,25,31] In one study,[31] the psychologists Matthew Lebowitz and Woo-kyoung Ahn asked psychologists and psychiatrists to reason about various case studies. In one, Terry, a 28-year-old woman, is said to be seeking treatment because she has felt deeply sad for the past four weeks. She has difficulty with her memory and concentration, an overwhelming sense of fatigue, hopelessness about the future, and feelings of worthlessness. One group of clinicians was presented with a biological explanation for the symptoms—they were told that Terry's father and grandparents had all struggled with similar problems, and that a recent brain scan using functional MRI revealed some structural abnormalities in Terry's brain, as well as a chemical imbalance involving serotonin and, possibly, other neurotransmitters. Another group was given a psychosocial explanation, which noted that Terry had experienced consistent sadness during her childhood after the death of her father. More recently, it continued, she had been through a difficult breakup with her boyfriend and experienced increased stress at work, while receiving little support from her mother, who presented as judgmental, critical, and nonnurturing. When the clinicians were asked to evaluate a clinical plan for Terry, the group that had received a biological evaluation considered psychotherapy to be less useful than the group that had received a psychosocial one. Similar results obtained for patients who had been described as presenting social phobias and obsessive-compulsive disorders. Strikingly, clinicians showed less empathy for the patients whose symptoms had a biological basis compared to those whose exact same symptoms received a social explanation.

To summarize, laypeople, patients, and even clinicians are systematically biased in their reasoning about mental disorders. First, they draw a false dichotomy between the brain/genes on the one hand and the psyche on the other, and they wrongly assume that one factor (be it a cause or a remedy) precludes the other. Second, they believe that brain disorders are more severe than psychosocial disorders and that their prognoses are poorer. Finally, patients with brain disorders elicit more negative reactions (albeit less blame) for their condition. The question is why.

***

The presumed dichotomy between psychological and biological causes and treatments is puzzling. It is one thing to assert that brain diseases require medical treatment; perhaps if a disease is "in the brain" its biological mechanism is better understood, so a targeted medical intervention would be more likely to succeed. But why should the presence of a brain basis for a disorder *preclude* psychotherapy? Nothing suggests that patients with diseased brains cannot benefit from "talk therapy" and, indeed, they do. By now, this kind of irrational reasoning should sound familiar, as it bears the distinct signature of Dualism.[4,5,24]

Dualism—the belief that the immaterial mind is distinct from the material body—leads us to consider immaterial mental properties as distinct from physical ones. If biogenetic and psychological conditions have different ontologies (the former material; the latter immaterial), then it stands to reason that they will each give rise to different disorders that are amenable to different forms of treatment. Ephemeral mental states cannot possibly be altered by material interventions, Dualism supposes, whereas conditions that reside in the material body can only be changed by material means. Dualism, then, explains why we are blind to the origins of mental disorders and why we wrongly assume that they cannot be helped by psychotherapy.

But the influence of Dualism extends much further. As Paul Bloom suggests, for most of us, Dualism not only describes us; it defines who we are. We believe that it is the possession of a mind that is altogether distinct from the body that sets us apart from nonhuman animals and objects.[26] Moreover, we believe that it is our immaterial minds, and not our physical bodies, that are the homes of the "self," and hence the basis of our free will (our capacity to determine our own actions).

By blurring the mind–body divide, the medicalized view of mental disorders threatens this view of the self. If someone's mind can be profoundly altered by a pill, the thinking goes, then it is their brain chemistry, and now a pill that controls their actions, rather than their immaterial self. The fact that the pill works, that it changes thoughts and behavior, exempts the patient from culpability for their actions, but it comes with a hefty price tag. Suggesting that a patient is materially controlled is dehumanizing—the material modification of the psyche not only challenges the belief that patients possess free will but that they possess a distinct, irreducible self. The psychiatrist Hannibal Lecter takes dehumanization to its horrific extreme by demonstrating that his victims are ingestible meat. Pills obviously do not annihilate the patient's body, but, in the eyes of Dualism, they threaten the patient's psyche and the unique human self. Setting the patient apart in this way gives rise to stigma, distancing, and fear, as the actions of a materially controlled creature are seen as mysterious and unpredictable.[4,5,17,20]

Failure to adhere to a medication regimen—noncompliance, as it is called—is a thorny challenge in treating mental disorders, and well-educated patients are not immune to this problem. Dualism helps explain it. To be sure, patients state multiple reasons for failing to take their medications, including side effects, stigma, and the belief that the medication is not required.[27] Kay Redfield Jamison explains that "once I felt normal again, it was very easy for me to deny that I had an illness that would come back. Somehow, I was convinced that I was an exception to the extensive research literature."[7] Some psychotic patients say that they miss their psychotic state, that their medication makes them numb.[27] Others,[28,29] like Jamison, state that "I ought to be able to handle whatever difficulties come my way without having to rely upon crutches such as medication."[7] Sentiments like these can and do come from many places. But worries about the inauthenticity or even the annihilation of the immaterial self is surely one of them. The capacity of a material medication to control our moods and thoughts throws the notion of an immaterial self into doubt: *What good does it do to cure my schizophrenia if doing so erases me?*

Thankfully, our Dualist bias is not our destiny; education can counter most of its errors. For example, when people who suffer from depression were presented with audiovisual materials explaining that the genetic and biochemical causes of depression are malleable (e.g., that gene expression can be modulated by experience), people reported more optimism about their prognosis and their sense of agency and a greater sense of hopefulness.[22] Simply recognizing a patient's agency and the biases that threaten it can help to strengthen it.

***

One aspect of our attitudes toward mental illness is not captured by Dualism, however, and that is our mistaken belief that "materially based" disorders have more severe symptoms and worse prognoses than those that are strictly psychological. One reason for this may be the belief that diseases that strike the brain are inherently more severe. But this explanation is difficult to sustain, given that the symptoms described in the aforementioned experiments were identical for the "biogenetic "and "psychological" conditions.

Perhaps it's because people assume that if a disease is innate (i.e., genetically caused), its course is also predetermined and thus less amenable to treatment. Innateness could also explain our negative reactions to patients. Being born with the illness would set them apart from typical individuals, which would promote stigma and social distancing.[4,5,17,20] Additionally, the notion that our psyche defines the self—who we really are—provides an explanation for why psychiatric patients resist treatment.[30] Presumed innateness seems to explain many of our biases. But before we declare the question settled, we must overcome one seemingly insurmountable challenge: Why would a person believe that a mental disorder that ravages the material body is innate?

At first, the answer would appear to be trivial: Isn't that what they're told? After all, the notion of a "biogenetic" explanation implies a genetic cause, and in many of the experiments, the biogenetic explanation "implanted" a genetic origin (e.g., by stating that the disease runs in the patient's family).[31] "Gene talk," however, is not necessary to make people slip to the false equivalency of "biological" and "innate." In one recent review of the literature, the psychologists Amy Loughman and Nick Haslam found that people (laypeople, clinicians, and patients alike) maintain the same biases, even when they are merely told that a disease is "brain-based" (e.g., affecting the brain's functional anatomy or chemistry).[20] For example, participants are more likely to state that their depression is chronic and uncontrollable when they are presented with bogus test results suggesting that their symptoms originate from a biochemical imbalance in their brain.[23] To be perfectly clear, this belief is entirely false—all psychological states reside in the brain; the tracing of psychological symptoms to a biochemical imbalance says nothing about whether or not the underlying condition is innate or even chronic.

Some researchers have suggested that merely mentioning the brain suggests that patients share an underlying feature that lumps them together.[4,5,17,20] But lumping people together does not explain why it is believed that their symptoms and prognoses would be worse. Missing is a *mechanism* that spells out why presumed materiality (a disease that is "in the brain") goes along with a presumed genetic cause, which, in turn, gives rise to our misconceptions concerning the severity of the disease and its prognosis.

Stated this way, the problem should now seem familiar. We have seen both its exact simile and its mirror image when we discussed our reasoning about ideas and emotions in the healthy psyche (in Chapters 3–9 vs. 10). When we reason about ideas, we are blind to innateness. For healthy emotions we presume the opposite, and this same bias also explains our unjustified pessimism about what we intuitively consider "affective" psychiatric disorders— we are too quick to presume that emotions (typical or atypical) *are* innate. (Note that our notion of "affective disorders" may not necessarily align with psychiatric classifications. For example, in psychiatry, major depression is an affective disorder, whereas schizophrenia is considered a psychotic disorder, but laypeople seem to treat them alike, possibly because they modulate affect. My reference to psychiatric disorders as "affective" strictly refers to this intuitive understanding.)

Our troubles with Essentialism can be traced to the bidirectional links it forms between innateness and materiality. Innateness, as we saw, requires essentialist biological traits to be material. And since immaterial ideas violate this condition, we conclude that ideas cannot be innate. In the case of emotions (typical or atypical), we readily presume a material basis in the body, and learning that affective disorders reside "in the brain" further exacerbates this tendency. But, as we saw in previous chapters, in our Essentialist mind, not only are innate traits material, but material (e.g., being "in the brain") traits are innate. So when we learn that a mental disorder is "in the brain," Essentialism automatically leads us to presume that the disorder is genetic. The materiality–innateness link (courtesy of Essentialism) thus solves the puzzle. "Brain" diseases are perceived as severe and immutable, not simply because they are material but because, in our Essentialist mind, being "in the body" (materiality) implies being "innate."

The proposal that people consider brain-based disorders as innate can also explain the stigma and distancing. If schizophrenia is "in your genes," then, on the one hand, you are not to blame, as your condition is predetermined. But, on the other hand, your different genetic profile means that your essence is different from mine, and, from there, the road to stigma and distancing is quite short.[32] The presumption that material disorders are innate can also explain why similarly negative attitudes extend to patients' families. Granted, some mental disorders like schizophrenia *are* highly heritable, so the innateness presumption is not necessarily irrational. What *is* irrational, however, is to presume (as people in fact do) that a disease is *more* likely to be genetic just because it is linked to the brain. But if (per Essentialism) material (brain) disorders are innate, then by sharing genes, your family members are immediately put at higher risk of exhibiting the same set of shunned symptoms. Essentialism thus accounts for the presumed link between the brain and heritability.

Our misreasoning about mental illness illustrates how a theory we built to explain one aspect of our mental life (our faulty reasoning about innate ideas) can explain a seemingly unrelated phenomenon—our faulty reasoning about mental illness. In the first case, we fail to invoke the potential for innateness; in the second, we overapply it.

The same theory also extends to cognitive disorders—conditions that are linked to abstract, immaterial ideas. The material basis for a cognitive disorder is harder for us to grasp than that of an affective disorder, and for this reason, we are reluctant to accept that it could be innate. So the same forces that prevent us from acknowledging the potential for innate ideas in the "typical" mind also hinder our ability to understand these conditions in an atypical one. Here, we predict an underapplication of innateness and materiality for disorders that affect thinking. The next chapter tests this prediction.

References

1. Black A, Crancato C, Fuller B. *Buffet froid*. Sara Films; 2013.
2. Kandel E, R. *The disordered mind*. New York, NY: Farrar, Straus and Giroux; 2018.
3. Sullivan PF, Neale MC, Kendler KS. Genetic epidemiology of major depression: review and meta-analysis. *The American Journal of Psychiatry*. 2000;157(10):1552–1562.
4. Haslam N, Kvaale EP. Biogenetic explanations of mental disorder: the mixed-blessings model. *Current Directions in Psychological Science*. 2015;24(5):399–404.
5. Ahn W-k, Kim NS, Lebowitz MS. The role of causal knowledge in reasoning about mental disorders. In: Waldmann MR, ed. *Oxford library of psychology. The Oxford handbook of causal reasoning*. Oxford, England: Oxford University Press; 2017:603–617.
6. Pescosolido BA, Martin JK, Long JS, Medina TR, Phelan JC, Link BG. "A disease like any other"? A decade of change in public reactions to schizophrenia, depression, and alcohol dependence. *American Journal of Psychiatry*. 2010;167(11):1321.
7. Jamison KR. *An unquiet mind*. 1st Vintage Books ed. New York, NY: Vintage Books; 1996.
8. Pryor L. How to have a better conversation about mental illness. *The New-York Times*. July 11, 2018.
9. Link BG, Yang LH, Phelan JC, Collins PY. Measuring mental illness stigma. *Schizophrenia Bulletin*. 2004;30(3):511–541.
10. O'Connor C, Rees G, Joffe H. Neuroscience in the public sphere. *Neuron*. 2012;74(2):220–226.
11. Racine E, Waldman S, Rosenberg J, Illes J. Contemporary neuroscience in the media. *Social Science & Medicine*. 2010;71(4):725–733.
12. Schomerus G, Schwahn C, Holzinger A, et al. Evolution of public attitudes about mental illness: a systematic review and meta-analysis. *Acta Psychiatrica Scandinavica*. 2012;125(6):440–452.
13. United States, Public Health Service, Office of the Surgeon General, Center for Mental Health Services. *Mental health: a report of the surgeon general*. Rockville, MD: Department of Health and Human Services, U.S. Public Health Service; 1999.
14. Harrington A. *Mind fixers: psychiatry's troubled search for the biology of mental illness*. New York, NY: Norton; 2019.
15. Kvaale EP, Gottdiener WH, Haslam N. Biogenetic explanations and stigma: a meta-analytic review of associations among laypeople. *Social Science & Medicine*. 2013;96:95–103.
16. Kvaale EP, Haslam N, Gottdiener WH. The "side effects" of medicalization: a meta-analytic review of how biogenetic explanations affect stigma. *Clinical Psychology Review*. 2013;33(6):782–794.
17. Dar-Nimrod I, Heine SJ. Genetic essentialism: on the deceptive determinism of DNA. *Psychological Bulletin*. 2011;137(5):800–818.
18. Bennett L, Thirlaway K, Murray AJ. The stigmatising implications of presenting schizophrenia as a genetic disease. *Journal of Genetic Counseling*. 2008;17(6):550–559.
19. Deacon BJ, Baird GL. The chemical imbalance explanation of depression: Reducing blame at what cost? *Journal of Social and Clinical Psychology*. 2009;28(4):415–435.
20. Loughman A, Haslam N. Neuroscientific explanations and the stigma of mental disorder: a meta-analytic study. *Cognitive Research: Principles and Implications*. 2018;3(1):43.

21. Lam DCK, Salkovskis PM. An experimental investigation of the impact of biological and psychological causal explanations on anxious and depressed patients' perception of a person with panic disorder. *Behaviour Research and Therapy*. 2007;45(2):405–411.
22. Lebowitz MS, Ahn W-k, Nolen-Hoeksema S. Fixable or fate? Perceptions of the biology of depression. *Journal of Consulting and Clinical Psychology*. 2013;81(3):518–527.
23. Kemp JJ, Lickel JJ, Deacon BJ. Effects of a chemical imbalance causal explanation on individuals' perceptions of their depressive symptoms. *Behaviour Research and Therapy*. 2014;56:47–52.
24. Ahn W-k, Proctor CC, Flanagan EH. Mental health clinicians' beliefs about the biological, psychological, and environmental bases of mental disorders. *Cognitive Science*. 2009;33(2):147–182.
25. Kim NS, Ahn W-k, Johnson SGB, Knobe J. The influence of framing on clinicians' judgments of the biological basis of behaviors. *Journal of Experimental Psychology: Applied*. 2016;22(1):39–47.
26. Bloom P. *Descartes' baby: how the science of child development explains what makes us human*. New York, NY: Basic Books; 2004.
27. Moritz S, Peters MJV, Karow A, Deljkovic A, Tonn P, Naber D. Cure or curse? Ambivalent attitudes towards neuroleptic medication in schizophrenia and non-schizophrenia patients. *Mental Illness*. 2009;1(1):e2.
28. Mojtabai R, Olfson M, Sampson NA, et al. Barriers to mental health treatment: results from the National Comorbidity Survey Replication. *Psychological Medicine*. 2011;41(8):1751–1761.
29. van Beljouw I, Verhaak P, Prins M, Cuijpers P, Penninx B, Bensing J. Reasons and determinants for not receiving treatment for common mental disorders. *Psychiatric Services*. 2010;61(3):250–257.
30. Nyholm S, O'Neill E. Deep brain stimulation, continuity over time, and the true self. *Cambridge Quarterly of Healthcare Ethics: CQ*. 2016;25(4):647–658.
31. Lebowitz MS, Ahn W-k. Effects of biological explanations for mental disorders on clinicians' empathy. *Proceedings of the National Academy of Sciences of the United States of America*. 2014;111(50):17786–17790.
32. Haslam N. Dehumanization: an integrative review. *Personality and Social Psychology Review*. 2006;10(3):252–264.

13

Decoding Dyslexia

The Diagnostic and Statistical Manual of Mental Disorders (DSM), the set of diagnostic criteria used by clinicians (e.g., psychologists and psychiatrists) to identify mental disorders, is the "Bible" of the mental health profession. And, according to the DSM, severe difficulties with reading, number cognition, and language are all aspects of a "Specific Learning Disorder." Since reading disability, or dyslexia, is listed in the DSM, dyslexia is technically a mental disorder.[1]

Dyslexia affects between 5% and 17% of the general population.[2] It is typically characterized by an unexpected difficulty in acquiring reading skills, despite otherwise normal "intelligence, motivation, and schooling considered necessary for accurate and fluent reading."[2] Like major depression and schizophrenia, dyslexia is a brain-based disorder[3] that is highly heritable (genes are believed to account for about 58% of the variability between individuals that have it and those who don't).[4]

Granted, the effect of dyslexia on a person's daily life is by no means comparable to what a sufferer of major depression or schizophrenia experiences. But as with the psychiatric disorders discussed in the previous chapter, the public's reaction to dyslexia is fraught with misconceptions. Remarkably, those errors are the mirror images of the ones seen in the context of affective psychiatric disorders.

***

Many people think of reading as a process of visual pattern recognition, for example being able to consistently register the contrast between symmetrical letters, such as *d* and *b*. If that is the case, then it stands to reason that when reading goes awry, the culprit is a visual deficit. But in reality, visual patterns are just a means to an end, which is language. Reading is a technology that gets you there.

You, the reader, can comprehend the words printed on this page because they convey a linguistic message. This becomes immediately apparent when

The Blind Storyteller. Iris Berent, Oxford University Press (2020). © Iris Berent, 2020.
DOI: 10.1093/oso/9780190061920.001.0001

you encounter a word in an unfamiliar orthography. For most readers of the English language, בלכ is just a visual scribble, markedly distinct from *dog*, which they readily recognize as a word. But if you know a little Hebrew, you will instantly consider both words the same. By contrasting the two cases (בלכ vs. *dog*), you can appreciate the power of reading. Reading renders visual scribbles into vehicles of language.

It is language that allows you to extract the syntactic structure of this sentence and comprehend its meaning, just as you would if you heard me utter these words out loud. To analyze a spoken sentence (*This is a dog*), you engage not with visual patterns but with phonology, that is, with abstract patterns of speech sounds. For example, when you hear the word *dog*, you notice that its first sound is /d/ (the tilted lines indicate phonemes, abstract sound units of language) and its last one is /g/ (which happen to be the same sounds as in *God*; the difference is just in their sequencing). Think of syntax like a locked door; phonology (speech patterns) is the code you need to unlock it, and in spoken language, that code is extracted naturally.

Reading requires that you pass through the same linguistic "gateway," or else you won't be able to glean any meaning from text. But now the entrance code—patterns of speech sounds—is no longer given naturally. So, when you read, a conversion must first take place. Printed words must be converted from visual symbols into a format that can open the language gateway. And that code is speech-based.[5,6]

To get from letters to speech patterns, you must decode their sound. Much as beginning readers learn to do in phonics, you associate each letter with its corresponding sound. You recognize that the *c* in *cat* is a /k/ sound, as in *kitten*, whereas *phrase* and *face* both begin with an /f/ sound. For skilled readers, this decoding process is so automatic that they are not even aware that it is taking place. But a small experiment can help you get a glimpse of the process.

Which of the following words is a vegetable? Respond "yes" or "no," as quickly as you can. Ready? *Tomato, bike, potato, pear, carat, banana, kite.*

Did you just fall for *carat*? Most people do, even when they are perfectly skilled readers. In fact, it is precisely *because* they are skilled readers that they get tripped up. You might think the culprit is its spelling, for *carat* and *carrot* share many letters. But the letters are only part of the story. If I were to replace *carat* with *carst* (which shares an equal number of letters with the target), you wouldn't get nearly as confused. What "gets you" is not just the letters; it's that the words are homophones—they share the same sound pattern. From such "glitches," it becomes evident that the reading code is sound-based; a *carat* is a *carrot,* a *kat* is a *cat* and a *roze* is a *rose.*[7-9] Being a skilled reader means that your letter-to-sound conversion process is automatic; it becomes second nature, almost a reflex. Literally hundreds of research papers have demonstrated this phenomenon in tightly controlled experiments. This letter-to-sound process occurs even when people read silently.[9-12]

And it is primarily this process that goes awry in most people with dyslexia. This breakdown of decoding has been as well established experimentally as its routine workings in typical readers.[13-19] It is particularly easy to see when people are presented with novel letter strings, like *blif* or *wug.* For skilled readers, decoding these strings is trivial. Not so for most people with dyslexia. Their difficulties do not usually concern letter recognition (many have no visual problems), and they certainly do not result from insufficient instruction or practice. Rather, it is their ability to carry out letter-to-sound conversions that is impaired, and this is borne out by both behavioral and brain studies. The culprit is the networks that support sound conversion in their brains.[16,20-22]

At first blush, this seems like a strange assertion, as most people with dyslexia have no overt difficulties with spoken language. But a subtle speech deficit nonetheless exists, and it is demonstrably linked to reading.[18,23-31] To recognize speech sounds, people sort them into distinct categories (phonemes). Like most automatic processes, this one typically goes on "beneath the radar"; people are normally unaware of the hard work that their brain is doing. But they can get a glimpse of it when they encounter an obstacle. Just try talking to a telemarketer over a noisy phone line. When I give them my last name, I have to explain that it's spelled with a *b* as in *boy,* not *p* as in *Paul.* This is because spoken words are not simply registered as unanalyzed wholes. Instead, we categorize their speech sounds into buckets. The "p" bucket, for instance, holds a wide array of slightly different speech sounds that are distinct from "b." Although you think of the *p* in *pie* and *spy* as "the same sound," in reality, they are different; we only treat them the same because, as English speakers, our brain assigns them both to a single category. If you were a speaker of Gujrati, for instance, those two sounds would seem completely distinct, akin to the contrast between the English *pea* and *bee.* Our mind thus imposes a sharp boundary between these two speech categories, /b/ and /p/,[32-34] and this is how we perceive speech from birth.[35,36]

For people with dyslexia, this classification process is slightly different; the boundaries between categories are fuzzier.[18,23,37-43] Infants who are at risk for dyslexia (because dyslexia runs in their families) exhibit subtle abnormalities in their processing of speech sounds from close to birth, which are evident in their brain responses.[28,44-46] In one study, the psychologist Dennis Molfese presented newborns with speech sounds like "*bi*" or "*gi*." The brains of "at risk" infants showed a different response to these sounds than members of a "not-at-risk" control group. Moreover, the patterns of brain response at birth predicted the reading ability of these children at eight years of age.[46-48] To be sure, dyslexia can also compromise other systems, including vision,[49] attention, and motor processing.[22] But, contrary to popular belief, the most prevalent deficit in dyslexia is in letter-to-sound conversion,[22,50,51] and this problem is typically associated with subtle difficulties in the perception of speech.

At this point, you might be wondering: How does a subtle abnormality in speech perception affect reading? After all, reading and speech are not one and the same. But they are related nonetheless, and the link is found at levels of both cognition and brain.

To acquire reading, children must recognize that spoken words are comprised of parts—*d*, for instance, is the first sound of *dog*; if children fail to identify the *d* sound (as distinct from *t*, for instance), then they would fail to recognize what the function of the letter *d* is.[6] And there is indeed ample evidence that children with dyslexia struggle to gain awareness of the components of spoken language.[18,50,52] This is the cognitive part of the story.

At the level of the brain, there is an abundance of evidence that the reading brain system is parasitic on the system that analyzes speech.[24,50,51,53-56] Like maps and numerals, reading is a cultural invention, not an innate instinct. But when we come to invent such technologies, we typically do so by relying on related cognitive systems of core knowledge.[55,57,58] In the words of the neuroscientist Stanislas Dehaene, the brain is a "recycler"—it forms new systems by adapting and reusing pre-existing ones.[55] The reading network in the brain capitalizes on many of the pathways that mediate the perception of speech. Reading recycles speech.

Now we can tie together all the loose ends and see how a subtle speech disorder can lead to difficulties with reading. Because reading must be linked to (abstract patterns of) speech, and because the brain hardware that supports speech perception and reading are partly shared, the inborn deficit of speech perception impairs the acquisition of reading in children and the reading skills of adults.

And while English orthography is notoriously difficult (the correspondence between spelling and sound can be capricious—consider *touch* and *couch*, for example, not to mention *yacht, knowledge,* and *psychology*), dyslexia is by no means unique to English. Italian orthography is much more sensible than English orthography, and Chinese has no letters at all. But there are Italian-[30] and Chinese-speaking[16] dyslexics. The specific symptoms of dyslexia and their severity might differ across orthographies, depending on their demands.[13] But dyslexia exists in every orthography, and it is always linked to difficulties in speech processing.[30,51] The "grammar" of reading is universal, and so are reading disabilities.[59]

***

The fact that dyslexia is a heritable brain disorder should be less-than-shocking shocking news to the general public. My informal survey of the U.S. media suggests that in the past 10 years, *The New York Times* published 24 stories linking dyslexia to the brain, NPR had 16 reports, and *USA TODAY* ran five such stories. Moreover, across the three sources, the number of such reports has increased, from 3.4 stories per year between 2008 and 2011 to 5.7 yearly (from 2013 to October 2018).

The growing media coverage of dyslexia's basis in the brain parallels the increase in public discussion of the biogenetic basis for major psychiatric disorders, discussed in the previous chapter. One would expect this increased media coverage to have similar effects in both cases. People should realize that dyslexia is a brain disease, presume that it is hereditary, and thus become less likely to blame the affected individuals. At the same time, they should show greater pessimism about sufferers' ability to overcome it and stronger endorsements of medical as opposed to cognitive/instructional approaches to its treatment.

But the actual state of affairs is mixed in curious ways. Emphatic denials of dyslexia are not uncommon, even among public figures. Richard Allington, a reading education researcher, recently told a group of Baltimore County public school administrators that "there is no such thing as a learning disability or dyslexia."[60] Across the Atlantic, Graham Stringer, a member of the British Parliament, argued[61] that dyslexia is "a cruel fiction" that is

> no more real than the 19th century scientific construction of "the æther"
> to explain how light travels through a vacuum . . . we should be dealing

with the problem, not incentivizing people to believe they have a condition which doesn't really exist.

The general public is typically more knowledgeable and kinder, and they correctly state that dyslexia is not due to a lack of trying. But they are systematically confused about the nature of the disorder. Many laypeople believe that dyslexia is a form of "word blindness"[62] that results from "troubles with vision."[63] A recent large study found that fully 76% of its participants believe that a "common sign of dyslexia is seeing letters backwards."[64] Alarmingly, so did 58% of the educators that were included in the study. In a study of British student teachers,[65] the majority of participants incorrectly stated that "colored overlays and/or tinted glasses were helpful to individuals with dyslexia" and that "eye tracking exercises are effective in remediating dyslexia-caused difficulties." These erroneous beliefs are equally common in the United States.

Laypeople in the United States readily volunteer that dyslexia is hereditary,[63] and their U.K. counterparts tend to correctly state that "people cannot help being dyslexic—it is in their genetic make-up."[62] As expected in light of the literature on mental disorders, participants in a U.S. study tended to believe that dyslexia can be cured by drugs while expressing skepticism about a child's capacity to control their symptoms.[63] Further in line with the view that dyslexia is a genetic disorder, laypeople in the United Kingdom correctly indicated that dyslexia is found worldwide.[62] But, upon further probing, it appears that the public's understanding is rather shaky. Those student teachers, for instance, were not quite sure whether "dyslexic parents are more likely than non-dyslexic parents to have children with dyslexia."[65] And they tended to disagree with the statement that "dyslexia is caused by inherited, faulty genes with evidence coming from studies of twins."[62]

Most surprisingly, while laypeople tend to volunteer that dyslexia is a genetic disorder, they don't necessarily view it as a brain disorder.[62,63] U.S. participants in a study were uncertain about whether the disorder has "medical or neurological causes."[63] Likewise, U.K. participants did not endorse the statement that "brain scan studies show that dyslexics' brains work differently from those of non-dyslexics," instead endorsing diagnostics by educational tests—an attitude that is typically indicative of a psychosocial disease model rather than a biogenetic one.

This attitude is puzzling. As science tells us, *all* cognitive disorders, hereditary or not, are expressed in the brain, and the structure of the brain is partly determined by genes. So, if people think dyslexia is hereditary, then they must also assume that it alters brain function—there is no other biological mechanism through which a cognitive disorder could manifest itself. Yet it appears that laypeople fail to fully grasp the notion of dyslexia as a brain disorder. Additionally, they stubbornly stick to the view of dyslexia as a visual disorder.

To probe into the link between the biological view of dyslexia and the mistaken idea that it invariably turns on visual difficulties, my lab asked people to reason about two individuals that suffer from reading difficulties.[66] John is said to have difficulties in the conversion of letters to sound; for him, *kat* does not sound like an animal name. Jack, on the other hand, suffers from letter reversals, as he confuses *b* with its mirror image *d*. When asked how likely it is that these individuals suffer from a reading disorder, people thought that, compared to Jack (with his visual difficulties), John (with his decoding difficulties) was less likely to suffer from a real disorder, his disorder was less severe, it was less likely to result from his biological makeup, and it was less likely to run in his family. In line with the literature on psychiatric disorders, we also found that the more likely people were to consider the disorder to be "in the brain," the more likely they were to view it as innate (for example, as likely to emerge spontaneously in the person's offspring), and the less likely they were to hold John responsible for his predicament.

***

Why do these misconceptions exist, and why do they tend to cluster in this particular fashion? It may be because reading is an acquired skill. Since we know that reading depends on learning, it is tempting to attribute the difficulties of individuals with dyslexia to inadequate instruction, rather than to the biogenetic makeup of their brains. While this could certainly contribute to the confusion, it does not entirely explain people's responses. For one thing, this view should have led people to blame mental patients for their conditions, but this is not usually the case.

The persistence of the "word blindness" misconception may partly be the fault of science. "Visual" explanations of dyslexia dominated the scientific literature at the beginning of the 20th century, and some (albeit a small minority) of affected individuals do in fact exhibit visual challenges.[67] Still, it is puzzling that this view is still accepted by teachers and student teachers, who have been exposed to more recent literature. When surveyed, most of them correctly stated that dyslexia compromises the mapping of letters to sounds. So why should they still insist that dyslexia is a visual disorder?

Some researchers have argued that they lack sufficient training,[68] and others have blamed it on the controversy surrounding the definition of "dyslexia" itself.[69] The fact that educators, psychologists, neurologists, and research scientists are still arguing over its precise definition does not instill confidence in their understanding of the disorder. In fact, Mark Seidenberg, a renowned reading researcher, notes that the current DSM definition of dyslexia as a general category of learning disability "with manifestations in reading, writing, or math" is misaligned with the picture emerging from reading research.[50]

There is some truth in all of these explanations, and there may not be just one answer. But I lay the bulk of the blame on our core cognition—specifically, on the twin principles of Dualism and Essentialism.

Viewed from that perspective, dyslexia is a mystery marked by two irreconcilable facts. On the one hand, we are told that dyslexia compromises *knowledge*—the associations we have learned between letters and sounds. Per Dualism, all forms of knowledge are immaterial, which means that dyslexia cannot reside in the body. But we also recognize that dyslexia is a hereditary brain disorder. And we know all too well per Essentialism that our innate essence (whether typical or not) is material.

Each of these two beliefs are perfectly tenable in and of themselves. We can certainly accept the possibility that people with dyslexia lack some immaterial knowledge, and we can also grasp the possibility that a disease impairs the material brain. But the two beliefs don't mix and match. Having a material brain disorder affecting some ephemeral immaterial process makes no sense in our Essentialist eyes.

It is thus no wonder that people's characterizations of dyslexia are confused. From the perspective of Dualism, a disorder that compromises knowledge cannot alter the material body. In fact, it is difficult to see how a condition affecting an immaterial process could be a disease at all. Dualism thus explains why some people deny the very existence of dyslexia.

The same analysis can also shed light on the stubborn insistence on framing dyslexia as a visual disorder. As we saw in previous chapters, sensory traits are viewed as more material and hence more likely to be innate than cognitive traits. By framing dyslexia as a "visual" problem, people can salvage the conception of dyslexia as a "real" disorder of the material brain. And since (per Essentialism) disorders that are "in the brain" are considered innate, the visual account of dyslexia further implies that dyslexia is not under an individual's control, thus reducing stigma and blame.

The psychologist Simon Gibbs and his colleagues have likewise attributed dyslexia to Essentialism, but, in their view, people project an immutable essence onto dyslexia simply because it allows them to categorize it as a biological disorder.[69] We encountered this same assertion in the context of mental disorders in the previous chapter and noted that this approach, while generally on the right track, is missing a crucial logical step. Being "in the brain" does not necessarily predict innateness. Missing from this account is a mechanism that explains *why* the "brain" view is associated with innateness. In the case of dyslexia, there is the further question of why it is incorrectly linked to visual symptoms. The hypothesis that, per Essentialism, dyslexia is linked to an innate material essence and that, per Dualism, sensory visual conditions are more material explains both.

***

The last two chapters considered how we reason about two sets of mental disorders—those that meddle with our emotions and those that interfere with our cognition. In each case, public understanding of the disorder is systematically distorted. Some of those misunderstandings are shared across both sets of disorders, but others differ in interesting ways.

When we consider psychiatric conditions such as major depression or schizophrenia, people tend to attribute the disorder to the brain. When they do so, they are less likely to blame the patients for their conditions and, simultaneously, assume (albeit incorrectly) that the disorders are more severe than they are, less likely to improve, and less amenable to behavioral interventions by psychotherapy.

"Brain talk" has also led people to become relatively more open to the biological basis of cognitive disorders. So when people consider dyslexia, they are now more likely to attribute it to the sufferers' biology and less likely to blame them for it. In line with reasoning about affective disorders, a biological view of dyslexia tends to go along with a more pessimistic outlook about its potential for a cure.

But the biogenetic view of dyslexia is not universally accepted, and doubts about whether the disorder even exists are still vigorously expressed. Even those who are open to accepting dyslexia as a real disorder struggle to grasp its biogenetic bases, and their views on the topic are fraught with inconsistencies. While many people are willing accept that dyslexia is hereditary, they are reluctant to attribute it to the brain, and they also tend to characterize it as a visual problem, rather than a failure to properly link letters to sounds.

So the question is why our reasoning is biased in these particular ways: first, why all "brain-based" disorders (cognitive or affective) are perceived to be more severe and with poorer prognoses than non-brain-based disorders; second, why psychiatric disorders are readily linked to the brain but not dyslexia; and third, why dyslexia is systematically and wrongly classified as a visual disorder.

I suggest that our core knowledge of Dualism and Essentialism accounts for all three syndromes. Essentialism leads us to link the material brain-based source of the disorder with innate essence, and for this reason, brain-based disorders are incorrectly associated with a fatalistic destiny. Dualism likewise biases us to assume that the cure for a disorder must be commensurable with its cause, so once a brain origin is postulated, we wrongly assume that a disorder cannot benefit from behavioral interventions, such as psychotherapy or educational practice.

But, as we have seen, not all states of the mind are equally amenable to material explanations. Because affect is viewed as material, we are all too keen to assume that emotions reside in the brain, and, being material, we also leap toward the conclusion that emotions form part of our human essence and are innate. Knowledge, on the other hand, is immaterial, so we are far less likely to accept that cognitive disorders exist, and instead we attribute them to sensory causes. And what cannot exist materially in our brain cannot innately define our essence. Dualism and Essentialism predict both the similarities between our perceptions of affective and cognitive disorders and the differences.

The same core principles that blind us to our healthy nature also distort our understandings of the etiology and prognosis of disease. And if core knowledge blinds our view of *who we are* in life, it is only natural for it to meddle with our perception of what happens once we're no more. In fact, the casualties of core knowledge could extend even to our very notion of the self as a moral agent and our free will. These are the topics of the final two chapters.

References

1. American Psychiatric Association. *Diagnostic and statistical manual of mental disorders: DSM-5.* 5th ed. Washington, DC: American Psychiatric Association; 2013.
2. Shaywitz S. Dyslexia. *The New England Journal of Medicine.* 1998;338(5):307–312.

3. Galaburda AM, Sherman GF, Rosen GD, Aboitiz F, Geschwind N. Developmental dyslexia: four consecutive patients with cortical anomalies. *Annals of Neurology.* 1985;18(2):222–233.

4. Pennington BF, McGrath LM, Rosenberg J, et al. Gene × environment interactions in reading disability and attention-deficit/hyperactivity disorder. *Developmental Psychology.* 2009;45(1):77–89.

5. Perfetti C. *Reading ability.* New York, NY: Oxford University Press; 1985.

6. Liberman IY. Segmentation of the spoken word and reading acquisition. *Bulletin of the Orton Society.* 1973;23:65–77.

7. Van Orden GC. A ROWS is a ROSE: spelling, sound and reading. *Memory and Cognition.* 1987;15:181–190.

8. Van Orden GC, Johnston JC, Hale BL. Word identification in reading proceeds from spelling to sound to meaning. *Journal of Experimental Psychology: Learning, Memory, and Cognition.* 1988;14:371–386.

9. Van Orden GC, Pennington BF, Stone GO. Word identification in reading and the promise of subsymbolic psycholinguistics. *Psychological Review.* 1990;97:488–522.

10. Berent I, Perfetti CA. A rose is a REEZ: the two cycles model of phonology assembly in reading English. *Psychological Review.* 1995;102:146–184.

11. Seidenberg M, McClelland J. A distributed developmental model of word recognition and naming. *Psychological Review.* 1989;96:523–568.

12. Amenta S, Marelli M, Sulpizio S. From sound to meaning: phonology-to-semantics mapping in visual word recognition. *Psychonomic Bulletin & Review.* 2017;24(3):887–893.

13. Paulesu E, Demonet JF, Fazio F, et al. Dyslexia: cultural diversity and biological unity. *Science.* 2001;291:2165–2167.

14. Ramus F. Outstanding questions about phonological processing in dyslexia. *Dyslexia.* 2001;7(4):197–216.

15. Shaywitz SE, Shaywitz BA, Pugh KR, et al. Functional disruption in the organization of the brain for reading in dyslexia. *Proceedings of the National Academy of Sciences of the United States of America.* 1998;95(5):2636–2641.

16. Siok WT, Niu Z, Jin Z, Perfetti CA, Tan LH. A structural-functional basis for dyslexia in the cortex of Chinese readers. *Proceedings of the National Academy of Sciences of the United States of America.* 2008;105(14):5561–5566.

17. Ramus F, Ahissar M. Developmental dyslexia: the difficulties of interpreting poor performance, and the importance of normal performance. *Cognitive Neuropsychology.* 2012;29(1-2):1–19.

18. Berent I, Vaknin-Nusbaum V, Balaban E, Galaburda A, M. Dyslexia impairs speech recognition but can spare phonological competence. *PLoS ONE.* 2012;7(9):e44875.

19. Berent I, Zhao X, Balaban E, Galaburda AM. Phonology and phonetics dissociate in dyslexia: evidence from adult English speakers. *Language, Cognition and Neuroscience.* 2016;31(9):1178–1192.

20. Pugh KR, Mencl WE, Shaywitz BA, et al. The angular gyrus in developmental dyslexia: task-specific differences in functional connectivity within posterior cortex. *Psychological Science.* 2000;11(1):51–56.

21. Shaywitz BA, Shaywitz SE, Pugh KR, et al. Disruption of posterior brain systems for reading in children with developmental dyslexia. *Biological Psychiatry.* 2002;52(2):101–110.

22. Paulesu E, Danelli L, Berlingeri M. Reading the dyslexic brain: multiple dysfunctional routes revealed by a new meta-analysis of PET and fMRI activation studies. *Frontiers in Human Neuroscience*. 2014;8.

23. Ziegler JC, Pech-Georgel C, George F, Lorenzi C. Speech-perception-in-noise deficits in dyslexia. *Developmental Science*. 2009;12(5):732–745.

24. Gabrieli JDE. Dyslexia: a new synergy between education and cognitive neuroscience. *Science*. 2009;325(5938):280–283.

25. Boets B, Ghesquiere P, van Wieringen A, Wouters J. Speech perception in preschoolers at family risk for dyslexia: relations with low-level auditory processing and phonological ability. *Brain and Language*. 2007;101(1):19–30.

26. Tallal P. What happens when "dyslexic" subjects do not meet the criteria for dyslexia and sensorimotor tasks are too difficult even for the controls? *Developmental Science*. 2006;9(3):262–264.

27. Serniclaes W, Van Heghe S, Mousty P, Carré R, Sprenger-Charolles L. Allophonic mode of speech perception in dyslexia. *Journal of Experimental Child Psychology*. 2004;87(4):336–361.

28. Leppänen PHT, Richardson U, Pihko E, et al. Brain responses to changes in speech sound durations differ between infants with and without familial risk for dyslexia. *Developmental Neuropsychology*. 2002;22(1):407–422.

29. Brandt J, Rosen JJ. Auditory phonemic perception in dyslexia: categorical identification and discrimination of stop consonants. *Brain and Language*. 1980;9(2): 324–337.

30. Paulesu E, Démonet JF, Fazio F, et al. Dyslexia: cultural diversity and biological unity. *Science*. 2001;291(5511):2165–2167.

31. Perrachione TK, Del Tufo SN, Gabrieli JDE. Human voice recognition depends on language ability. *Science*. 2011;333(6042):595–595.

32. Liberman AM, Cooper FS, Shankweiler DP, Studdert-Kennedy M. Perception of the speech code. *Psychological Review*. 1967;74(6):431–461.

33. Liberman AM, Harris KS, Kinney JA, Lane H. The discrimination of relative onset-time of the components of certain speech and nonspeech patterns. *Journal of Experimental Psychology*. 1961;61(5):379–388.

34. Lisker L, Abramson A. A cross-language study of voicing in initial stops: Acoustical measurements. *Word*. 1964;20:384–422.

35. Eimas P, Seidenberg M. Do infants learn grammar with algebra or statistics? *Science*. 1997;284:433.

36. Bertoncini J, Bijeljac-Babic R, Blumstein SE, Mehler J. Discrimination in neonates of very short CVs. *The Journal of the Acoustical Society of America*. 1987;82(1):31–37.

37. Blomert L, Mitterer H, Paffen C. In search of the auditory, phonetic, and/or phonological problems in dyslexia: context effects in speech perception. *Journal of Speech, Language, and Hearing Research: JSLHR*. 2004;47(5):1030–1047.

38. Robertson EK, Joanisse MF, Desroches AS, Ng S. Categorical speech perception deficits distinguish language and reading impairments in children. *Developmental Science*. 2009;12(5):753–767.

39. Hazan V, Messaoud-Galusi S, Rosen S, Nouwens S, Shakespeare B. Speech perception abilities of adults with dyslexia: is there any evidence for a true deficit? *Journal of Speech, Language, and Hearing Research: JSLHR*. 2009;52(6):1510–1529.

40. Werker JF, Tees RC. Speech perception in severely disabled and average reading children. *Canadian Journal of Psychology*. 1987;41(1):48–61.

41. Mody M, Wehner DT, Ahlfors SP. Auditory word perception in sentence context in reading-disabled children. *Neuroreport*. 2008;19(16):1567–1571.
42. Berent I, Vaknin-Nusbaum V, Balaban E, Galaburda A. Phonological generalizations in dyslexia: the phonological grammar may not be impaired. *Cognitive Neuropsychology*. 2013;30(15):285–310.
43. Serniclaes W, Seck Mb. Enhanced sensitivity to subphonemic segments in dyslexia: a new instance of allophonic perception. *Brain Sciences*. 2018;8(4).
44. Guttorm TK, Leppänen PHT, Poikkeus A-M, Eklund KM, Lyytinen P, Lyytinen H. Brain event-related potentials (ERPs) measured at birth predict later language development in children with and without familial risk for dyslexia. *Cortex*. 2005;41(3):291–303.
45. van Leeuwen T, Been P, van Herten M, Zwarts F, Maassen B, van der Leij A. Cortical categorization failure in 2-month-old infants at risk for dyslexia. *Neuroreport*. 2007;18(9):857–861.
46. Molfese DL. Predicting dyslexia at 8 years of age using neonatal brain response. *Brain and Language*. 2000;72:238–245.
47. Molfese DL, Molfese VJ. Cortical response of preterm infants to phonetic and non-phonetic speech stimuli. *Developmental Psychology*. 1980;16(6):574–581.
48. Espy KA, Molfese DL, Molfese VJ, Modglin A. Development of auditory event-related potentials in young children and relations to word-level reading abilities at age 8 years. *Annals of Dyslexia*. 2004;54(1):9–38.
49. Stein J, Walsh V. To see but not to read: the magnocellular theory of dyslexia. *Trends in Neurosciences*. 1997;20(4):147–152.
50. Seidenberg M. *Language at the speed of sight: how we read, why so many can't, and what can be done about it*. New York, NY: Basic Books; 2018.
51. Bolger DJ, Perfetti CA, Schneider W. Cross-cultural effect on the brain revisited: universal structures plus writing system variation. *Human Brain Mapping*. 2005;25(1):92–104.
52. Manis FR, McBride-Chang C, Seidenberg MS, et al. Are speech perception deficits associated with developmental dyslexia? *Journal of Experimental Child Psychology*. 1997;66(2):211–235.
53. Raschle NM, Zuk J, Gaab N. Functional characteristics of developmental dyslexia in left-hemispheric posterior brain regions predate reading onset. *Proceedings of the National Academy of Sciences of the United States of America*. 2012;109(6):2156–2161.
54. Perfetti CA, Sandak R. Reading optimally builds on spoken language: implications for deaf readers. *Journal of Deaf Studies & Deaf Education*. 2000;5(1).
55. Dehaene S. *Reading and the brain: the science and evolution of a human invention*. New York, NY: Viking; 2009.
56. Dehaene S, Cohen L. The unique role of the visual word form area in reading. *Trends in Cognitive Sciences*. 2011;15:254–262.
57. Carey S. *The origin of concepts*. Oxford, U.K.: Oxford University Press; 2009.
58. Carey S, Spelke E. Science and core knowledge. *Philosophy of Science*. 1996;63(4): 515–533.
59. Perfetti CA. The universal grammar of reading. *Scientific Studies of Reading*. 2003;7(1):3–24.
60. Gencer A. National reading expert comes to Baltimore County. *The Baltimore Sun*. Feb. 13, 2009.
61. Dyslexia is "a cruel fiction," says Manchester Blackley MP *The Guardian*. Jan. 13, 2009.

62. Furnham A. Lay knowledge of dyslexia. *Psychology*. 2013;04(12):940–949.
63. Castillo A, Gilger JW. Adult perceptions of children with dyslexia in the USA. *Annals of Dyslexia*. 2018;68(3):203–217.
64. Macdonald K, Germine L, Anderson A, Christodoulou J, McGrath LM. Dispelling the myth: training in education or neuroscience decreases but does not eliminate beliefs in neuromyths. *Frontiers in Psychology*. 2017;8:1314.
65. Washburn EK, Binks-Cantrell ES, Joshi RM. What do preservice teachers from the USA and the UK know about dyslexia? *Dyslexia*. 2014;20(1):1–18.
66. Berent I, Platt M. Laypeople's misconceptions about dyslexia. Unpublisehd raw data, Northeatsern University, 2019.
67. Ramus F, Rosen S, Dakin SC, et al. Theories of developmental dyslexia: insights from a multiple case study of dyslexic adults. *Brain*. 2003;126(4):841–865.
68. Hurford DP, Hurford JD, Head KL, Keiper MM, Nitcher SP, Renner LP. The dyslexia dilemma: a history of ignorance, complacency and resistance in colleges of education. *Journal of Childhood & Developmental Disorders*. 2016;2(3).
69. Gibbs S, Elliott J. The differential effects of labelling: how do "dyslexia" and "reading difficulties" affect teachers' beliefs. *European Journal of Special Needs Education*. 2015;30(3):323–337.

D. While We're Here and Once We're No More

14

Once We're No More

As a cognitive scientist with expertise on language, I'm often approached by people at cocktail parties. Bilingualism is a popular topic. "Would growing up with a second language hurt/help my child?" So are dreams. "What language do I dream in?" I always try to reply politely, to the best of my ability. But one question I got on a recent trip to Israel left me stumped. "Have you heard? It was on Chanel 10! The news headline says it all: *A Druze child speaking fluent English in a British accent—amazing reincarnation!*[1] How do you explain *that*?"

At the center of all the excitement was three-and-a-half-year-old O'Neal Mahmoud, a cute, sociable boy who lives in a Druze community in the Golan Heights. O'Neal's parents are Arab speakers who hardly know a word of English. But their son's language development has been highly unusual. Typically, before children produce their first words (around their first birthday), they pass through a period of articulatory experimentation known as babbling (sign language learners likewise babble; they just use their hands). Normally, babbling sounds much like the child's target language.[2] But O'Neal didn't begin to babble until he was two, and when he finally did, it didn't sound like his parents' Arabic but made-up gibberish. Then, all of a sudden, he opened his mouth, and out came complete phrases in *English*.

Assisted by members of the family, neighbors, and a crew of experts that ran the gamut from a speech and language specialist to a spiritualist, the TV reporters diligently tried to explain how this otherwise normal-seeming child could have learned to speak English. The mystery, they concluded, could only have one explanation: O'Neal's "inborn" command of English was conveyed through the spirit of a Druze ancestor who had lived in the South of London.

The Druze are a religious group whose secretive faith is said to combine elements from Islam with Greek philosophy. I grew up near some Druze villages, so the report naturally piqued my curiosity. No, I didn't believe that reincarnation was the only possible explanation for O'Neal's

The Blind Storyteller. Iris Berent, Oxford University Press (2020). © Iris Berent, 2020.
DOI: 10.1093/oso/9780190061920.001.0001

linguistic abilities—a boy who is named after Shaquille O'Neal, the legendary American basketball player, has likely had at least *some* exposure to English. What surprised me was why the investigative team caved in to mysticism. Granted, Channel 10 is commercial TV, but it's still a mainstream channel in Israel, a country with a booming high-tech economy and widespread scientific literacy.

But on further consideration, I realized I shouldn't have been so surprised. TV executives might or might not be scientifically literate, but they are no fools when it comes to business. They know all too well what their audience wants, and, without a doubt, the supernatural sells. People are universally fascinated with what happens after they die, in the Levant and elsewhere, which is why there is no dearth of shows starring souls without bodies (and vice versa) on American TV. To name just a few, there is *Ghost Hunters, The Scariest Places on Earth, A Ghost Story*, and *Ghost Asylum*. On the big screen, there are classics like *The Shining* and *Hereditary*. On the other side of the coin (bodies without souls), there is the ever-popular *The Walking Dead, World War Z*, and *The Night of the Living Dead*. The real puzzle, then, is not what network producers are thinking but the viewers—you and me. Why are we so fascinated by what obviously *doesn't* happen when we're dead?

Who Believes in the Afterlife?

Oh, well, you might reply, don't be so serious. Ghosts are just fun! They walk through walls, give you something to dress up as when you go out trick-or-treating, and scare you a bit at night, even when you're old enough to know better. Religious people, of course, might actually believe this stuff, as did our ancient ancestors, and as some remote hunter-gatherers still do ("silly them!"). But we educated 21st-century Westerners are just amused. We recognize that thinking and feeling all happens "up north" in the brain—that without pulsing meat in the skull, none of this mental stuff can really happen. We know better than to believe in ghosts, reincarnation, and the afterlife.

I wouldn't be so sure. As we have seen thus far, our self-reflective capacities are limited; when it comes to our own minds, there is a lot that we are blind to. The air may be clear in Death Valley, but it hardly improves our visual acuity.

Don't get me wrong. I'm not questioning your rational, scientific understanding of the finality of death. Rational understanding, however, does not close the door on our intuitive beliefs. Blindness and enlightenment can live happily side by side; when it comes to the afterlife, we are remarkably good at holding more than one idea in our heads at once. Usually it's our reason that does the "talking." But our intuitive understanding constantly whispers in our ears, and we do listen. Science bears it out.

In one study, the psychologist Jesse Bering asked college students to rate how likely it is that a dead person would exhibit a number of biological and psychological traits.[3] When asked "Would the dead person need to eat?" or "Would they feel hunger?" the participants readily said "no." But for epistemic states ("Will he know that he's dead?" and "Is he still thinking about his wife?"), the participants were less certain. Some openly said they believe that consciousness survives death or reincarnates into another body; in their view, Richard would know he's dead and he would still be thinking about his wife—all those epistemic states would be preserved, along with some desires and even emotions. This is a remarkable result, given that the participants were college students in South Florida, but it is perhaps not entirely unexpected. After all, they had explicitly defined themselves as believers in an afterlife.

But even some participants who were agnostic about the supernatural or who had described themselves as outright certain that the self is utterly extinguished at death still leaned toward "yes" (about 20% of their responses). Strikingly, when these agnostics/extinctivists did say "no" (e.g., "Richard won't be thinking about his wife"), they took twice as long to respond as they did to the biological questions. The longer response time implies that, despite their explicit beliefs to the contrary, these staunch naturalists were closet supernaturalists. Although they say that they don't believe in afterlife, their behavior showed that they weren't so sure, at least when it came to epistemic states.

Why epistemic states are so special in the afterlife is a question that I will consider shortly (hint—recall our misconceptions regarding the innateness of cognitive traits in the living, in Chapters 2–8). But for now, we note that similar results obtain when people are asked to reason about a hypothetical situation in which the mind of one person miraculously "migrates" into the body of another—a situation that invites people (college students in Northern Ireland and Oxford, U.K.) to reason about minds without invoking death. Once again, it is psychological (mental) properties (e.g., storytelling), not physical properties (e.g., sprinting) that transfer to the host body.[4,5]

Further evidence that people are tacit or subconscious supernaturalists is presented by a study that compared reasoning about the dead to reasoning about people whose brains were damaged to a point that they were in a permanent vegetative state. Compared to people in vegetative states, the dead were actually quite lively—participants rated them higher on multiple cognitive capacities (e.g., being aware of their environment; knowing right from wrong; being able to influence situations, remember events, possess personality, have emotions). Once again, these participants were U.S. college students from New England—one of the most liberal and highly educated regions in the United States.[6] When another study informed participants (students from the University of Arkansas) that the ghost of a dead student had been seen in the testing room, they were less likely to cheat on a test, even when no experimenter was present.[7] So yes, ghosts are funny indeed. But when mortals' extinctivist beliefs are put to the test, it is the ghosts that have the last laugh.

Bodies and Minds

Why, then, do educated college students lean toward the supernatural? Cultural and religious experience would seem to present an obvious explanation. Even if you are a firm extinctivist, with no religious beliefs whatsoever, it is likely that you have been exposed to various religious traditions that profess a belief in the afterlife. So when we consider the beliefs of Western adults, it is difficult to rule out their cultural experiences entirely; young children and people from other cultures offer critical insights on the origins of afterlife beliefs, and we will consider them shortly. Returning to our Western adults, however, it is hardly obvious that institutional religion provides the sole explanation for their intuitions about the afterlife.

First, reasoning about the afterlife parallels reasoning about mind migration—a scenario that does not have explicit roots in religion.[4,5] Second, our reasoning about the supernatural does not faithfully follow the dictums of institutional religions.[8,9] For example, while people profess to believe that God is omnipotent, their implicit beliefs are quite anthropomorphic. Thus, when the psychologists Justin Barrett and Frank Keil asked Western participants to recall a narrative about God's failure to intervene on behalf of a drowning child, their answers implied that they believed that there was a limit to how many prayers God could attend to at once.[10] Similar questions presented to Hindu participants suggested that they viewed God (e.g., Brahman) as moving from one place to another, in marked contrast to their explicit account.[11] So when we do observe a correlation between people's religions and their implicit beliefs about the afterlife, we shouldn't jump to assume causation. In fact, scholars like Dan Sperber,[12] Pascal Boyer,[8,9,13,14] Steven Pinker,[15] Justin Barret,[16] and Paul Bloom[17] have turned the argument on its head: it is not cultural and institutional religion that shapes people's intuitive understanding of the afterlife. Rather, people are naturally prone to presuppose the supernatural; it is this natural predisposition (courtesy of our core cognition) that primes us for our belief in the afterlife as it is described in institutional religion, and not the other way around.

Dualism presents an obvious explanation for these supernaturalist intuitions. As Paul Bloom notes, if you think of your body as merely the vessel of the actual "you," then the belief in an afterlife emerges "for free." People don't need to be told that the soul survives the body; this notion follows logically from the belief that the material body and immaterial mind/soul are distinct.[18] Dualism, then, would lead you to assume that the self continues to exist immaterially in the afterlife. And since the immaterial self is automatically endowed with cognitive capacities, these same traits will continue to exist posthumously.

Dualism, moreover, can explain both why we identify "John's ghost" as "John," even though it lacks John's body, and how we relate to the converse situation with zombies. In the macabre duel between ghosts and zombies, ghosts would win any day. Yes, ghosts are scary; zombies, however, are viscerally repugnant. Dualism explains why. If John is more strongly associated with his mind/soul than with his body, then his ghost (a disembodied "John") is unnatural but conceivable. In fact, some people would pay a fortune to preserve only their brains after they die in the hope that science will endow them with a physical afterlife in a new body.[19] Zombies get the wrong part of the bargain. A functional body without a fully sentient mind is an imposture—it looks like a person, but it lacks its defining feature, the self.

Moving back to science, Dualism sheds further light on the experimental findings discussed in the previous section. People, as you might recall, believe that epistemic traits are more likely to be maintained in the afterlife than physical and perceptual ones. Dualism presents a ready explanation. As we saw in the context of reasoning about living beings (Chapters 2–8), people consider epistemic cognitive traits as less material than sensory and motor traits. If epistemic cognitive states are not grounded in the material body, then it stands to reason that when the body no longer functions, epistemic states could still exist. Indeed, when I asked participants to reason which traits might transfer to the afterlife, they responded that cognitive traits are the most likely to be maintained (these findings are discussed in Chapter 8).

Jesse Bering, however, proposes another explanation for the results. Since no one really knows what happens when we die, the only way for us to respond to questions about the afterlife is by putting ourselves in the dead person's "shoes," so to speak, by vicariously simulating their mental condition.[20] In other words, we try to imagine what it would "feel" like to not hear or to not think. Critically, according to Bering, our conclusion that "hearing" is implausible in the afterlife is based not on the Dualist view that hearing is more associated with the material body (as I suggest) but because it is easier for us to imagine the cessation of hearing than thinking. We have all experienced "not hearing," but we cannot fathom what "not thinking" even means. It is a "lack of imagination" rather than a "lack of materiality" that leads us to conclude that the dead can think.

While the "simulation" strategy is not unreasonable, I don't think it provides the right explanation. First, "simulation" fails to explain the mirror symmetry between reasoning about the origins of knowledge (at birth) and its demise (after death). If people approached such questions by simulating cessation ("what it feels like not knowing/not hearing"), then their conclusions about the two "endpoints" of our existence should converge. If I cannot conjure up "not thinking" at death, then I should also fail to grasp the possibility of "not thinking" at birth. "Simulation," then, should have led us to conclude that epistemic states are prevalent not only in the afterlife but also innately, at birth. And the results reported in Chapters 6 and 8 clearly counter this prediction. The alternative "materiality" explanation handles both phenomena naturally. In fact, the results of the afterlife and the innateness scenarios bolster each other. Finding that people *shift* their response to the same trait depending on the context (innateness/afterlife) shows that people know what they are doing. It's not a lack of imagination that leads them to conclude that epistemic states transfer to the afterlife but are not innate. Rather, their responses in the two contexts are guided by a single cause: the (perceived) immateriality of epistemic states.

Other evidence for the link between afterlife beliefs and Dualism is presented in a study that correlated people's beliefs in the afterlife with their explicit beliefs in Dualism, by measuring the extent to which they endorsed statements such as "the body is material and the mind is immaterial."[21]

Results showed that people who were highly Dualist were also likely to express beliefs about the afterlife. These people, however, were apparently also confused about other natural facts, as they had some trouble contrasting facts from metaphors ("stars live in the sky"), so given these results alone, it's possible that their afterlife beliefs are grounded not just in Dualism but in a broader "ontological confusion."

The psychologist Nathan Heflick and his colleagues, however, found that Dualism directly promotes a belief in the afterlife.[22] The logic is simple: if Dualism causes afterlife beliefs, then situations that enhance Dualism should enhance belief in the afterlife. And since people are overall more likely to consider the afterlife when death is salient, the effect of Dualism should be strongest when people are thinking about their own deaths. Several experiments test this premise and the results are generally consistent with it.

One manipulated Dualism across two groups of participants. People in one group were asked to focus on their immaterial selves (by thinking about their minds and personalities, in line with Dualism); a second group was instructed to think about their physical bodies and experiences (in line with Physicalism). Results showed that when death was salient, people in the Dualism condition showed stronger beliefs in the afterlife relative to those in the Physicalist condition.

Another experiment manipulated the role of Dualism implicitly, by providing people with direct evidence for the causal powers of their minds. Participants were fitted with a brain–computer interface that allowed them to type words merely by thinking. The contraption was not magical. Rather, the researchers capitalized on the fact that unexpected events elicit a specific electric "signature" in the brain (the P300), so the detection of the P300 can indicate what people think. The experiment showed participants that their thoughts were powerful indeed—so much so that they elicited whole words spelled out on their computer screens.

In the experiment, people imagined a specific target letter (e.g., say, a *d*) while they saw arrays of letters flashing on the computer screen. By simple laws of probability, most letters did not match the target, so when a match did occasionally occur, this event was unexpected, and a P300 was detected by electrodes placed on the subject's scalp. In this manner, P300 by P300, the device detected whole words that the participant had in mind. Now, for various technical reasons, this procedure did not work equally accurately for all participants. But for the participants who attained high accuracy, the device presented palpable evidence that their mental powers were real. The critical manipulation concerned the word imagined—either *death* or *dealt*. Results showed that for the "high accuracy" participants, afterlife beliefs (as gauged by a questionnaire) were stronger when participants spelled *death* (relative to *dealt*). This increase is not simply due to the word *death* itself (specifically, the association of *death* with the afterlife), as the "low accuracy" group did not show the same increase. It thus appears that it is selective to people who witnessed the power of their mind. When death became salient to those participants (by the act of spelling the word *death*), their belief in the afterlife increased.

Summarizing, then, adult Western participants hold strong tacit beliefs about the afterlife, and these beliefs are evident even among staunch extinctivists. These beliefs, moreover, are linked to Dualism. First, we believe that only immaterial epistemic traits are maintained in the afterlife. Second, when death is salient, our beliefs in the afterlife are causally enhanced by Dualism.

Around the Globe—Afterlife Beliefs
in Young and Old

Given the prominence of the belief in the afterlife in Western culture and religion, the Dualist explanation for it is admittedly open to question. If it is our intuitive core knowledge that promotes our belief, however, then we should see similar beliefs in young children, who presumably have had less exposure to culturally and religiously imparted notions than adults. Moreover, similar attitudes should be evident across the globe. For the most part, the experimental evidence bears these assumptions out.

In a seminal study, Jesse Bering and David Bjorklund compared the afterlife beliefs of young children and adults.[23] The experiment was conducted in South Florida, so naturally, an alligator featured prominently among the protagonists. The lead character, Mr. Mouse, was having a really bad day—he had lost his way and was sick, hungry, and thirsty. Adding injury to insult, he got eaten by Mr. Alligator. Children were told that Mr. Mouse was no longer alive, and the message got through. Even the youngest, the four-year-olds, stated that Mr. Mouse is no longer alive and that he will no longer grow up or go to the bathroom. Children (kindergarteners, early- and late elementary school children) nonetheless believed that Mr. Mouse will maintain some functions in the afterlife; for comparison, the study also included a group of adults.

You might recall that adults believe that epistemic (immaterial) states continue to exist in the afterlife more than (material) psychobiological capacities, and this contrast is the telltale of Dualism. The question is whether children would spontaneously do the same. If adults' Dualist beliefs in the afterlife are solely acquired from experience, then continuity (between the traits in the afterlife and before) should gradually increase with age. The youngest four-year-olds would thus be the least likely to endow dead Mr. Mouse with any of his previous capacities (i.e., show the weakest continuity), affording no special status to epistemic states. But in the study, continuity was actually strongest in kindergarteners, and it was stronger still for epistemic states ("Knows he is not alive") compared to psychobiological states (e.g., "He is still hungry"), which in turn, showed greater continuity than biological states ("Needs to eat food again"). The latter comparison was especially telling, as the two types of states were closely matched. Thus, young children were more likely to ascribe "hunger" to the dead mouse than to say, "He needed to eat." In fact, four-year-olds were more likely than adults to project epistemic beliefs onto Mr. Mouse. These striking results suggest that afterlife beliefs are prominent early in development.

Subsequent research has replicated these findings with other U.S. children[24,25] and Catholic children in Spain.[26,27] In all cases, psychological traits were considered more likely to transfer to the afterlife than biological states. Other studies in non-Western cultures, including the Vezo people of Madagascar[28] (adults and older children), found the same. Similarly, when adult natives of Marajo Island in Brazil were asked to imagine that they were to leave their body, participants showed greater continuity of epistemic states (e.g., *hope, learn, understand*) relative to perceptual states (e.g., *feel itchy, dirty, bloated*).[4,5]

But the literature also presents several challenges to the universality of Dualist afterlife beliefs. First, many of these judgments are context-dependent. For example, Vezo,[28] Spanish,[27] and U.S.[24,25] participants showed a greater continuity when death was depicted in a religious context (e.g., in the presence of a priest or a tomb) than in a biological context (when a hospital or a corpse is depicted). Context, moreover, can further shift the continuity of psychological relative to biological states. When death was depicted in a medical setting, participants from Vanuatu in the Melanesian archipelago, both 7-year old children and adults, showed greater continuity of psychological relative to biological traits. But when the context was religious (invoking God and a funeral), it was biological traits that showed greater continuity, possibly because the Vanuatu have a literal interpretation of Christianity that assumes the resurrection of the body.[24] Finally, 4-year old children in China showed greater afterlife continuity than adults (in line with children in the United States), but they did not differentiate between psychological and biological states.[25]

Whether these discrepancies are mere "wrinkles" or a death sentence for Dualism is not entirely clear. First, these studies did not all use the same age groups, and there is evidence that age matters, as children's understanding of death changes in a nonlinear fashion.[29] Second, the studies used different methodologies, and, most critically, they did not classify traits in a uniform fashion. For example, in the Vezo study in Madagascar, half of the "mental" states were actually psychobiological (*feel hungry/cold*) and sensory capacities (*see, hear*),[28] so their discontinuity could be due to the materiality of these specific traits, rather than a lack of Dualism. Third, non-Western participants (especially children) might decline to consider epistemic states in the afterlife because they have trouble discussing mental states in the living. For example, when compared to U.S. children, young Chinese children were less likely to attribute psychological traits to people who were either dead or alive.[25]

Westerners are obsessed with their psychological well-being, and as we will see in the next chapter, inferences about the mental states of others are critical to their reasoning about moral responsibility (e.g., was it an accident or a premeditated crime?). It is thus difficult for them to imagine a society in which the psyche is not the topic of public discourse. But anthropologists have documented several societies in which it is inappropriate to talk about the minds of others. Some researchers, however, believe that members of these societies not only refrain from talking about the minds of others but are also unable to *understand* them. They develop "mind opacity"—meaning that they do not ascribe mental states to others.[30,31] If we don't think others have minds, Dualism cannot arise. The cross-cultural variation in how people talk about the afterlife could thus be a symptom of a deeper divide, namely, the possibility that core knowledge itself is not universal.

Several observations counter this position. First, while the literature on "mind reading" is complex, some studies have demonstrated that the sensitivity to the minds of others emerges in young infants,[32] and it is implicated in members of small-scale societies that are expected to exhibit "mind opacity."[33] In fact, we saw (in Chapter 7) that 5-month-old infants exhibit mind–body Dualism: while they know that objects are cohesive and they move in continuous paths, they seem to suspend this expectation for human agents.[34] These results call into question the possibility that sensitivity to the minds of others (and, by extension, Dualism, and beliefs in the afterlife) require extensive enculturation and explicit learning.

Second, returning to the Chinese children, other results suggest that Dualism does play a role in Chinese culture, at least historically. The study analyzed historic changes in the meaning of the word for heart (*xin*) in ancient Chinese texts (1500–221 BCE). Results showed that, with time, the meaning of *xin* bifurcated to contrast mind and body. There was an increase in the use of *xin* to indicate the locus of cognition, accompanied by a corresponding decrease in its use to reference emotion and the physical organ.[35] These results open up the possibility that the failure of Chinese children to differentiate between epistemic and biological states could be partly due to their reluctance to discuss psychological states, rather than to their indifference to Dualism.

Finally, an ingenious recent study by the psychologist Maciej Chudek and his colleagues documents beliefs in reincarnation in a small-scale society with "mind opacity."[36] The study was conducted on the Yasawans, indigenous residents of iTaukei Fijianian. Yasawans are discouraged from reasoning about the mental states of others as an explanation for their behavior. If Dualism, and, by extension, beliefs in the afterlife result from culture (specifically, the Western obsession with understanding others' minds), then the Yasawans should show no beliefs in the mind as distinct from the body, and, consequently, they would lack the basis to represent the notion of reincarnation.

To dissociate beliefs in reincarnation from people's willingness to merely talk about the minds of others, the study gauged rencarnation implicitly, using a nonverbal task. Participants (Yasawans and Canadians, both children and adults) watched multiple animated scenes featuring Penny the Pentagon, who was attempting to reach a cake. In the critical condition, the path to the cake was blocked by a barrier with a gap too narrow for Penny to pass through (see Figure 14.1). Having attempted to traverse the gap multiple times, Penny eventually gives up, moves away from the gap, and stops gazing at the cake. A moment later, a triangle, which has so far been stationary and inanimate (without eyes), suddenly gazes toward the cake and proceeds through the gap toward the cake. At the start of the trial, all the children identified "Penny" as

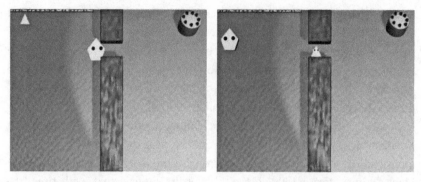

Figure 14.1. Penny the Pentagon and the triangle. The left figure depicts Penny's unsuccessful attempt to reach the cake through the gap; the right panel depicts the animated triangle approaching the cake.
Adapted from Chudek et al. (2018),[36] with persmission.

the pentagon. But after seeing the animation, most particiapnts—adults and children—now pointed toward the triangle, as did Candian children.

A number of control conditions suggest that the shift was specifically informed by cues related to animacy. For example, people did not shift their repsonse when the appearance/disappearance of the eyes (a valid cue for agency) was replaced with the appearance/disappearance of a bowtie (an invalid cue for agency). Similarly, people were more likely to shift their response when these animacy cues were strong (the eyes on the triangle appeared only after they had appeared on the pentagon) compared to when they were minimal (both figures had eyes throughout).

The most likely explanation for the shift, then, is that people assumed that the mind of the pentagon agent migrated to the triangle. The fact that people inferred such mind switching in a soceity that exhibits mind opacity suggests that Dualistic beliefs in reincarnation are not learned by cultural transmission. In fact, Yasawan adults were more likely to infer mind-switching than adult Canadians. So, while the cross-cultural results are not all consistent with Dualism, there is nonetheless strong evidence that beliefs in Dualism and reincarnation may not require that our culture exposes us to beliefs in Dualism.

Dualism alone, however, does not explain the full range of beliefs associated with the afterlife. A closer look at the skeletons in our closet suggests that, in death and in life, we are still at the mercy of Dualism's twin co-conspirator, Essentialism.

The Essentialist Skeleton in the Closet

Hungry Travelers

If you have ever been in Mexico for the Day of the Dead, it is an experience you will never forget. If you haven't, the Pixar movie *Coco* depicts it quite accurately. The Day of the Dead is actually two days rather than one. During this period, entire families spend the night at the graves of their loved ones and celebrate their expected brief visits to earth. To entice their loved ones' spirits to show up and support them on their journey, people build gorgeous altars at the graves, decorate them with the traditional yellow marigolds, and lay out sugar skulls, food, and drinks. When I lived in Mexico, my first encounter with the tradition was when a coworker unexpectedly walked into the office carrying a large pink skull, which, thanks to his skills in ventriloquism, appeared to be spontaneously laughing and talking. The prank worked its magic—I was utterly horrified.

The dates of the holiday (November 1–2) coincide with the Catholic All Saints' and All Souls' Days. The Mexican anthropologist Claudio Lomnitz has artfully shown how the significance of this event (indeed, of death as a Mexican national symbol) has been shaped by history, spanning the genocidal Spanish conquest of the Aztecs between 1519 and 1595 (death estimates range from 22% to 95%) to modern sociopolitical conditions.[37] As a social scientist, Lomnitz naturally focuses on history and sociology, but core knowledge may well play a secondary, perhaps even primary, role.

Before considering core knowledge, let us first inspect the cultural raw materials. Lomnitz notes that the Days of the Dead tradition is principally rooted in the Catholic notion of Purgatory (inflected by pre-Hispanic indigenous traditions and local postcolonial developments). In the Catholic religion, Purgatory is a "detention" center for dead souls who perished in good standing with the church yet are not quite "ready" to transfer to heaven. To hasten their transfer, families are encouraged to perform masses, prayers, fasting, and acts of charity. Since spirits in Purgatory are tortured by fire, they are invariably thirsty and hungry when they visit Earth, a presumption that is clearly evident in the lavish food and drink that people provide for their loved ones on their altars. Lomnitz describes how children in contemporary Tlayacapan chant in the streets on the eve of All Souls Day, begging for food for the dead.[37pp108–109]

The skull is hungry,
Is there no bread around here?
Don't finish all of it!
Leave one half of it.
Bread, bread, for the little skull,
Bread, bread, for the little skull,
A little bit of mole for the souls
A little mole for the bells friar

A hungry soul? How is that possible? Cultural traditions are unquestion-
ably real, but to hold such beliefs in our heads, we need to reconcile those
notions with the constraints imposed by core knowledge. And per intuitive
psychology (courtesy of Dualism), souls are immaterial, and they are entities
devoid of any biological functions. So why, then, would spirits on the Day of
the Dead require food?

Picky Relocators

When a dead soul visits us on Earth, it is not only hungry but apparently
in need of a new habitat. That an immaterial being would require shelter is
itself puzzling. As it turns out, however, souls won't just settle for any new
residence; they are picky relocators. Such care for matters of matter is truly
bizarre.

In the Aztec tradition, for instance, the soul is a three-part entity, and
each part is associated with a different material substance (*teyolia* is associated with the heart; *tonali* is associated with the blood; and *ihiyotl* is linked to
breath and bodily gases). Not only does the soul occasionally leave the body
while it is still living (in dreams and during sex), but it can transfer to other
material things after death. For example, the *teyolia* of a dead child can reside
in a particular bird (*yolototl*, "the bird of the heart") or in other children.[37]
So the spirit cannot be utterly devoid of material substance. Rather, its material essence in life continues to guide its choice of a reincarnation vessel.

Moving to an utterly different tradition, remember O'Neal, the
reincarnated boy who was "born speaking English"? Well, a belief in reincarnation is highly prominent in the Druze tradition, and several children have
proclaimed themselves to be the reincarnations of specific Druze individuals
(apparently encouraged by adults).[38] The religious belief in reincarnation

thus provides a natural (albeit unusual) motivation for O'Neal's family's claims about his behavior, and it is possible that exposure to English (e.g., via TV) has provided the means for it. Since I don't possess the full facts about O'Neal, I can only speculate about the specifics. What's interesting for our purposes, however, are the beliefs of his community.

On the one hand, the Druze view the soul as a single, indivisible, ephemeral entity, distinct from the material body—the quintessential hallmark of Dualism. Also, the reincarnated soul maintains a memory of its previous life, and the continuity of epistemic states is exactly what Dualism predicts. Yet, in the same tradition, reincarnation is constrained to preserve both ethnicity and gender: A Druze soul can only reincarnate in another Druze; a man can only reincarnate in a man and a woman in a woman.[38] How come? If the soul is immaterial, distinct from the body, how could the biological essence of the body constrain the soul's choice of a new vessel?

These constraints on the association of the soul with matter are also supported by experimental findings. In a clever set of experiments, the anthropologist Emma Cohen and her colleagues asked participants to imagine that their spirits left their bodies to migrate to other entities—either a plant (biological) or a rock (physical).[5] Participants were presented with a large list of traits and indicated which ones would move to the plant and which would move to the rock. Another question asked people to reason about migration without any vessel (the control condition). These questions were presented to two groups of participants, native residents of either the Brazilian Amazon (Marajo Island) or of Oxford, U.K.

In the control condition, both groups showed greater continuity of epistemic states (e.g., *hope, learn, understand*) relative to perceptual states (e.g., *feel itchy, dirty, bloated*).[5] This is in line with the original findings of Jesse Bering, and since (as we saw in previous chapters) epistemic states are less material than perceptual ones, their stronger propensity for continuity outside the body is exactly what you'd expect in Dualism.

Dualism, however, would further lead you to predict that the soul is utterly immaterial. So, if soul/mind were to relocate, the material properties of the new vessel should be, well, immaterial: stones shouldn't be any worse than plants, for instance. At first, this statement might appear surprising, given that we have just argued that epistemic states should show greater continuity in the afterlife. Allow me to spell out the logic.

Migration is a two-part problem: (a) Will the trait leave the original body? and (b) Will it reincarnate in another? To determine whether a given trait is a candidate for reincarnation, we need to consider whether it can dissociate from the material body in the first place; here it would make sense that only immaterial traits could have a disembodied existence in the afterlife/migration. Once departed, however, the traits are expected to remain immaterial, utterly devoid of any material embodiment. So when we move to the second question—what new "vessels" are appropriate for reincarnation?—the new vessel should be irrelevant. Participants, however, insisted that the medium mattered, and its effect was quite systematic.

Cohen and colleagues considered the migration of two types of traits, defined by their propensity to migrate away from the body in the control ("no vessel") condition. The first type included the traits that are prone for migration (mostly epistemic traits), suggesting that these traits are body-independent; the second included traits that are relatively body-dependent and hence resistant for migration (mostly perceptual bodily states). It turns out that the propensity of a trait to relocate to a new vessel depends on its propensity to migrate out from the body in the control conditions. When perceptual (body-dependent) traits are offered an appropriate new vessel, they become more likely to migrate relative to the no-vessel (control) condition, and this result obtained for both Brazilian and British participants. In contrast, epistemic (body-independent) traits show the opposite pattern: they are *less* likely to migrate to the appropriate material vessel relative to the control condition (although this latter result was significant only with the U.K. participants).

		Likelihood of Migration	
		Appropriate Vessel	No vessel
Trait	*Material*	+	–
	Immaterial	–	+

These results establish a remarkable double dissociation between the materiality of the trait (before it leaves the body) and its propensity for material reincarnation thereafter. Traits that are bodily dependent (i.e., material) favor an "appropriate" material vessel for reincarnation; those that are immaterial (i.e., bodily independent) favor nonmaterial reincarnation (without a vessel). Now what counts as an "appropriate" vessel varied across the two cultures. The U.K. participants insisted on a biological medium (plant); for the Brazilian participants, plants and rocks (biological and physical) were equally appropriate vessels. Critically, once the appropriate vessel is identified, its role in migration is quite consistent across the two cultures, and it systematically depends on the materiality of the traits. This outcome is unexpected by Dualism.

Contagious Spirits

Not only do spirits require food and shelter, but much like the living, their essence can contaminate material objects. The psychologist Paul Rozin has famously shown that people believe in magical contagion.[39-41] For example, they would resist wearing a sweater that belonged to a murderer (even after the sweater is thoroughly laundered). Although the contagion logic defies science, it is entirely consistent with intuitive psychology. Presumably, the murderer possessed some negative physical essence, capable of contaminating the garment and transferring to another person by physical contact. Paul Rozin and Carol Nemeroff make it clear that physical contact is absolutely necessary for contagion,[40] and this requirement bears the telltale of Essentialism. Since the murderer's essence is material, its transmission to another person's body can only occur by physical contact.

But it turns out that in naïve psychology, contagion applies to both living bodies and souls. My 19-year old daughter Alma insists on buying her clothes from consignment sales (she is conscious about the environmental footprints of fashion); my father-in-law, however, reacts to the notion with visceral disgust. He is appalled that his lovely granddaughter is "wearing the clothes of the dead." I very much doubt he would lift his objection if he were assured that their original owner had died in their pajamas.

This makes no sense. Once a person dies, they don't change their outfits, so there is unlikely to have been any physical contact between the corpse and a garment from their closet. If people still believe that a dead owner's essence is contagious, then the contagion must occur in the afterlife. But "contagion by spirit" is an oxymoron. Per Dualism, the soul (and, posthumously, the spirit) is immaterial; whereas per the laws of contagion, contagion requires physical contact. So if the spirit is contagious, then, per naive cognition, the soul must possess some properties that are material.

Do Westerners (my father-in-law notwithstanding) really believe in "contagion by spirit"? The experimental findings on this question aren't clearcut, but there are some hints. The psychologist Jesse Bering reports that participants rated a donated organ from a suicide victim as significantly less desirable than an organ from the victim of an accident or homicide. Moreover, people believed that the characteristics of the dead person (enjoying spicy food, color preferences) would transfer along with the organ.[42] Leaving aside the question of why people find suicide so aversive (for this, I refer you to Bering's book), what's remarkable for our purposes is the contagion mechanism. It's one thing to avoid objects that were in direct physical contact with a corpse; discrimination between different causes of death is another matter. Causes of death aren't necessary imprinted on the dead body—the body of a person who took their life with a gun does not differ from that of a murder victim who was also shot to death. So if the organs of the suicide victim are more "contagious," then the contagion must be due to a posthumous property of the spirit. The capacity of immaterial spirit to transmit material contagion is an utter mystery for Dualism.

Spirit Ontology: Soul and Matter

I think by now you are getting the picture. Dualism predicts that the potential of a trait to emerge in the afterlife should depend on the extent that it is distinct from the physical body, that is, its immateriality, and we have indeed seen that, per intuitive psychology, immaterial (e.g., epistemic) states are the most likely to "live on" in the dead. By the same token, Dualism should further predict that once the immaterial soul/spirit reaches its destination in the afterlife, it should be utterly free of any of the material biological constraints that define living things. Spirits should thus have no biological needs (no hunger and thirst), no need for a material bodily, and, certainly, no preference for one particular vessel over another (biological vs. physical; member of the same ethnic group or not). Finally, souls cannot be contagious, and contagion certainly shouldn't depend on the cause of death. None of this agrees with Dualism.

All of these biologically inclined properties of the dead, however, sound very much like those of the living. In fact, this line of reasoning directly mirrors Essentialism. It's the biological essence of living things that determines their immutable distinct character—the essence of John is distinct from Jim, and it is decidedly material. All of this would make sense for the living. But if upon his demise, John's spirit sheds off his body much as we throw our dirty shirt into the laundry, then why do we insist that some of his body's material essence transfers to the afterlife?

Perhaps this incongruous notion of the afterlife lies in the conflicting notions of the "self" and "agency" in the living offered by Dualism and Essentialism. Per Dualism, the body is merely a vessel, so once it is shed after death, dead John's spirit is still his good old self, even if his body is no longer functioning. This immaterial notion of agency, however, presents a problem for Essentialism. As noted, living agents possess a material essence—even young infants would be surprised to discover that agents are hollow.[43] So our concept of the afterlife is doomed to permanent oscillation between these two conflicting poles.

When we approach the notion of death from the perspective of the Dualist pole, we emphasize the permanence of the spirit afterlife and focus on its immaterial properties. But when we consider spirits as agents, we cannot help but endow them with the Essentialist material properties of living creatures, and with them come biological constraints, embodiment, and contagion. As we will see in the next chapter, these conflicting notions of the afterlife directly reflect our divided understanding of the self in the living. And that understanding is jointly shaped by Dualism and Essentialism.

References

1. Levy A. A Druze boy speaking fluent English in a British accent: amazing reincarnation! Chanel 10. 2018.
2. Petitto LA, Holowka S, Sergio LE, Ostry D. Language rhythms in baby hand movements. *Nature*. 2001;413(6851):35–36.
3. Bering JM. Intuitive Conceptions of Dead Agents' Minds: The Natural Foundations of Afterlife Beliefs as Phenomenological Boundary. *Journal of Cognition and Culture*. 2002;2(4):263–308.
4. Cohen E, Barrett J. When minds migrate: conceptualizing spirit possession. *Journal of Cognition & Culture*. 2008;8(1/2):23–48.
5. Cohen E, Burdett E, Knight N, Barrett J. Cross-cultural similarities and differences in person-body reasoning: experimental evidence from the United Kingdom and Brazilian Amazon. *Cognitive Science*. 2011;35(7):1282–1304.
6. Gray K, Knickman TA, Wegner DM. More dead than dead: perceptions of persons in the persistent vegetative state. *Cognition*. 2011;121(2):275–280.
7. Bering J, McLeod K, Shackelford T. Reasoning about dead agents reveals possible adaptive trends. *Human Nature*. 2005;16(4):360–381.
8. Boyer P, Baumard N. The diversity of religious systems across history: An evolutionary cognitive approach. In: Shackelford TK, Liddle JR, eds. *The Oxford Handbook of Evolutionary Psychology and Religion*. 2016. doi:10.1093/oxfordhb/97801993.
9. Baumard N, Boyer P. Religious beliefs as reflective elaborations on intuitions: a modified dual-process model. *Current Directions in Psychological Science*. 2013;22(4):295–300.

10. Barrett JL, Keil FC. Conceptualizing a nonnatural entity: anthropomorphism in God concepts. *Cognitive Psychology.* 1996;31(3):219–247.

11. Barrett JL. Cognitive constraints on Hindu concepts of the divine. *Journal for the Scientific Study of Religion.* 1998;37(4):608–619.

12. Sperber D. Apparently irrational beliefs. In: Hollis M, Barnes B, Bloor D, et al., eds. *Rationality and relativism.* Cambridge, MA: MIT Press; 1982:149–180.

13. Boyer P. Cognitive constraints on cultural representations: natural ontologies and religious ideas. In: Hirschfeld LA, Gelman SA, eds. *Mapping the mind: domain specificity in cognition and culture.* New York, NY: Cambridge University Press; 1994:391–411.

14. Boyer P. Minds make societies: how cognition explains the world humans create. New Haven, CT: Yale University Press; 2018.

15. Pinker S. *How the mind works.* New York, NY: Norton; 1997.

16. Barrett JL. Exploring the natural foundations of religion. *Trends in Cognitive Sciences.* 2000;4(1):29–34.

17. Bloom P. Religion is natural. *Developmental Science.* 2007;10(1):147–151.

18. Bloom P. *Descartes' baby: how the science of child development explains what makes us human.* New York, NY: Basic Books; 2004.

19. Knapton S. Cryogenically frozen brains will be "woken up" and transplanted in donor bodies within three years, claims surgeon *The Telegraph.* April 27, 2017.

20. Bering JM. The folk psychology of souls. *Behavioral and Brain Sciences.* 2006;29(5):453–462.

21. Riekki T, Lindeman M, Lipsanen J. Conceptions about the mind-body problem and their relations to afterlife beliefs, paranormal beliefs, religiosity, and ontological confusions. *Advances in Cognitive Psychology.* 2013;9(3):112–120.

22. Heflick NA, Goldenberg JL, Hart J, Kamp SM. Death awareness and body–self dualism: a why and how of afterlife belief. *European Journal of Social Psychology.* 2015;45(2):267–275.

23. Bering JM, Bjorklund DF. The natural emergence of reasoning about the afterlife as a developmental regularity. *Developmental Psychology.* 2004;40(2):217–233.

24. Watson-Jones RE, Busch JTA, Harris PL, Legare CH. Does the body survive death? Cultural variation in beliefs about life everlasting. *Cognitive Science.* 2017;41(Suppl 3):455–476.

25. Lane JD, Zhu L, Evans EM, Wellman HM. Developing concepts of the mind, body, and afterlife: exploring the roles of narrative context and culture. *Journal of Cognition and Culture.* 2016;16(1–2):50–82.

26. Bering JM, Blasi CH, Bjorklund DF. The development of "afterlife" beliefs in religiously and secularly schooled children. *British Journal of Developmental Psychology.* 2005;23(4):587–607.

27. Harris PL, Giménez M. Children's acceptance of conflicting testimony: the case of death. *Journal of Cognition & Culture.* 2005;5(1–2):143–164.

28. Astuti R, Harris PL. Understanding mortality and the life of the ancestors in rural Madagascar. *Cognitive Science.* 2008;32(4):713–740.

29. Panagiotaki G, Hopkins M, Nobes G, Ward E, Griffiths D. Children's and adults' understanding of death: cognitive, parental, and experiential influences. *Journal of Experimental Child Psychology.* 2018;166:96–115.

30. Robbins J, Rumsey A. Introduction: cultural and linguistic anthropology and the opacity of other minds. *Anthropological Quarterly.* 2008;81(2):407–420.

31. Mayer A, Träuble BE. Synchrony in the onset of mental state understanding across cultures? A study among children in Samoa. *International Journal of Behavioral Development*. 2013;37(1):21–28.

32. Onishi KH, Baillargeon R. Do 15-month-old infants understand false beliefs? *Science*. 2005;308(5719):255–258.

33. Barrett HC, Bolyanatz A, Crittenden AN, et al. Small-scale societies exhibit fundamental variation in the role of intentions in moral judgment. *Psychological and Cognitive Sciences*. 2016;113(17):4688.

34. Kuhlmeier VA, Bloom P, Wynn K. Do 5-month-old infants see humans as material objects? *Cognition*. 2004;94(1):95–103.

35. Slingerland E, Chudek M. The prevalence of mind-body dualism in early China. *Cognitive Science*. 2011;35(5):997.

36. Chudek M, McNamara RA, Birch S, Bloom P, Henrich J. Do minds switch bodies? Dualist interpretations across ages and societies. *Religion, Brain & Behavior*. 2018;8(4):354–368.

37. Lomnitz-Adler C. *Death and the idea of Mexico*. New York, NY: Zone Books; 2005.

38. Halabi R, Horenczyk G. Reincarnation beliefs among Israeli Druze and the construction of a hard primordial identity. *Death Studies*. 2019:1–10.

39. Nemeroff C, Rozin P. The contagion concept in adult thinking in the United States: transmission of germs and of interpersonal influence. *Ethos*. 1994;22(2):158–186.

40. Rozin P, Nemeroff C. Sympathetic magical thinking: The contagion and similarity "heuristics." In: Gilovich T, Griffin D, Kahneman D, eds. *Heuristics and biases: the psychology of intuitive judgment*. New York, NY: Cambridge University Press; 2002:201–216.

41. Rozin P, Markwith M, McCauley C. Sensitivity to indirect contacts with other persons: AIDS aversion as a composite of aversion to strangers, infection, moral taint, and misfortune. *Journal of Abnormal Psychology*. 1994;103(3):495–504.

42. Bering J. *Suicidal: why we kill ourselves*. Chicago, IL: University of Chicago Press; 2018.

43. Setoh P, Wu D, Baillargeon R, Gelman R. Young infants have biological expectations about animals. *Proceedings of the National Academy of Sciences of the United States of America*. 2013;110(40):15937–15942.

15

Land of the Free

As we have seen time and time again, people are prolific storytellers. We tell a story about what physical objects are and how they move; about living things and how they inherit their essential biological properties; and about agents and what makes them tick. Above all, there is the story we tell about the storyteller—the self.

Looking at our own lives, we identify a single protagonist that occupies the center stage, from infancy to old age. The picture album tells it all. There is your baby self, smiling in the crib; the toddler you, taking her first steps; a carefree child in a field of blooming daisies; the shy awkward teenager; the confident young adult. Here is your wedding day, and all of a sudden, a bunch of new kids are in the album too.

Who is the actor that plays the lead role? Strangers looking at your photos may not always discern the similarities between the infant and the grown-up you; biologists would point out that most of the cells in your adult body are new; and feminist scholars and philosophers might quibble about whether the obedient girl in the classroom and the activist marching in the #MeToo rally are truly one and the same person. But there is no question in your mind. All of them are the same unique "me."

One defining characteristic of the protagonist is her capacity to choose at will. It is "you," the kid, who decided to get control of the ball and kick it through the goal in that soccer tournament. The same self also made the decision to major in psychology and not humanities, and to marry her spouse. All of these decisions were made freely, at will. And it is that same willing self who continues to choose on a daily basis, from "Americano" versus "Latte" to "Democrats" versus "Republicans." Some of these choices are made arbitrarily, at the flip of a coin. Others are deliberate and reflect aspects of your personality and values that are deeply rooted and that you might not even be consciously aware of. But all of them are yours and only yours to make. It is precisely because you choose freely that you bear the responsibility for your actions.

The Blind Storyteller. Iris Berent, Oxford University Press (2020). © Iris Berent, 2020.
DOI: 10.1093/oso/9780190061920.001.0001

So, who is "the decider?" Who is "you"—the self? In our minds, the answer is as certain as the light of day. That willing self is the protagonist "me"— a single, coherent entity that exists continuously throughout my life. That this thinking, willing "self" exists is perhaps the only conclusion we can deduce with any certainly by relying on the force of reason—so thought Rene Descartes, at least.[1] Everything else could be an illusion. My eyes can mistake a patch of light on the desert sand for a spring of water; I might remember seeing you yesterday, while in reality you visited only my dreams. But so long as I recognize that I think, I cannot go wrong. The thinker must be "me."

Our narrative not only identifies the protagonist but further reasons about her qualities. In our minds, that willing self—me—isn't my flesh and bones. My body as an adult is vastly different from my baby body, but inside that fleshy package the true immaterial me remains unchanged. It is that immaterial self that has made all those decisions at will. In fact, it is precisely because that self is immaterial that it can will and choose, rather than simply follow the laws of nature that define every physical entity. That immaterial self is the author of every one of the thoughts and feelings that I had throughout my whole life, and the choices that I made because of them. Come to think of it, however, that is not exactly true. That willing self is certainly the author of my benevolent actions—my acts of kindness, charity, and consideration toward others. But our deeds of lesser perfection—the occasional untruth that we tell, let alone theft and murder—must be products of some temporary weakness or temptation, a "suspension" of our true selves. Those aren't the real "me."

But in all likelihood, all three of these assumptions—that the "moral self" is good, immaterial, and singular—are our biggest illusion of all. Our beliefs in the self are not only mistaken, but in the spirit of Greek tragedy, they are likely our destiny too. They are fictional creations of Dualism and Essentialism, the principles of core knowledge that we almost certainly carry with us from birth.

In this chapter, we will briefly examine our beliefs in the freely willing "self." Given the confinement of a single chapter, we can only skim the surface—what follows is a "taster" of a topic that has generated a vast literature in psychology and philosophy. We first examine what laypeople mean by "free will" and why this particular view of free will is an illusion. We next move to inspect our assumptions about our singular willing selves.

My Choice

What do you want to do this evening? Go out for dinner? Or spend a cozy evening at home with a book and a nice cup of tea? If you're debating the question, you must have options. Whatever you end up doing, you know that things could have gone differently; your choice was not predetermined. But perhaps other universes do not offer this option. In the movie *Groundhog Day*, a TV weatherman (played by Bill Murray) is trapped by a blizzard in a weird small town, where the exact same series of events repeat themselves every day—he wakes up to the same precise song on the radio, the same person greets him in the lobby of his hotel and tells him exactly the same story he told him yesterday.

In such a fully deterministic universe, all events are fixed in advance. You might *think* you chose to take the stairs rather than ride the elevator, or select a chocolate ice cream for dessert, but in reality, this choice results from some previous events, which, in turn, were predetermined by others, going back all the way to your conception. In fact, a powerful computer could predict each of these actions with perfect certainty. So while *you* believe you chose freely, these events could not have possibly gone any differently—everything was predetermined at your birth.

Most people believe that this fully deterministic universe is monstrous and different from their own; this was the opinion expressed by test subjects in America,[2,3] China, Colombia, and India.[3] When they were asked to judge actors in this universe, they responded that they are not morally responsible for their actions.[2-5] Now whether they are actually right is a totally different question, which philosophers have pondered for centuries and one that I will not discuss here. For our purposes, what matters is whether we *believe* we can act freely. And most laypeople feel that the universe of *Groundhog Day* is not their own. So, when people consider responsibility "in the abstract," they view free will as incompatible with determinism (more on this question later).

Moreover, challenging free will promotes antisocial behavior. When people are told that free will is an illusion, that every one of their acts is predetermined, they become more selfish. In one study, people read a passage indicating that human actions occur before we can control them. When these participants were next asked to divide a pot of money under time pressure, they became more likely to claim the money for themselves.[6] Determinism further reduced people's willingness to help others,[7] promoted cheating in an arithmetic task[8] and aggressive behavior (treating a fellow participant to hot, spicy food despite being explicitly told that the person disliked such food),[7] and reduced people's tendency to assign retributive punishments to offenders.[9]

The antisocial consequences of determinism are also evident in real life. A comparative study of 65,000 people in 46 countries found that reactions to ethical violations varied depending on the integrity of the social institution in the participants' countries. In countries with accountable public sectors that are free of corruption, strong beliefs in free will were associated with intolerance of unethical behavior. But when social institutions were corrupt or dysfunctional, this correlation was absent. Presumably, when corruption is rampant, people attribute unethical behavior to external circumstances, rather than to the individual's inherent moral character.[10]

To act freely, however, one needs not only the *potential* to choose an option but also to realize it. Moreover, the act must be intended by the self. If someone forcefully placed you next to a bank teller with a gun in your hand and programmed your mouth to shout "Give me the money or I shoot," you would not be held responsible for the robbery. Acts that are externally controlled aren't acts of free will. It is disturbing to think that you can be controlled like a puppet on strings. But in "the age of the brain" this can be science, not fiction. Transcranial magnetic stimulation of the brain—a technique we mentioned in earlier chapters—can force you to move a limb or make you go temporarily dumb. The action is all yours, but since the control is external, you wouldn't consider it willed.

In fact, some internally controlled acts wouldn't count as free either. When the comedian Mark Birbiglia gets anxious, he becomes prone to sleepwalking. One night, he jumped out of his hotel room window without even opening it.[11] The hotel might charge him for the broken glass, but in the eyes of most people, Birbiglia was neither malicious nor culpable.

To be held responsible for one's acts, the act must be evitable, it must be internally willed, and it must be preceded by a conscious intention. As for the notion of "intention," circumstances matter too. Many people will argue that it's OK to shoot an armed burglar who invades your home. Although the shooting is intentional, the intention is self-defense, not aggression per se.

This is not only the case with Westerners. A survey of eight traditional small-scale societies,[12] from hunter-gatherers to pastoralists and
horticulturalists, found that their moral judgments were mitigated by their
understandings of actors' intentions. The weight they put on intent varied
greatly. The Himba people, for example—the seminomadic pastoral group
from Namibia we encountered in Chapter 10—are hardly talkative when it
comes to their emotions. But when they evaluate acts that inflict physical
harm, the Himba judge their perceived "badness" (the extent that they reflect on the perpetrator's reputation and merit punishment) according to his
or her intent, much like their U.S. counterparts. Good intentions, however,
do not always excuse one's actions. For severe transgressions, like poisoning,
the Himba held the perpetrator responsible irrespective of intent, and for the
Yasawa of Fiji, intentions didn't matter at all. But in all eight cultures, acts
committed in self-defense and from necessity were universally viewed as less
culpable than intentional acts.

Summarizing our discussion so far, it seems that, in the layperson's view,
free will is intimately linked to moral responsibility. To determine whether
a person is morally responsible for their actions, we evaluate whether they
acted freely. Free acts, in turn, are caused by the conscious intentions of the
self. The sequence of events is simple: the self first wills, and in so doing, it
causes an act to unfold. Our naïve account of free will can be summarized as
follows:

Self → conscious intentions → action

So to ascertain whether a given act was freely willed, all we need to do is determine the actor's intentions and whether those intentions were the cause
of their actions. But knowing the will of others can be a thorny problem;
their intentions can be hard to discern. How can I tell what goes on in your
mind, or for that matter, whether you (let alone nonhuman agents, such as
Apple and Google) even have minds and intentions at all?[13] So to keep things
simple, let's just focus on the agents we know and love the best—ourselves.

Surely, I can judge my own actions and determine with perfect accuracy
whether or not they are willed. But as we'll see, I cannot really. Whether "I
intended to do it" is not always obvious; in fact, it is not always clear whether
"I did it." Our troubles, moreover, are not limited to judging intentions and
actions. And the root cause for this lies in our shaky notion of "me."

Did I Do It?

RT, an intelligent 55-year-old engineer, was sitting comfortably in his doctor's office. "Could you please move both your arms?" asked the doctor. "Could you clench and unclench your fists?" "How about extending and flexing your wrist in a circular movement, as if you were conducting an orchestra—can you do that?" RT responded to each of these commands. He moved his right arm, circled his right hand, and unclenched it, and he reported doing the same with his left hand.

This would all seem unremarkable if it wasn't for the fact that RT has no left hand. RT's left arm was amputated six inches above the elbow. Remarkably, RT (as well as many other amputees) reported voluntary control of his missing limb. He reported being able to move it at will and noted a sense of touch. RT senses willful control of his actions, but this sense is clearly illusory when it comes to his left hand.

This illusion of control was demonstrated by the neuroscientist Vilayanur Ramachandran[14,16] using a low-tech contraption consisting of a simple wooden box partitioned by a vertical mirror (see Figure 15.1A). The patient places their healthy arm in one chamber, and upon seeing its mirror image, the missing limb feels as if it were resurrected. When asked to move "both hands," the patient moves the healthy arm, which in turn, makes them see "their" left hand move. Upon seeing "their" missing limb move at will, they conclude, "I did it." Similarly, when they see their healthy arm being touched, they report the same tactile sensation in their phantom limb.

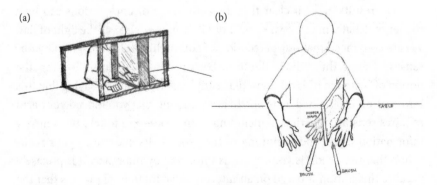

Figure 15.1. The mirror box (a) and the rubber hand illusion (b).
(a) Redrawn, from Ramachandran et al. (1996)[14]; (b) Peled et al. (2000).[15]

Several control conditions show that the illusion of control is not merely a confabulation. Patients reported no control of the phantom limb when their eyes were shut. This finding demonstrates that people do not invariably report a phantom limb whenever they move their healthy arm. In fact, some patients experienced the illusion of a phantom limb even when the arm reflected in the mirror belonged to the experimenter. So, to resurrect the phantom limb, people need visual evidence that the two arms move in tandem, and this information is apparently both necessary and sufficient for the illusion of control to emerge.

But you need not lose your arm to have a phantom limb experience. In one study, healthy individuals were asked to place both their arms on a table. Their left arm was hidden from view behind a barrier, and in its place, they saw a life-size rubber replica (see Figure 15.1b). The researchers then stroked both hands simultaneously, the rubber hand and the hidden real one, with a paintbrush. In a matter of minutes, people began to "sense" the rubber limb as their own.[17] They said they "felt" the touch in the rubber hand, and when asked to shut their eyes and point to their left hand, they tended to veer rightwards, toward the rubber hand. Once again, the rubber hand illusion isn't a fabrication. A control group for whom the induction procedure was changed minimally (the two hands were brushed asynchronically) did not experience the same illusion. In fact, the illusion of the rubber hand is evident physiologically. When the rubber hand is "threatened" (by pulling back one of the fingers), people not only reported a subjective sense of pain but they also exhibited it in their skin conductivity.[18]

These results make it clear that the authorship of one's actions can be a matter of debate. In our own eyes, "I did it" seems as clear as the light of day. We are convinced that our perception of authorship is directly given by our senses—I see it, thus I did it. But these illusory cases of control show that the notion of "who did it" is not sensed directly. I'm obviously not saying that this information is obtained by telepathy; recognizing that you moved your arm requires sensory experience, including both vision and touch. But sensory information is just the beginning of the process. Its endpoint—your realization that the action is your own—is informed by inference. It is precisely because this notion is based on an interpretative inferential process that the reckoning can go wrong. Whether "you did it" and whether you *think* you did it are quite distinct.

Did I Mean To?

OK, you might reply, perhaps I can sometimes be tricked about which arm I'm moving, I get it. But this is no serious threat to my free will. After all, these illusory actions are rare. Moreover, for my sense of free will, it is really the intention that counts. It is my conscious willful command that makes my action happen. First, I will—I consciously command my arm to move. Then, the action follows as a result. So, for free will, it is the causal role of my intention that is paramount. And when it comes to judging my own intention, I'm the ultimate expert.

Am I? Consider another psychological test. JW is seated near a display that flashes simple commands, like "laugh" and "walk," for a fraction of a second.[19,20] When JW sees words on the right side of the display, he is able to read them with no difficulty and perform the action as requested. When similar commands appear on the left side, however, JW says he sees nothing. But surprisingly, JW still acts as instructed. When "walk" flashes, JW stands up and starts to leave the testing room. He has a perfectly good explanation for his action: "I'm going into the kitchen to get a Coke," he says.

JW was certain that his conscious wishes were the cause of his act. In his mind, the sequence of events was exactly the same as in a decision that you might make to lift your hand. First came the conscious intention, then the act. But JW clearly got the order wrong. Yes, he acted and he expressed a conscious intention. But the expressed intention occurred *after* the action, so it could not have possibly been its cause.

JW's confusion is the result of a brain operation that severed his corpus callosum, a solution of last resort to alleviate severe epileptic seizures. You might know that each hemisphere of the brain gets its sensory input from the opposite side of the body: information from the left eye first arrives at the right hemisphere, whereas information from the right eye goes to the left half of the brain. Each hemisphere, however, "shares" its information with the other through the corpus callosum. For example, linguistic processing relies predominantly on the left hemisphere, so when words are presented to your left eye, the information is first registered in the right hemisphere (the point of entry into the brain) and next travels to the left hemisphere (where most linguistic processing occurs). In JW's brain, however, the connection between the left and right hemispheres was broken. These so called "split brain" patients experience difficulty in processing linguistic information that is presented to their right hemisphere via the left visual field, and they also fail to gain conscious awareness of it. The information is clearly processed by the right hemisphere, but it is not consciously registered.

Given his neurological condition, the fact that JW cannot gain conscious awareness of information presented to his right hemisphere is perhaps not surprising. What's telling for our purposes is that he claimed authorship for actions he hadn't consciously intended. This case of mistaken authorship should give you pause. If JW can be fooled about his own intentions, how can you be certain about yours?

The late Harvard psychologist Daniel Wegner[21-23] asserted that free will is an illusion. Marshalling a vast array of cases, Wegner demonstrated that we can not only be wrong about what we do (as shown in the previous section) but also about our conscious intentions. Some of these examples border on the bizarre.

Wegner notes, for example, that post-hypnotic suggestions can direct a person's actions when they are otherwise fully conscious. In one case, a woman under hypnosis was instructed to take a book from the table and place it on a shelf. When she woke up, she dutifully did just that. What's remarkable is her explanation for her action. Like JW, she credited her actions to her own conscious intention ("I don't like to see things so untidy," she said.[22p149]). In cases of schizophrenia and trance, the opposite phenomenon occurs, with people misattributing their own intentions to external sources that "command" them to do something—via either voices (in schizophrenia) or virtual spirits (in trance).

You and I are likely to experience the very same kinds of cognitive "mishaps," and they can be just as "exotic." The other day, I was emailing an acquaintance from 30,000 feet on my flight back to Boston. This was just a couple of days after the disastrous crash of an Ethiopian Boeing 373 MAX. When the person jokingly replied that he hoped I wasn't flying on a 373 MAX myself, his remark didn't feel funny at all. In fact, it felt threatening, like it was tempting fate. We all know, of course, that the "evil eye" is a myth. But even otherwise nonsuperstitious people can take the magical powers of thought quite seriously.

In one series of experiments,[24] participants carried out a voodoo rite that involved sticking pins in a doll representing a victim. When the victim (one of the experimenters) later reported feeling a headache, participants thought that the headache was their own doing. As it happens, that same experimenter had treated some of them rudely before the experiment, and the event naturally prompted negative thoughts toward that person. People who had experienced those negative interactions were more likely to believe they had caused the headache compared to participants who had not had the negative interaction and whose thoughts were therefore neutral.

Positive thoughts can seem magical too. Do you ever find yourself trying to "help" your favorite team by imagining them scoring a winning goal? People apparently believe the visualization helps. In another experiment,[24] a group of participants were asked to engage in hopeful visualization while they watched a basketball player shoot hoops. When the shooter had a run of good luck, these participants were more likely to claim credit for the shooter's success than controls (e.g., participants who had been told to visualize the shooter lifting a dumbbell). These participants consciously willed, but they commanded no action at all.

In another study, people assumed credit for an action that they had not consciously commanded. The act was mundane, the mere pressing of a button, and the instructions simply asked them to act (e.g., move their finger) spontaneously, whenever they felt the desire or urge to do so. People reported that they were quite certain that they had consciously willed the action. But they were wrong. They had indeed willed it, but not until after it had been launched. The psychologist Benjamin Libet arrived at this conclusion by comparing the time course of two events. The first was the characteristic brain response that was recorded on the scalp about 550 milliseconds prior to the initiation of the action (pressing the button); Libet's interpreted this signature as a "readiness potentital " (RP), signaling the subconscious initiation of action by the brain. The second was the onset of the conscious will to act, which Libet termed "W." To estimate the timing of that second event, Libet asked them to report the position of a spot of light that was moving in a steady circular motion at the precise moment when they willed the action. Remarkably, the conscious willful "feel" of wanting to act (W) happened well after RP—the presumed moment at which the action had been initiated by their brains (by about 345 milliseconds).[25]

Could this discrepancy have occurred simply because the experiment is inaccurate? Perhaps people take too long to *report* their conscious experience, but the actual conscious "feel" occurs "just on time" (exactly when their brains indicated they were ready to push the button). This possibility was addressed by several control conditions that asked people to report the timing of two other mental events—a slight stimulation of their skin (delivered at random intervals) and the time at which they actually moved their finger (as opposed to when they had commanded the move). Both reports require monitoring of one's conscious mental life, and when those reports were compared to the actual event (the sensory stimulus or the initiation of movement), it turned out that they indeed lagged behind. All this suggests that reporting one's own mental states takes time and that delay introduces a measurement error in estimating the timing of our conscious will to act. But even when this "measurement error" is taken into account, the conscious will to act is felt well after the action was initiated by the brain. Libet thus concludes that conscious will to act occurs after the fact, and so it cannot be the cause of the action.

The lagging of W (the presumed onset of conscious volition) behind RP was observed in many studies,[26] and it was even evident in intracranial recordings from single neurons.[27] In fact, an fMRI study found that W (the onset of conscious volition) is preceded by brain activity that occurs as long as 10 seconds earlier.[28] Nonetheless, Libet's interpretation of two landmarks—the RP and W—has been challenged.[26]

If the RP indeed reflects the subconscious decision to respond, then the RP should be restricted to volitional actions. But subsequent research by Aaron Schurger and his colleagues found a similar RP signature even when the action was triggered by an external auditory signal that occurred randomly.[29] Schruger and colleagues suggested that the RP does not signal an unconscious decision to act. Rather, it merely signals the setting of an internal gauge, much like you set the sand timer when you are preparing to cook your eggs. You turn over the timer, and once the sand crosses some threshold, you launch the action (taking the eggs off the stove, or the button press, in the Libet task). Critically, what the gauge actually monitors (the "sand" in the cooking metaphor) is neural activity that builds up in the motor cortex *spontaneously*, irrespective of any prior volitional decision to act. This means that, if we were given an instruction to respond by some external signal and that signal came just as the neural gauge approached the threshold (i.e., our maximal readiness to respond), the response time should be faster compared to when the neural gauge runs "low." In line with this prediction, Schurger and colleagues observed that RP brain signatures with stronger amplitude (i.e., indicating "high" readings of the neural gauge) were associated with faster responses to an external auditory signal.[29] So under this more recent reconceptualization, the RP is not the signature of a fully formed unconscious decision, and its dissociation with W is not as sharp as Libet had originally envisioned.[30]

For some, this new interpretation vindicates conscious volition. After all, my conscious sense that "I willed my finger to move" is lawfully linked to the subconscious RP signal that preceded this response. Others might view the "half empty" side of the equation. If the timing of my decision to lift my finger is determined by the accumulation of spontaneous neural activity, then the notion that I lifted my finger *because I consciously willed it* gets more murky.

But even if we put aside the mental events that precede the conscious decision to act, it is evident that the timing of this conscious response is not as clear we might think. One study, for example, has shown that people's estimate of the timing of their intention to act is based on the consequence of their actions. In the experiment, participants were asked to estimate the onset of their will to act (just as in the previous studies by Libet) and given feedback (via a computer beep) on when their action, a button press, had presumably occurred. The button, however, was designed to provide no visual or tactile feedback on when the press was completed, and, unbeknownst to the participants, the timing feedback provided by the computer was delayed by 5 to 60 milliseconds. Results showed that as the computer feedback was delayed, so was participants' estimates (the exact moment at which "I willed").[31,32]

Another study[33] found that people can be led to initiate an act despite having no sense of conscious will. Participants were given a post-hypnotic suggestion to squeeze a ball. When they woke up, they acted as instructed, and they demonstrably had no recollection of the instructions—they believed that they were being stimulated to squeeze the ball by jolts of electricity that were fed through electrodes attached to their arms. In reality, however, their response was entirely volitional, and the brain signatures indicating the initiation of the act were indistinguishable from the signatures that accompanied acts that they performed without having received hypnotic suggestions.

Together, these experiments show systematic dissociations between our reports of our conscious intentions to act and the real causes of our actions (as judged by our best estimates). Sometimes we claim control of actions that we committed but could not have consciously commanded—either because we couldn't (the cases of RT and JW), or because we could not have done so on time (prior to the action). In other cases, we claim it is not "me" who willed the act but some external source that is real (the electrodes attached to my arm), or virtual (the "voices" heard by schizophrenic patients or spirits and ghosts in the case of trance), whereas in others, we claim we magically willed an action that we did not (a voodoo curse or a basketball player's successful shot).

The Illusion of Free Will

The lesson we learn from these examples is sobering: We are not trustworthy judges of our own conscious will. We believe we consciously will and that our will causes actions to follow.[23] We think "I want coffee" and when we subsequently reach for our cup, it is our conscious intention that *caused* the action. But as we saw, we aren't so good at keeping track of our conscious intentions and actions. As Wegner argues, our "free will" equation (*self→conscious will→action*) is wrong.[22]

None of this negates our potential to exercise free will or to carry out deliberate intentions. It does not mean that people cannot act freely or that their intentions are irrelevant to their actions. On the contrary, cognitive science tells us repeatedly that our intentions and goals crucially determine each and every one of our behaviors. But having intention and having *conscious* intention are two different things. We experience this distinction every time we wonder "Did I turn off the stove?"; "Did I lock the front door?"; or "Did I take my daily baby aspirin?" You often discover that yes, you did act, and yes, the action was intended, but the intention went entirely "under the radar," leaving no conscious recollection of either your action or your will. The real drivers of our acts are intentions that, for the most part, are unconscious. Now, it's true that some of our intended actions are associated with a distinct "feel" of "I willed." So yes, your action was probably intended ("under the hood"), and yes, it probably happened. But your conscious experience of willing it could well have occurred after it started, as a consequence of the action rather than its trigger.

Our multiple "short circuits" in reasoning about our intentions, our actions, and the causal links between them suggest to Wegner that *conscious free will* is an illusion. To reiterate yet again—the emphasis is on *conscious*; this says nothing about our intentions generally, and it does not negate free will. It is only our intuitive notion of free will that is at stake. In our naïve minds, it is the consciously willing self that is the cause of our action. "I did it" *because* "I *consciously* meant to." That notion is apparently the fruit of our imagination—it's the wrong story about how our actions really occur.

Deconstructing the Illusion: The Role of Core Knowledge

So why do we insist that our conscious intentions are the cause of our actions? As noted, our concern here is with our reasoning about our actions, not with whether actions are in fact free. Reasoning, moreover, can proceed along multiple routes. One possibility is that people are equipped with a moral instinct—an inborn system that is specialized for reasoning about morality, including reasoning about free will.[2,34-36] Another possibility is that our moral intuitions are based on systems that are not specialized to the domain of morality specifically. And of course, these two routes could work in parallel, in a hybrid-like fashion. This book, however, is concerned not with the moral instinct but rather with the casualties of Dualism and Essentialism. For this reason, I now explore how our two old friends could conspire to derail our intuitions about free will; whether a moral instinct also has a contribution to make is not a question I consider here.

Wegner's seminal work provide some crucial leads. Wegner believes the culprit is our intuitive sense of agency (a system of core knowledge that does not concern moral reasoning specifically). We view agents as driven by mental states—I look for the keys where *I think* I left them, not where they actually are.

Following the philosopher David Hume,[37] Wegner suggests that we infer mental causation based on the same principles we use to guide our reasoning about physical causation. Remember the launching balls from Chapter 3? People, as you recall, assume that one ball can cause another to change its trajectory, and the change will only occur upon such causation; a moving ball will not simply veer off its track all by itself.

How do we infer causation in the physical domain? Answer: by inspecting whether (a) the changed trajectory of ball A was preceded by the collision with ball B (*priority*) and whether (b) It was *not* preceded by a collision with any other ball (*exclusivity*). Had ball A collided with both balls B and C, you couldn't have determined which one was the true cause of its new trajectory.

Now when we reason about physical events, we probably don't need to learn the link between cause and effect from experience; as we saw, newborns show knowledge of those principles from birth. But if you had to learn about causality in a new domain—say, the link between inflation and the stock market—then your inference about causality (e.g., inflation lowers stocks) would require not only priority (inflation preceded the drop in share values) and exclusivity (inflation is the only plausible reason for the drop) but also *consistency*: a single occurrence may get you thinking, but it is the consistent link between inflation and the stock market that cements your belief.

To summarize, core knowledge makes us expect that the actions of agents are caused by their goals, and causality, in turn, is inferred by principles of priority, consistency, and exclusivity. And it is possible that we apply these two principles—of intentional agents and causation—when we reason about our selves. We expect our actions to be caused by our intentions, and we establish internal causality by the same principles that drive our interpretation of external events (by priority, consistency, and exclusivity). But for internal events, our reckoning suffers from a fatal design flaw.

While we know that reasoning about others' intentions is elusive, when it comes to the self, we assume expertise. Our conscious thoughts are all too salient. Moreover, we all have plenty of experiences in which our conscious intention (*I am going to drink some coffee*) precedes action (*proceed to Starbucks*) in a consistent manner, just as required by our intuitive understanding of causality. The problem is that we aren't so good at registering our conscious life, and to add insult to injury, we are utterly unaware of all the unconscious mental events that drive our actions "under the hood" in blatant violation of exclusivity. Blinded by the conscious "me," we conclude that our conscious intention is the sole cause of our action.

Wegner presents results from numerous ingenious experiments that show how the principles of causality can promote the illusion of conscious free will. In one study,[38] loosely modeled after the "rubber hand" phenomenon, people stand in front of a mirror and are instructed to perform a repeated sequence of actions with "their" hand ("snap your fingers," "wave," etc.). But the hand shown in the mirror isn't theirs; it belongs to an experimenter standing behind them, hidden from their view. Since the experimenter and the participants are both wearing the same dark robe and the same plastic gloves, the experimenter's hand in the mirror appears to be an integral part of the participant's body. When asked to rate their sense of authorship of their actions ("How much control did you feel you had over the arm's movements?" and "To what degree did you feel that you were consciously willing the arm to move?"), participants who consistently heard the instructions before the hand moved (in line with priority and consistency) reported a greater sense of control than those who didn't hear the instructions or heard them only after the action had occurred. Similarly, when the foreign hand was "insulted" (by snapping a rubber band on the wrist), participants who heard the instructions prior to the actions were more threatened (i.e., more likely to show an increase in their skin conductivity) than those who were given no instructions or instructions that were incongruent with the movement. Presumably, hearing the congruent instructions prior to movement generated a greater sense of control of the foreign arm and, with it, a greater sense of empathy. These results reaffirm the conclusion that people can assume authorship of acts they did not perform and that the attribution of authorship depends on priority and consistency.

Another set of experiments demonstrates the role of exclusivity.[23] Here, participants' sense of authorship of their action (pointing to a sequence of letters) was diminished when the experimenter pointed to or gazed at the target prior to the participants' own action. This, again, is an illusion—the experimenter's action changed neither the participant's action nor their intention, but the sense of authorship (the perception of will as the cause of action) was diminished by the possibility that the experimenter was the instigator of the action.

These core knowledge biases can explain why we misattribute some of our own actions to external forces and why we reclaim others' actions as our own. For schizophrenia patients, for instance, the sudden radical shifts in their own mental states lead them to attribute their thoughts to an external agent (the "voices"). The rubber hand and phantom limb present the opposite challenge. Here people need to reconcile their conscious intention to act with the incomplete cues for action offered by vision alone; the assumed causal volition ("I moved the rubber arm") resolves this conflict.

Wegner thus concludes that the notion of free will is a construction of the self, a reality that stands in stark contrast to our naïve notion of free will. Per our naïve psychology, free will is perceived by the senses, much like we perceive light or sound—*I willed, so I made actions happen.* In reality, each of these notions (conscious intention, action, and causality) is obtained by inference. When the facts mismatch our expectations, we fill in the blanks post hoc, and our illusion of a conscious free will emerges.

Who's "Me"?

So far, we have considered three components of the self-made notion of conscious free will: the notion of self-action ("I did it"), conscious intention ("I meant to"), and the causal inference that links intention to action. Missing from the equation is the fourth secret ingredient: the inference-maker, the self. And as we will see, when we come to reason about our conscious free will, the self is not an unbiased observer. Rather, we come equipped with pre-conceived notions about the willing self, and those notions guide our under-standing of free will. We assume that a true self that is good, immaterial, and unitary lies at our core—that there is only one single self. It won't be the first time our bets are off, but this time, the stakes couldn't be higher, and the blow couldn't hit us any closer to home.

A Free Self

Want to make a blockbuster science fiction movie? A best-selling novel? Let me suggest a winning formula. The main character is an all-powerful villain—a mad scientist, an alien, or an out-of-control robot. The plot follows the villain's evil attempts to take over the world by robbing us humans of the ability to exert our free will and control our destiny. Fortunately, a hero foils the villain's plot at the last moment. Some scholars actually believe that this formula could play out in real life. The Oxford philosopher Nick Bostrom warns about the takeover of humanity by artificial intelligence.[39,40] The historian Yuval Harari, on his part, predicts that, now that science has "proven" that free will is dead, and that people are "mere" biological algorithms, we are doomed to a future in which we are slaves to the new religion of "Dataism."[41] No wonder we get scared. These horror scenarios deny us a capacity that, in our minds at least, is our innate birthright.

Our belief in the free-willing self—one that can exert the magic of action by the mere force of its conscious intention—is at the heart of the numerous illusions of control described in the previous section. Other evidence for our belief in a free-willing self is evident in another set of seemingly irrational behaviors that we exhibit in our moral reasoning.

Earlier, we noted that free will is paramount to moral responsibility. So when asked to evaluate responsibility in a deterministic universe in which "everything that happens is completely caused by whatever happened be-fore," people are less likely to state that a person acted on his or her own free will, and they are also less likely to hold them morally responsible for their actions.[2] In other words, people believe that free will is incompatible with de-terminism. At least that is what they say when you ask them "in the abstract." But like Groucho Marx said, if you don't like these principles, well, we have others. When the problem hits "closer to home," people will now state that free will and determinism are compatible.

The conditions that prompt this retreat from the moral high ground don't seem to follow any particular rational pattern. People are willing to suspend "incompatibilism" (and maintain free will) when prompted to reason about their own world (as compared to some other universe),[2,4,42] when presented with a concrete case (compared to one in the abstract[2,42]), especially when the case depicts a heinous crime like rape and robbery[43]—events that play on one's emotions, compared to less-charged infractions like tax evasion.[2] In fact, people were more likely to assign free will to nonhuman primates when told that free will in animals speaks to the presence of free will in humans.[42] The only common denominator that unites these various responses is our belief in the free-willing self.[42] When this belief is threatened, we step in to defend our turf by downplaying the significance of determinism and upholding the free-willing capacities of the self. All of these various "exceptions" prove the rule: in our minds, free will is the birthright of the self.

A Good Self

Anne Frank (1929–1945) famously wrote that "in spite of everything, I still believe that people are really good at heart."[44] Coming as it does from a girl who spent her teenage years hiding from the Nazis, and who was subsequently murdered in a concentration camp, this unqualified endorsement of human nature is especially striking. But her sentiments seem to be quite widely shared.

When asked to determine whether John is still "the same person" after he has had a partial brain transplant, taken a magic pill that induces a personality change, undergone reincarnation, or simply succumbed to aging, people considered John's moral characteristics as diagnostic for the continuity of the self.[45] So long as he maintains his moral fiber, then his self is "the same." When further probed as to which moral traits define the self, people considered positive moral traits as more probative than negative traits. When asked to determine whether Jack was "the same as before" after undergoing a brain surgery that triggered a personality change, the answers depended on the valence of the change. People perceived greater continuity between the pre- and post-surgery person when the moral change was for the better (Jack is now kinder) compared to when it got worse (Jack is now more cruel).[46]

People reach the same conclusion when they reason about changes in themselves. They were more likely to state they would "still be themselves" when the change improved their moral characteristics compared to when there was a moral deterioration.[47] Similar results obtained across the three countries where this experiment was carried out (the United States, Singapore, and Colombia) despite marked differences in the participants' beliefs about the degree of the self's independence of others.[48] In fact, the belief in a good "true self" was so strong that it was evident even in misanthropes—those who hold negative beliefs about humankind.[48] People were further willing to extend it to outgroups that they usually perceive as stereotypically threatening. In those experiments, U.S. participants were invited to reason about Alhadin, an Arab immigrant (or a native Arab) who has experienced a behavioral change. When asked to determine what aspects of his personality drive the change, people were still more likely to credit it to Alhadin's "true self" when the change resulted in an improvement (e.g., becoming a more caring father) as opposed to a deterioration.[49]

Interestingly, what counts as "good" depends on people's own beliefs. For liberals, traits that reflect liberal views (e.g., concern about global warming) are viewed as more likely to reflect the true self than those reflecting conservative views (e.g., patriotism); conservative participants show the opposite judgment.[50] Moreover, our belief in the "good self" colors our reasoning about other people's mental states and the causes of their actions.

People, as we know, sometimes act on a momentary urge that conflicts with their core beliefs. Josh, for instance, believes in racial equality, but he sometimes commits acts of racial discrimination. Paul, on the other hand, is a racist, but he occasionally commits acts that promote racial equality. In each case, there is a conflict between the agent's beliefs and an act committed on a whim. But when asked to evaluate the person's "true self," people interpret the positive act as more indicative of who this person is "deep down." This belief further led them to assume that Paul must have "valued" his morally positive actions more than Josh valued his morally negative ones.[51] The belief in the true self also affects our inferences as to whether people's actions originate from internal or external sources. We apparently assume that the agent is morally good (where "good" depends on our own perspective), so when the actions mismatch those beliefs, we assume the causes of actions are external.[52]

The roots of the belief in the "good self" are found in early childhood; in fact, children were more optimistic than adults. Children stated that negative psychological traits would change over time into positive traits, whereas existing positive psychological traits will be maintained.[53] As you might recall, when a "helper" is contrasted with a "hinderer," even 3-month old infants prefer "the good guy."[54]

The cognitive scientists Nina Strohminger, Joshua Knobe, and George Newman[55] and Julian De Freitas and colleagues[56] thus propose that we each possess a notion of a "true self"—my real essential self, distinct from just "me." While the actual person can act in either moral or immoral ways, deep down, the "true self" is moral. Like Anne Frank, we believe our "true self" is fundamentally good.

Why do we contrast our "true self" from the "self"? According to these scholars, the "true self" is the "brainchild" of Essentialism—our intuitive belief in the innate immutable essence.[55] In line with this position, Nick Haslam and colleagues found that "desirable" personality traits are linked to a number of characteristics that are associated with Essentialism (discreteness, biological basis, immutability, informativeness, consistency, and inheritability).[57] But whether these particular results speak to the moral self is uncertain. For one thing, Haslam and colleagues examined personality traits (e.g., moody, tense), not moral traits, so their presumed Essentialism does not necessarily speak to our core moral character. Moreover, it is unclear that Essentialism can singlehandedly capture our notion of the "true self." Granted, "true self" and "essence" both speak to our "core." But as the next section shows, what lies at the core of my material body may not overlap with the immaterial "me."

An Immaterial Self

Jeff isn't a "nice guy." He is rude to his friends, he cheats on his taxes, he never lifts a finger to help his spouse, and he abuses the neighbor's cat. But is he actually morally responsible for his actions? Given our "free will" formula (*Self* → *conscious intentions* → *action*), it seems like he is. It is Jeff's conscious intentions that led him to commit these acts. You willed it, so you're responsible.

But suppose you now learn that a recent brain scan revealed that Jeff exhibits various abnormalities in brain centers associated with emotion and action control. Who's in charge now? Several studies have shown that the brain scan is a game changer. The mere mention of brain or biochemical explanations for a crime leads laypeople to view the defendant as less blameworthy,[58,59] and when asked to assign a sentence, the severity of the verdict is reduced.[59] Remarkably, people—laypeople and even judges—do the same, even when they are explicitly asked to judge legal responsibility.

Legal responsibility, to be sure, is defined by strict criteria that can differ from moral standards. In the eyes of the American law, a person is responsible for a crime if their mental state at the time was that of a "guilty mind" (*mens rea*)—meaning that they either intended to commit the act or they acted recklessly. Two conditions can exonerate a person from responsibility for a criminal act. One is duress—you robbed the bank because someone held a gun to a loved one's head; the other is insanity, which (per the M'Naghten standard) means that at the time you committed the crime, you either (a) did not know what you were doing or (b) did not know that the act was wrong.[60-62] Per these strict standards, a person with severe mental illness could still be held legally responsible for their actions. The case of Andrea Yates illustrates this point.

Yates, a 37-year-old mother of five, suffered from severe postpartum psychosis. Her medical condition was so grave that her psychiatrist had warned that she must be under constant supervision.[63] But in the span of the 1 hour that separated the departure of her husband for work and the arrival of a family member, Yates drowned each of her five children in a bathtub in order to protect them from the torments of Satan. Yates, no doubt, was psychotic, but she demonstrably knew what she was doing and knew that it was wrong. So her first trial found her legally sane and hence guilty for her action (this decision was overturned in a second trial).[60]

All this is to show that legal responsibility is a rigid notion. But while the law may not be moved by cases of even severe psychosis, it yields to the brain. A landmark Supreme court case (*Roper vs. Simmons*, 2004) banned the execution of a minor accused of a heinous premeditated crime on the grounds that a teenager's brain is biologically immature.[61] Subsequent research found that brain-related information had significant effects on the sentencing decisions of judges. When a group of 181 U.S. judges were presented with expert testimony that a psychopath convicted of aggravated battery exhibited brain abnormalities, the assigned sentence was reduced from an average of 13.93 years to an average of 12.83 years.[64] Similarly, a mock jury presented with a murder case along with detailed jury instructions were more likely to deliver a "not guilty by reason of insanity verdict" if they'd heard neurological testimony documenting a brain abnormality.[65] If the brain lit, you must acquit.

Why should a brain abnormality matter? Brain scans do not directly demonstrate that a person is more likely to meet the legal criteria for insanity. Similarly, per our "free will" formula, to be culpable for an act, all that is required is that the act is consciously intended. The last time I checked, my brain was still very much attached to my body. Why, then, would an action controlled by my brain not be controlled by "me"?

Yes, you've guessed it; this form of twisted reasoning bears the fingerprints of Dualism. The link between Dualism and mental disorders was considered in detail in Chapter 12. As we saw, people view brain-based disorders as even more severe and immutable than psychological ones, and, for this reason, they are less likely to hold patients responsible for their actions. Although the brain doesn't speak for or against the legal definition of insanity, Dualism insists that it must.

Dualism can likewise explain why brain explanations attenuate moral responsibility. According to Dualism, we are comprised of a material body and an immaterial mind. The body acts, but it is the mind that intends the action. And to will freely, the mind must be free not only from external constraints (no one put a gun to my head) but also from its material bodily confines (having a head). In the words of the philosopher Joshua Greene and the neuroscientist Jonathan Cohen,[62] the mind, per naïve psychology, is an "uncaused causer." If mental acts can be traced to the material brain, then the agent cannot will freely. So when it comes to my moral self, it's my immaterial mind that is the real "me."[55]

This immaterial view of the true self is also supported by experimental manipulations of "compatibilism." Earlier, we saw that people tend to remove blame and moral responsibility if a person's action was predetermined by external forces; for example, if every one of their actions could have been clearly traced to earlier events in their lives and predicted by a powerful computer. Similarly, the mention of determinism elicits antisocial behavior, including selfishness,[6] cheating,[8] and a lesser willingness to assign retributive punishment.[9] Interestingly, similar results obtain when the challenge to free will is presented not by external causes but by the brain. For example, people who had been informed that human decisions are the product of complex brain interactions that occur before we can control them were more likely to exhibit selfishness (i.e., less likely to contribute money to the public good).[6] Similarly, people who read a passage about the brain, or who have enrolled in a semester-long neuroscience course, are less likely to require retributive punishments.[9] These results are in line with the possibility that the home of the free will is the immaterial self, not the brain.

The Dualist view of the true self is not without its challenges. First, the belief in an immaterial moral self is not absolute: people would still conclude that a person has acted on his accord even if they are told that each of their acts could be predicted with full certainty from their previous brain states.[66] Second, people project free will to "soul-less" creatures—a cyborg consisting of a human brain placed in a robotic body, as well as an AI "brain" implanted in a human body. People categorically denied that these two creatures possess a soul, yet they believe they exert free will in their actions.[67]

But these challenges do not necessarily present a fatal blow to Dualism. The finding that people are "OK" with the fact that "my brain made me do it" is not utterly surprising. Recall that people are also biased to believe that the self is free, and they are willing to go to great lengths to uphold this belief against various challenges.[42] So when Dualism is pitted against free will, people uphold freedom above the immaterial self. This result, however, only suggests that the immaterial view of the self is violable; it does not show that it does not exist. The same holds for the free will of soulless creatures. An immaterial self, as discussed so far, is only endowed with the capacity for a mind: it exhibits mental states that can magically cause an action. Soul, by contrast, is associated with religious, rather than cognitive functions,[68] so per naïve psychology, it is perfectly possible for intentional beings to will freely even if they lack a soul.

The discussion in previous chapters, however, presents a deeper challenge to the immaterial notion of the moral self. That challenge is linked to a second aspect of our core cognition—Essentialism. People, as we saw, believe that moral character is in our essence. But as previous chapters have demonstrated, Essentialism requires a material mechanism of inheritance. People assume that innate essentialist traits are in the material body—if a trait is innate, then it must be localized in the body and realized in some material physical substance.

So once again, we witness a collision between the two titanic forces of our core cognition—Dualism and Essentialism. Per Dualism, we expect the moral self to be immaterial, but per Essentialism, it must be materially embodied. Who is the true self, then? And how can it be simultaneously immaterial and material, ephemeral and embodied?

A Unitary Self

Summarizing the discussion so far, we believe our moral self is free, good, and immaterial. But there is a tension between this view of our "essential self" and our material notion of biological essence. So who's the real me: is it good or bad? Material or immaterial? And is there indeed a single unitary notion of "me"?

To address these questions, we[69]presented people with the fictional case of a college student we called "John," who, we said, is a modern-day reincarnation of the famous Dr. Jekyll and Mr. Hyde.[70] John exhibits erratic changes in behavior. He can be quite kind and generous; he would stop to help an elderly person cross the street, donate money to the needy, and assist a fellow student with difficult course material. But at other times, he can show inexplicable aggression. He posts nasty hate messages on Facebook, exhibits cruelty to animals, and randomly bullies strangers that he runs into on campus.

John is unaware of his condition, but, on the advice of his family, he approaches a psychologist who refers him for testing to a nearby hospital. The evaluation includes two tests—a behavioral test and a brain test. The idea, as you might have guessed (from Chapter 11), is to contrast two measures of John's inner self. The brain test evaluates the representation of the moral self in the body; the behavioral test evaluates cognition. Otherwise, the two tests are entirely comparable. Each presents John with a series of pictures; to proceed to the next, he has to press a computer key. Some of the pictures depict aggression; others present acts of kindness. John's reactions to these two types of pictures is compared using both his behavioral responses (how fast he presses a key in response to each type of picture) and his brain activity (how fast his brain spikes in response to each type of picture).

People are further informed on how to interpret the test results. Past research, they are told, has shown that people who suffer from aggression exhibit atypical responses to aggressive images, whereas people singled out for their kindness show atypical responses to kind images. Moreover, people are informed that the outcomes of the behavioral tests and the brain scans usually agree. But in John's case, they differ markedly. The precise nature of the disagreement was described differently to two groups of participants.

One group was told that the behavioral test shows strong benevolence and no aggression, while the brain test shows the opposite—strong evidence of aggression and not even a hint of benevolence. A second group was presented with the opposite outcome (the behavioral test shows aggression; the brain test shows benevolence). Participants in both groups were told that, in light of these conflicting outcomes, the psychologist is naturally stumped, and the participants were invited to come to the rescue.

At this point, we presented the participants with two questions. One inquired about free will—when John commits acts of benevolence/aggression, does he perform those acts of his own free will? Another asked participants to determine John's real essence: at his core, is he a benevolent or an aggressive person?" (Participants read both questions, counterbalanced for order.)

So in this experiment, we sought to gauge John's true self "here and now" (as opposed to some idealized future "me") and to allow people to choose between a positive and a negative moral self. If our "true" self is uniformly good, then people should invariably choose the test that presents John as benevolent; if our notion of the true self is more nuanced, then it's conceivable that evidence for both positive and negative traits would arise.

The contrast between the brain and behavioral measures allows us to further gauge the materiality of the self: if the self is immaterial, then people should prefer the outcomes of the behavioral tests (especially when the behavioral test is positive), but if some aspects of the self are material, then those should be best reflected in the brain test.

Finally, there is the question of whether the free-willing self indeed reflects John's essence. If it does, then the two questions ("Did John act of his free will?" vs. What is John's essence?") should yield a similar outcome; a divergence would suggest that there isn't a single unitary self.

The hypothesis that the true self is in our essence, and that it's unitary, good, and immaterial would predict a uniform preference for "benevolent John" in both tests (free will and essence), but it should only arise when benevolence is gauged by the behavioral measure; the true self, in this view, is immaterial, so it's not "in the brain." But the results suggest otherwise. Reasoning about John's free will and essence differed, and these results were further modulated by the trait (benevolence vs. aggression) and test (behavior vs. brain). When asked to reason about John's free will, people always rated acts of benevolence as more likely to be performed freely compared to acts of aggression, and that was the case irrespective of the test (brain or behavior). But when asked to reason about John's essence, the results differed markedly. Now people always accepted the outcome of the brain over the behavioral test. When the brain result indicated John was aggressive, aggression was rated higher; when the brain indicated John was benevolent, benevolence was rated higher. In other words, people believed that John's free-willing self is good, but his essence is material and is devoid of any particular moral valence—good or bad.

The finding that people believe that John's essence is material is in line with the hypothesis that, per naïve psychology, the immutable essence of living things is material. People, in this view, believe that the brain test better speaks to John's essence because they believe that "what's in the brain is innate."

To further test this possibility, we asked another group of participants to directly consider this question. Participants were presented with the same information about John's puzzling behavior, along with the conflicting outcomes of his brain and behavior tests. Their task now was to determine how likely it is that the results of each test (brain or behavior) mean that John exhibited that trait (benevolence or aggression) from birth. Results clearly showed that people believed that the results of the brain test reflect on John's character from birth. Regardless of whether the test indicates evidence for benevolence or aggression, what's "in the brain" is what's innate.

So who is our "true self"? The answer, it appears, is "it depends." When invited to reason about a person's free will, people decidedly chose "good" over "bad," and they maintained this belief irrespective of whether goodness was manifested in the material brain or behavior. These results suggest that the true moral self is not necessarily immaterial,[66] but it is decidedly good.

This, however, doesn't necessarily mean that goodness is our biological essence. When asked about a person's essence specifically, people now seem to access a different aspect of themselves, the "essential self," and, per Essentialism, our innate essence is in the material body. Here, the true self is not ephemeral but embodied, and it encompasses both good and bad.

In our mind, then, the true moral "I" is both good and bad, material (as required by Essentialism) and immaterial (in line with Dualism), and the side of me that I access depends on whether the question flags moral reasoning explicitly (by asking about free will) or implicitly (by asking about our essence). So perhaps the biggest illusion of all is our belief in a single, unitary, moral "me."

Conclusions

Our intuitive notion of free will is ill-formed. We believe our acts result from the conscious intentions of the self. But in reality, conscious intentions are often the consequence of actions, rather than their cause. We are likewise not the best judges of what we actually did and what we consciously intended. Worst of all, our notion of the moral self is misinformed. We believe in a single unitary notion of "me," distinct from our bodies—a true self that is good and freely-willing. But we appear to simultaneously hold multiple conflicting notions—an idealized, good, free-willing "me" lives side by side with my true embodied self, which includes both good and bad. To add insult to injury, the instigators of the free will illusion are none other than Dualism and Essentialism—the two core principles of core knowledge that are likely innate.

With this conclusion looming, one cannot help but wonder whether free will exists—a question distinct from our intuitive beliefs about free will, which form the topic of this chapter. I do not presume to advance the discussion of this age-old question, let alone solve it. But here, I would second Steven Pinker,[71] who, in the best Jewish tradition, counters the "are we free?" question with another question: "why do you care?"

One reason to care, Pinker notes, is the social consequences of responsibility. In order for our society to function, we need effective methods of deterrence: if someone robs you of your money, you want them sanctioned, so that robbery doesn't turn into a fad. Free will seems relevant to how we set our social sanctions, inasmuch as we don't hold people responsible for unintentional accidents or for acts that they committed under mortal threat. But we don't quite need to decide the philosophical question of free will to establish an effective deterrence system. In fact, free will is a rather dubious notion. As the philosopher David Hume has shown,[37] if our actions are predetermined, then we aren't responsible for them; on the other hand, if our actions result from random events, then we aren't responsible for them either. So, from the pragmatic social standpoint, it is not free will but the agent's intention that is paramount. If our universe were deterministic, Pinker notes, we would still hold your robber just as responsible for their actions as we would if we believed that the robber was an "uncaused causer," operating in an utterly free universe.

But I believe that our fear of determinism concerns not only our actions but also our minds. We worry that, like the shackled slaves in Plato's cave, we might be leading a blind life. Are our worries justified?

The answer, I think, depends on what we worry about. If our concern is with physicalism—the notion that our mental life is shaped by the material processes operating in our brains—then we should probably relax. In the words of Paul Bloom, "It is wrong, then, to think that one can escape from the world of physical causation—but it is not wrong to think that one can think, that we can mull over arguments, weigh the options, and sometimes come to a conclusion."[72] On the other hand, if we worry about being in the grip of innate knowledge, here the answer is less optimistic. The multiple instances of self-blindness discussed in this book suggest that these concerns are not unfounded. Dualism and Essentialism keep "whispering" in our ears, and we keep marching to their sound.

The push and pull between these two forces appear to shape every aspect of our mental lives, from how we reason about the origins of our knowledge to what we think a "cup" is and what we mean by "love." Core knowledge makes us fall for our brain; it distorts our understanding of mental health, and now it derails our reasoning about our moral life, twisting the very notion of the self.

Can we free ourselves from the spells of core knowledge? I doubt we can fully. In fact, I'm not sure it's even a worthy goal—we rely on these principles for every one of our daily actions, from recognizing a solid object to identifying a human face. So "turning them off" is probably neither practical nor desirable. But perhaps we can start by simply listening to what they whisper.

References

1. Descartes R. *Meditations and other metaphysical writings*. Reprinted with corrections. New York, NY: Penguin; 2003.
2. Nichols S, Knobe J. Moral responsibility and determinism: the cognitive science of folk intuitions. *Noûs*. 2007;41(4):663–685.
3. Sarkissian H, Chatterjee A, De Brigard F, Knobe J, Nichols S, Sirker S. Is belief in free will a cultural universal? *Mind & Language*. 2010;25(3):346–358.
4. Roskies AL, Nichols S. Bringing moral responsibility down to Earth. *The Journal of Philosophy*. 2008;105(7):371–388.
5. Nichols S. Experimental philosophy and the problem of free will. *Science*. 2011;331(6023):1401.
6. Protzko J, Ouimette B, Schooler J. Believing there is no free will corrupts intuitive cooperation. *Cognition*. 2016;151:6–9.
7. Baumeister RF, Masicampo EJ, DeWall CN. Prosocial benefits of feeling free: disbelief in free will increases aggression and reduces helpfulness. *Personality and Social Psychology Bulletin*. 2009;35(2):260–268.
8. Vohs KD, Schooler JW. The value of believing in free will: encouraging a belief in determinism increases cheating. *Psychological Science*. 2008;19(1):49–54.
9. Shariff AF, Greene JD, Karremans JC, et al. Free will and punishment: a mechanistic view of human nature reduces retribution. *Psychological Science*. 2014;25(8):1563–1570.

10. Martin ND, Rigoni D, Vohs KD. Free will beliefs predict attitudes toward unethical behavior and criminal punishment. *Proceedings of the National Academy of Sciences of the United States of America.* 2017;114(28):7325–7330.
11. Gross T. Spending the night with sleepwalker Mike Birbiglia. NPR. October 18, 2010.
12. Barrett HC, Bolyanatz A, Crittenden AN, et al. Small-scale societies exhibit fundamental variation in the role of intentions in moral judgment. *Psychological and Cognitive Sciences.* 2016;113(17):4688.
13. Knobe J. Finding the mind in the body. In: Brockman M, ed. *Future Science: Essays from the Cutting Edge.* New York, NY: Vintage Books; 2011:184–196.
14. Ramachandran VS, Synaesthesia in phantom limbs induced with mirrors. *Proceedings: Biological Sciences.* 1996;263(1369):377–386.
15. Peled A, Ritsner M, Hirschmann S, Geva AB, Modai I. Touch feel illusion in schizophrenic patients. *Biological Psychiatry.* 2000;48(11):1105–1108.
16. Ramachandran VS, Rogers-Ramachandran D, Cobb S. Touching the phantom limb. *Nature.* 1995;377(6549):489.
17. Botvinick M, Cohen J. Rubber hands "feel" touch that eyes see. *Nature.* 1998;391(6669):756.
18. Armel KC, Ramachandran VS. Projecting sensations to external objects: evidence from skin conductance response. *Proceedings: Biological Sciences.* 2003;270(1523):1499.
19. Gazzaniga MS. Right hemisphere language following brain bisection: a 20-year perspective. *American Psychologist.* 1983;38(5):525–537.
20. Funk CM, Putnam MC, Gazzaniga MS. Consciousness. In: Berntson GG, Cacioppo JT, eds. *Handbook of neuroscience for the behavioral sciences.* New York, NY: Wiley; 2009:482–506.
21. Wegner DM. The mind's best trick: how we experience conscious will. *Trends in Cognitive Sciences.* 2003;7(2):65–69.
22. Wegner DM. *The illusion of conscious will.* Cambridge, MA: MIT Press; 2002.
23. Wegner DM. Self is magic. In: Baer J, Kaufman JC, Baumeister RF, eds. *Are we free? Psychology and free will.* New York, NY: Oxford University Press; 2008:226–247.
24. Pronin E, Wegner DM, McCarthy K, Rodriguez S. Everyday magical powers: the role of apparent mental causation in the overestimation of personal influence. *Journal of Personality and Social Psychology.* 2006;91(2):218–231.
25. Libet B. Unconscious cerebral initiative and the role of conscious will in voluntary action. *Behavioral and Brain Sciences.* 1985;8(4):529–566.
26. Brass M, Furstenberg A, Mele AR. Why neuroscience does not disprove free will. *Neuroscience and Biobehavioral Reviews.* 2019;102:251–263.
27. Fried I, Mukamel R, Kreiman G. Internally generated preactivation of single neurons in human medial frontal cortex predicts volition. *Neuron.* 2011;69(3):548–562.
28. Soon CS, Brass M, Heinze H-J, Haynes J-D. Unconscious determinants of free decisions in the human brain. *Nature Neuroscience.* 2008;11(5):543.
29. Schurger A, Sitt JD, Dehaene S. An accumulator model for spontaneous neural activity prior to self-initiated movement. *Proceedings of the National Academy of Sciences of the United States of America.* 2012;109(42):E2904.
30. Schurger A, Mylopoulos M, Rosenthal D. Neural antecedents of spontaneous voluntary movement: a new perspective. *Trends in Cognitive Sciences.* 2016;20(2):77–79.
31. Banks WP, Isham EA. We infer rather than perceive the moment we decided to act. *Psychological Science.* 2009;20(1):17–21.

32. Rigoni D, Brass M, Sartori G. Post-action determinants of the reported time of conscious intentions. *Frontiers in Human Neuroscience.* 2010;4:38–38.

33. Schlegel A, Alexander P, Sinnott-Armstrong W, Roskies A, Tse PU, Wheatley T. Hypnotizing Libet: readiness potentials with non-conscious volition. *Consciousness and Cognition.* 2015;33:196–203.

34. Bloom P. *Just babies: the origins of good and evil.* 1st ed. New York, NY: Crown; 2013.

35. Nichols S. Folk intuitions on free will. *Journal of Cognition and Culture.* 2006;6(1–2):57–86.

36. Hauser MD. *Moral minds: how nature designed our universal sense of right and wrong.* 1st ed., Ecco, 2006.

37. Hume D. An enquiry concerning human understanding. In: Millican PF, ed. *Oxford world's classics.* Oxford, U.K.; New York, NY: Oxford University Press; 2007.

38. Wegner DM, Sparrow B, Winerman L. Vicarious agency: experiencing control over the movements of others. *Journal of Personality and Social Psychology.* 2004;86(6):838–848.

39. Bostrom N. When machines outsmart humans. *Futures.* 2003;35(7):759–764.

40. Bostrom N. *Superintelligence: paths, dangers, strategies.* 1st ed. Oxford, U.K.: Oxford University Press; 2004.

41. Harari YN. *Homo Deus: a brief history of tomorrow.* 1st U.S. ed. New York, NY: Harper; 2017.

42. Clark CJ, Winegard BM, Baumeister RF. Forget the folk: moral responsibility preservation motives and other conditions for compatibilism. *Frontiers in Psychology.* 2019;10(215).

43. Nahmias E, Morris S, Nadelhoffer T, Turner J. Surveying freedom: folk intuitions about free will and moral responsibility. *Philosophical Psychology.* 2005;18(5):561–584.

44. Frank A. *The diary of a young girl.* 1st ed. Garden City, NY: Doubleday; 1952.

45. Strohminger N, Nichols S. The essential moral self. *Cognition.* 2014;131(1):159–171.

46. Tobia KP. Personal identity, direction of change, and neuroethics. *Neuroethics.* 2016;9(1):37–43.

47. Molouki S, Bartels DM. Personal change and the continuity of the self. *Cognitive Psychology.* 2017;93:1–17.

48. De Freitas J, Sarkissian H, Newman GE, et al. Consistent belief in a good true self in misanthropes and three interdependent cultures. *Cognitive Science.* 2018;42(Suppl 1):134–160.

49. De Freitas J, Cikara M. Deep down my enemy is good: thinking about the true self reduces intergroup bias. *Journal of Experimental Social Psychology.* 2018;74:307–316.

50. Newman GE, Bloom P, Knobe J. Value judgments and the true self. *Personality and Social Psychology Bulletin.* 2014;40(2):203–216.

51. Newman GE, De Freitas J, Knobe J. Beliefs about the true self explain asymmetries based on moral judgment. *Cognitive Science.* 2015;39(1):96–125.

52. Cullen S. When do circumstances excuse? Moral prejudices and beliefs about the true self drive preferences for agency-minimizing explanations. *Cognition.* 2018;180:165–181.

53. Lockhart KL, Chang B, Story T. Young children's beliefs about the stability of traits: protective optimism? *Child Development.* 2002;73(5):1408–1430.

54. Hamlin JK, Wynn K, Bloom P. Three-month-olds show a negativity bias in their social evaluations. *Developmental Science.* 2010;13(6):923–929.

55. Strohminger N, Knobe J, Newman G. The true self: a psychological concept distinct from the self. *Perspectives on Psychological Science*. 2017;12(4):551–560.

56. De Freitas J, Cikara M, Grossmann I, Schlegel R. Origins of the belief in good true selves. *Trends in Cognitive Sciences*. 2017;21(9):634–636.

57. Haslam N, Bastian B, Bissett M. Essentialist beliefs about personality and their implications. *Personality and Social Psychology Bulletin*. 2004;30(12):1661–1673.

58. Monterosso J, Royzman EB, Schwartz B. Explaining away responsibility: effects of scientific explanation on perceived culpability. *Ethics & Behavior*. 2005;15(2):139–158.

59. Heath WP, Stone J, Darley JM, Grannemann BD. Yes, I did it, but don't blame me: perceptions of excuse defenses. *Journal of Psychiatry & Law*. 2003;31(2):187–226.

60. Denno DW. Andrea Yates: a continuing story about insanity. In: White MD, ed. *The insanity defense: multidisciplinary views on its history, trends, and controversies*. Santa Barbara, CA: Praeger; 2017:367–416.

61. Satel SL, Lilienfeld SO. *Brainwashed: the seductive appeal of mindless neuroscience*. New York, NY: Basic Books; 2013.

62. Greene J, Cohen J. For the law, neuroscience changes nothing and everything. *Philosophical Transactions: Biological Sciences*. 2004;359(1451):1775–1785.

63. Lezon D. Yates not "grossly psychotic" before drownings, Dietz testifies. *Houston Chronicle*. July 13, 2006.

64. Aspinwall LG, Brown TR, Tabery J. The double-edged sword: does biomechanism increase or decrease judges' sentencing of psychopaths? *Science*. 2012;337(6096):846.

65. Gurley JR, Marcus DK. The effects of neuroimaging and brain injury on insanity defenses. *Behavioral Sciences & the Law*. 2008;26(1):85–97.

66. Nahmias E, Shepard J, Reuter S. It's OK if "my brain made me do it": people's intuitions about free will and neuroscientific prediction. *Cognition*. 2014;133(2):502.

67. Monroe AE, Dillon KD, Malle BF. Bringing free will down to Earth: people's psychological concept of free will and its role in moral judgment. *Consciousness and Cognition*. 2014;27:100–108.

68. Richert RA, Harris PL. Dualism revisited: body vs. mind vs. soul. *Journal of Cognition & Culture*. 2008;8(1–2):99–115.

69. Berent I, Platt M. "The 'true Me'—one or Many?" PsyArXiv. December 9. doi:10.31234/osf.io/tkur5.

70. Stevenson RL. *The strange case of Dr. Jekyll and Mr. Hyde*. New York, NY: Scribner's; 1888.

71. Pinker S. The fear of determinism. In: Baer J, Kaufman JC, Baumeister RF, eds. *Are we free? Psychology and free will*. New York, NY: Oxford University Press; 2008:311–324.

72. Bloom P. Free will does not exist. so what? *The Chronical of Higher Education*. March 18, 2012. Retrieved from https://www.chronicle.com/article/Paul-Bloom-Free-Will-Does-Not/131170

PART III
CODA

16

Why It All Matters

Conspiracy theories spark our imaginations. Some people are fascinated by allegations of political conspiracy, like those surrounding the Kennedy assassination; for others, conspiracy takes a cosmic scale, in tales of the alien invasion of Roswell.[1] This book, however, has plotted a conspiracy of a personal kind. I have unveiled hidden forces that distort our view of human nature. The culprits are not the inhabitants of an extraterrestrial planet or a massive government intrigue. Rather, our blindness springs from within—it emanates from human nature itself.

We humans are Intuitive Dualists and Essentialists. Dualism governs our grasp of the physical and psychological worlds; Essentialism, in turn, guides our understanding of living things. Indeed, there is some evidence that these principles appear in early development and are shared with our nonhuman relatives. So, in all likelihood, these twin forces were selected for good evolutionary reasons; they are not implanted in us by some vicious aliens. But when they collide, they give rise to a perfect storm, and we, the innocent bystanders, are the casualties.

We go through our lives looking through the lenses of Dualism and Essentialism, and these lenses systematically distort our view of our reality. They obscure who we think we are—they twist our account of concepts and emotions; they fuel our irrational fascination with the brain; they bias our understanding of its role in affective and cognitive disorders; they engender supernatural beliefs in the afterlife; and they plant misconceptions about free will and the self. The prisms of core knowledge also render us blind to the origins of our knowledge—to the possibility that some of our ideas are innate. And in the best tradition of Greek tragedy, we are entirely oblivion to our blindness. We are the victims of an epistemic conspiracy.

Faced with such charges, two different reactions might arise. One leads you to question the theory—*how do we know it's right*? The other leaves you wondering whether you should even care. Skepticism, of course, is healthy; it's the impetus for science. Yet each of these reactions can also be a form of

The Blind Storyteller. Iris Berent, Oxford University Press (2020). © Iris Berent, 2020.
DOI: 10.1093/oso/9780190061920.001.0001

denial, which is only to be expected under the circumstances. Self-blindness is tragic, and denial is a common reaction to grief. Let me address each of these questions in turn.

***

So how certain are we that we are biased by core knowledge? Although this book concerns a conspiracy, I hope it's clear that my theory is firmly grounded in science. Throughout the previous chapters, I have supported my claims by evidence, including findings from previous research as well as novel results from my own lab.

Science, however, always comes with limitations, and the present theory is no exception; I would be remiss if I did not point them out. So let us take the magnifying glass, inspect the narrative I have woven, and identify the weakest links therein. As with every crime investigation, there are questions about the crime, the victims, and the suspects.

First, keep in mind that the multiple symptoms of blindness—our obliviousness to *what we know* and *who we are* each represents a novel proposal. To my knowledge, no one has ever considered the possibility that core knowledge renders us blind to innate ideas or analyzed our blindness to *who we are* in these specific ways. As I've shown, this conclusion is in line with a large body of existing evidence. But because the proposal is new and bold, I was compelled to further present direct experimental tests of its predictions. If nothing else, these results make it clear that each of these questions *can* be tested in a straightforward fashion, and, for the most part, the predictions are borne out by the results. But each of these demonstrations (especially for the case studies presented in the second part of the book) requires far deeper experimental scrutiny. So while there are reasons to believe that a crime took place (i.e., the conspiracy theory is plausible), I don't presume to have produced the smoking gun.

Now, the victims. My survey of the consequences of the conspiracy are based primarily on evidence from Western adults, so it's natural to wonder whether my findings also apply to non-Westerners and children. Here, the evidence is admittedly spotty. Throughout the book, I have examined the handful of studies that took a comparative cross-cultural perspective, investigating non-Western adults[2-7] and children,[2,5,8,9] and the results suggest that the hallmarks of Dualism and Essentialism are not a uniquely Western phenomenon. But whether the biases I have documented here extend to non-Westerners, and whether they are present in young children, is still a research program in progress.

In light of these limitations in my account of the crime and its victims, our understanding of the suspects must remain incomplete as well. At the heart of the conspiracy is the proposal that our blindness to human nature emanates from human nature. But the evidence here is circumstantial. In support of this view, I showed that (a) the chief suspects—Dualism and Essentialism—may well be involved in the crimes and (b) these two principles are possibly innate. The "possibly" qualification is important—let me spell it out again.

As we saw (in Chapter 3), there is strong evidence that newborns view objects as material, and, as discussed, it appears unlikely that they learn the notion of "object" from their experiences in utero. But when it comes to our intuitive psychology (*the mental states of agents are immaterial*) and biology (*the essence of living things is innate, immutable, and material*), here most of the evidence is obtained from older infants and children. As noted, this doesn't necessarily mean that these principles are learned from experience. Indeed, we saw that Dualism is documented even in societies with "mind opacity"; similarly, Essentialism is seen cross-culturally, and it is stronger in children than adults. Whether these twin forces are innate, however, is still very much an open question.

So while we have pretty good reasons to assume a crime was committed (yes, we are the victims of an epistemic conspiracy) and have identified a suspect and pressed charges (actually, two suspects, Dualism and Essentialism), we still don't quite hold the conviction in our hands. The investigation is still active.

***

Why should you care about all this? Why does blindness matter? I think the reasons are multiple.

First, blindness exerts a toll. *Where knowledge comes from* and *who we are* have been the topics of long scholarly debates, first in philosophy (at least from the era of the Ancient Greeks) and, subsequently, in the social sciences—in psychology, linguistics, anthropology, and sociology. Whether core knowledge actually sways these scholarly discussions is unknown. But to the extent that human reasoning is systematically biased by core knowledge, and scholars are humans, there are certainly reasons to worry.

Blindness, as we saw, could also interfere with our reasoning about topics that are at the heart of our social and political life. It derails our understanding of results from brain sciences in both health and disease, engendering stigma and discrimination against persons with mental disorders and systematic misunderstanding and underdiagnosis of congenital neurocognitive disorders, like dyslexia. Our difficulty in reconciling minds and bodies also interferes with our understanding of criminal responsibility and the notion of free will.

Blindness is further worth noticing because its engines not only distort our account of human nature but also of the natural world. For example, the notion of biological adaptation presupposes random mutations and selection, but our intuitive notion of an essence is immutable. If, in our minds, living things, like dogs and gray wolves, are invariant and immutable, then it is difficult for us to grasp how dogs could be the descendants of gray wolves. Essentialism thus interferes with our grasp of evolution, and this is a formidable challenge to science education.[10]

Finally, let us consider what happens when the blind ventures to devise a "golem" in his own image—the "thinking machines" of artificial intelligence (AI). Since we view human nature as a blank slate, the AI we design to mimic our own thinking is likewise devoid of "innate" concepts. These systems are typically engineered with none the concepts that are available to human newborn infants; their creators hope these notions will eventually emerge spontaneously, by learning, just as they believe infants acquire these concepts. But the cognitive scientist Gary Marcus and the computer scientist Ernest Davis argue that this approach is doomed; it will never deliver an AI we can trust.[11] In their words "we need to stop building computer systems that merely get better and better at detecting statistical patterns in data sets—often using an approach known as deep learning—and start building computer systems that from the moment of their assembly innately grasp three basic concepts: time, space and causality."[12] So in light of the multiple tolls of blindness—on scholarship, science education, AI, and societal matters—we had better become cognizant of our prisms.

A second reason to care is that blindness is in the air. In an era of "fake news," the systematic spreading of misinformation, and the denial of science, there is no better place to start clearing the public sphere than from within.

The third and most important reason to face our blindness is that we care. Our stories are the means by which we explore and define who we are, both personally and collectively, as a species. Stories are not easy to construct or tell, and yet, storytellers have always courageously looked within and spoken, even at the cost of their own lives. So getting the story right is a need that many of us value deeply. Blindness is in our way.

I doubt the culprits—the forces of Dualism and Essentialism—can be eliminated. Core knowledge is probably in our nature, and the notion that we can slip off our biological shackles at will is no more likely than the prospects of Remy the cat transcending his feline confinements. But while we are bound to think in the shadows of core knowledge, we are not necessarily doomed to utter blindness.

Core knowledge, to reiterate, is only one component in the rich suite of mechanisms that comprise human cognition; other rational capacities exist, and they allow us to look within, recognize the conspiracy, and begin to counteract it. Our path out of the cave begins with careful self-inspection. Perhaps this book could be a guide.

The Ancient Greeks, you might recall, inscribed the words "Know thyself" at the entrance of the temple of Apollo in Delphi. The deeper we dig into the spells of core knowledge, the wiser this advice seems.

References

1. Goldwag A. *Cults, conspiracies, and secret societies: the straight scoop on Freemasons, the Illuminati, Skull and Bones, Black Helicopters, the New World Order, and many, many more.* 1st Vintage Books ed. New York, NY: Vintage Books; 2009.
2. Chudek M, McNamara RA, Birch S, Bloom P, Henrich J. Do minds switch bodies? Dualist interpretations across ages and societies. *Religion, Brain & Behavior.* 2018;8(4):354–368.
3. Cohen E, Burdett E, Knight N, Barrett J. Cross-cultural similarities and differences in person-body reasoning: experimental evidence from the United Kingdom and Brazilian Amazon. *Cognitive Science.* 2011;35(7):1282–1304.
4. Martin ND, Rigoni D, Vohs KD. Free will beliefs predict attitudes toward unethical behavior and criminal punishment. *Proceedings of the National Academy of Sciences of the United States of America.* 2017;114(28):7325–7733.
5. Astuti R, Harris PL. Understanding mortality and the life of the ancestors in rural Madagascar. *Cognitive Science.* 2008;32(4):713–740.
6. Sznycer D, Xygalatas D, Agey E, et al. Cross-cultural invariances in the architecture of shame. *Proceedings of the National Academy of Sciences of the United States of America.* 2018;115(39):9702–9707.
7. Sznycer D, Xygalatas D, Alami S, et al. Invariances in the architecture of pride across small-scale societies. *Proceedings of the National Academy of Sciences of the United States of America.* 2018;115(33):8322–8327.
8. Atran S, Medin D, Lynch E, Vapnarsky V, Ucan Ek E, Sousa P. Folkbiology doesn't come from folkpsychology: evidence from Yukatek Maya in cross-cultural perspective. *Journal of Cognition & Culture.* 2001;1(1):3–42.
9. Sousa P, Atran S, Medin D. Essentialism and folkbiology: evidence from Brazil. *Journal of Cognition and Culture.* 2002;2(3):195–223.

10. Shtulman A. *Scienceblind: why our intuitive theories about the world are so often wrong.* New York, NY: Basic Books; 2017.
11. Marcus G, Davis E. *Rebooting AI: building artificial intelligence we can trust.* New York, NY: Random House; 2019.
12. Marcus G, Davis E. How to build artificial intelligence we can trust. *The New York Times.* Sept. 6, 2019.

Index

Figures and boxes are indicated by *f* and *b* following the page number

For the benefit of digital users, indexed terms that span two pages (e.g., 52–53) may, on occasion, appear on only one of those pages.